NARRATIVE OF WILLIAM W. BROWN, A FUGITIVE SLAVE (1848)

A moving portrayal of a man's life as a slave, William Wells Brown's first autobiography quietly, disarmingly recounts his early days, including his forced separation from his mother and siblings as a child, his sojourn on the Mississippi River as a handyman for a slave trader, and his final triumphant escape north where he becomes a conductor on the underground railway. This edition includes Brown's original dedication to the Quaker abolitionist who aided his escape and two later essays by the author.

MY SOUTHERN HOME (1880)

Brown's last autobiography tells of the struggle for power and prestige among whites and blacks in the antebellum South. Its deadpan, detached tone presents a complex, multilayered vision of the institution of slavery, one that represents a less emotional but unequivocally authentic picture of the dehumanization and cruelty of the buying and selling of humankind.

THE AUTOBIOGRAPHIES OF
William Wells Brown

WILLIAM L. ANDREWS is Joyce and Elizabeth Hall Professor of American Literature at the University of Kansas. A prize-winning scholar of African American literature, Andrews is the author of *To Tell a Free Story: the First Century of Afro-American Autobiography, 1760–1865* and the editor of *Classic American Autobiographies*, *The African American Novel in the Age of Reaction*, *Collected Stories of Charles W. Chesnutt*, and *Three Classic African American Novels*, all available in Mentor editions.

FROM
FUGITIVE SLAVE
TO
FREE MAN

THE AUTOBIOGRAPHIES OF
William Wells Brown

EDITED AND WITH AN
INTRODUCTION BY
William L. Andrews

A MENTOR BOOK

MENTOR
Published by the Penguin Group
Penguin Books USA Inc., 375 Hudson Street,
New York, New York 10014, U.S.A.
Penguin Books Ltd, 27 Wrights Lane,
London W8 5TZ, England
Penguin Books Australia Ltd, Ringwood,
Victoria, Australia
Penguin Books Canada Ltd, 10 Alcorn Avenue,
Toronto, Ontario, Canada M4V 3B2
Penguin Books (N.Z.) Ltd, 182–190 Wairau Road,
Auckland 10, New Zealand

Penguin Books Ltd, Registered Offices:
Harmondsworth, Middlesex, England

First published by Mentor, an imprint of New American Library,
a division of Penguin Books USA Inc.

First Printing, July, 1993
10 9 8 7 6 5 4 3 2 1

 REGISTERED TRADEMARK—MARCA REGISTRADA

Library of Congress Cataloging Card Number: 92-063389

Printed in the United States of America

CONTENTS

Introduction

Though traditionally regarded as the first African American man of letters, William Wells Brown has always stood in the shadow of his more famous contemporary, Frederick Douglass. Two years after his first autobiography, *Narrative of William W. Brown, A Fugitive Slave,* was published with considerable fanfare in 1847, a newspaper reporter characterized Brown as ''a good-natured fellow, of respectable talents, and one whose lectures are more calculated to do good than those of almost any other man''—any man except, the reporter went on to add, Frederick Douglass. In 1849 the first review of the most widely read slave narratives of the era, including those of Douglass and Brown, was published in *The Christian Examiner,* a popular liberal-minded journal. To the *Examiner,* Brown's narrative related what seemed typical of ''what must belong to the life of almost any fugitive slave.'' Douglass's story, by contrast, depicted ''the life of a superior man.'' By the time Brown's ground-breaking novel, *Clotel; or, The President's Daughter,* came out in 1853, reviewers of his books had taken to reciting, almost like a litany, the notion that Brown ''occupies a position in public esteem only second to that of his powerful-minded compatriot, Frederick Douglass.'' Although Brown would distinguish himself as the most prolific and multifaceted African American author of his era, he would never be lionized as *the* spokesman of black America. That distinction, dubious as many would see it today, was always reserved for Douglass.

Unlike Brown, Douglass the writer showed little interest in the traditional literary genres of poetry, drama, and fiction. Yet in the eyes of many literary critics Douglass's star has risen to truly astronomical heights, rivaling in brilliance some of the brightest of mid-nineteenth century white American writers. Brown's literary reputation glows much more faintly. Still, one of the most knowledgeable and astute historians of black American letters, J. Saunders Redding, has cautioned against making so much of Douglass's achievement that a writer like Brown inevitably falls into eclipse, along with much of what makes him truly significant. William Wells Brown was, in Redding's words, "historically more important in the development of Negro literature than any of his contemporaries." Perhaps more noteworthy, in light of the status conferred upon Douglass in our own time, Brown was in Redding's view "the most representative Negro" of his era. Douglass may have been the spokesman and exemplar of his people's aspirations, but he was "too exceptional" to embody what Brown's writing gave voice and articulation to: "the hope and despair, the thoughts and yearnings" of the masses of black people in the middle of the nineteenth century.

The lingering image of Brown as the most representative African American writer of his time depends in large part on his own careful self-fashioning in and through his autobiographies. Like Douglass, Brown was at his best when writing about himself. On numerous occasions on the platform and in print, Brown and Douglass capitalized on their inherently interesting lives and their rhetorically sophisticated styles of self-representation. On the strength of his remarkable triad of autobiographical accounts—*Narrative of the Life of Frederick Douglass, An American Slave* (1845), *My Bondage and My Freedom* (1855), and *Life and Times of Frederick Douglass* (1881, 1892)—Douglass is often credited with pioneering what is called today the "serial autobiography" in African American letters. It may be, however, that Douglass learned from Brown the advantages of self-revision for a fugitive slave who aspired to a career as a writer. It was Brown who led the way in adapting a variety of autobiographical forms to the expressive needs of his evolving sense of selfhood, both as an African American and a literary man. As a result Brown's experiments with the forms of life-writing, as well as with the interrelationships of personal myth and social history, were in some ways more radical than Douglass's—and more prophetic of the future of African American literature.

William Wells Brown was born in 1814 on a plantation near Lexington, Kentucky, the son of a white man and a slave woman. Light-complexioned and quick-witted, William spent his first twenty years mainly in St. Louis, Missouri, and its vicinity, working as a house servant, a field hand, a tavern-keeper's assistant, a printer's helper, an assistant in a medical office, and finally as a handyman for James Walker, a Missouri slave trader with whom Brown claimed to have made three trips up and down the Mississippi River between St. Louis and the New Orleans slave market. Before he escaped from slavery on New Year's Day, 1834, this unusually well-traveled slave had seen and experienced slavery from almost every perspective, an education that he would put to good use throughout his literary career.

After seizing his freedom, Brown (who received his middle and last name from an Ohio Quaker who helped him get to Canada) worked for nine years as a steamboatman on Lake Erie and a conductor for the Underground Railroad in Buffalo, New York. In 1843, the fugitive slave became a lecturing agent for the Western New York Anti-Slavery Society. Moving to Boston in 1847, he wrote the first, and still the most famous, version of his autobiography, *Narrative of William W. Brown, A Fugitive Slave, Written by Himself*, which went through four American and five British editions before 1850, earning its author international fame. Brown's *Narrative* was exceeded in popularity and sales only by the *Narrative of the Life of Frederick Douglass*.

In 1848 the second edition of Brown's *Narrative*, slightly but significantly revised, and expanded by a lengthy appendix, was published in a printing of two thousand, which quickly sold out. A third edition followed, and in May of 1849 a fourth, expanded once again. In the same year Brown went abroad to attend an international peace conference in Paris and to lend his voice to the antislavery crusade in England. In addition to his demanding speaking schedule, he found time to try his hand at a new form of first-person narrative, which he entitled *Three Years in Europe; or, Places I Have Seen and People I Have Met* (1852). This was the first travel book authored by an African American; it was favorably received by the British press in general, as well as by the American antislavery press. A year later *Clotel,* generally regarded as the first African American novel, was published, prefaced by a lengthy "Narrative of the Life and Escape of William Wells Brown." Although written in the third person as though by a biographer, this installment of Brown's life, which included a good deal of information on his experiences in the North and in England, was more than likely his own creation.

After returning to the United States in 1854, Brown continued his pioneering literary work, publishing *The Escape; or, A Leap for Freedom* (1858), the first drama by an African American. During the 1860s he published three more versions of *Clotel* and two volumes of black history, one of which, *The Negro in the American Rebellion* (1867), is the first military history of the African American in the United States. In *The Black Man: His Antecedents, His Genius, and His Achievements* (1863), Brown reworked parts of his life story once again, prefacing the book with a "memoir of the author" that shed new light on his boyhood experiences as the bodyservant of his master's son. *The Black Man* also contains "A Man without a Name," a short story premised on the biographical fact that the name Brown's mother gave him was later denied him by his owners. Through this fictionalization of his life as a slave and a fugitive, Brown revised his story into something that could represent the lives of many whose names would never be known to history.

Brown's final autobiography, *My Southern Home: or, The South and Its People* (1880), returned again to the scene of Brown's experience as a slave, not so much to retrace his own steps from bondage to freedom but rather to characterize from an intimate perspective the complex interrelationships between blacks and whites that made the South, both before and after the Civil War, the kind of "home" that Brown could neither embrace nor expunge from his memory. *My Southern Home* went through three editions in its first three years of existence. Historians of African American literature have praised *My Southern Home* as Brown's most finished book, a fitting capstone to the literary monument he built for himself during a writing career that spanned four of the most turbulent decades of American history. William Wells Brown died in Chelsea, Massachusetts, on November 6, 1884.

Perhaps more than any other text of its kind, the *Narrative of William W. Brown* typifies in its subject matter and development the basic plot structure of the antebellum slave narrative. Brown begins with three chapters on his childhood and gradual initiation into the horrors of slavery. In Chapters 4 through 7 he comes to a mature realization of his condition as a slave, which leads to his resolution to try to seize his freedom. Chapter 8 ends with a failed escape attempt that testifies not only to Brown's dedication to freedom but also to his commitment to his mother. Brown then recalls a kind of dark night of the soul in Chapter 9, occasioned by his visit to his mother just before she is to be sold away from him forever. Although profoundly desperate over the loss of his mother and sister, Brown still does not give up hope. Instead he plots his climactic escape, which is recounted in suspenseful detail in Chapters 10 and 11. With freedom attained, the narrative concludes with Brown actively engaged in antislavery work as a lecturer for a branch of William Lloyd Garrison's American Anti-Slavery Society.

Though in many ways Brown's story may be read as a paradigm of the genre in which he wrote, his manner of telling that story is more distinctively his own. Compared to the highly self-conscious rhetorical flourishes of Frederick Douglass's narrative, Brown's decidedly understated, restrained, almost deadpan manner of recounting his life seems artless. The letter from abolitionist Edmund Quincy that serves as an introduction to Brown's *Narrative* stresses how much the white man "marvelled at" Brown's "simplicity and calmness" in describing scenes that cried out for powerful feeling. Anyone familiar with Brown's antislavery speeches knew that he was quite adept at verbal appeals to the moral outrage of his readers. But as J. C. Hathaway comments in his preface to the *Narrative,* Brown also understood that by writing with "simplicity and ingenuousness" he could set forward "many harrowing scenes" of slavery without jeopardizing his reader's "conviction of the truthfulness of the picture."

Brown's manner of self-presentation also resisted the example set by the *Narrative of the Life of Frederick Douglass*. More than any previous writer, Douglass had engendered what a later critic has called "the heroic fugitive school of American literature," in which a black rugged individualist struggles against the oppressiveness of bondage, dedicates himself single-mindedly to freedom, and overcomes all obstacles that stand between him and the goal of his indomitable striving. The turning point of Douglass's story evokes the traditional heroic ideal of male combat: the teenaged Douglass battles hand-to-hand with the slave-breaker Edward Covey, with nothing less than what Douglass termed his "manhood" hanging in the balance. Having wrested his sense of potential, pride, and worthiness for freedom from the tyrannical white man, the formerly humiliated slave is transformed into a heroic resister, a man with a mission that must inevitably triumph.

Brown seems to have almost deliberately refused to identify himself according to Douglass's myth of the heroic resister. From the outset of Brown's *Narrative*, the reader encounters admirable black men who pit themselves physically and morally against ruthless slave-owners in an effort to attain human dignity. Yet invariably they fail. The slaves who succeed against these overwhelming odds are those who learn how to use guile and deception to protect and advance their interests. Brown makes it clear that he too was a slave trickster, savvy enough to profess to his master's wife a matrimonial desire for a slave woman whom he did not love in order to divert his owners' attention away from his much stronger attachment to the idea of freedom. Even after an abortive escape attempt, when confronted with an exasperated, threatening master, Brown refuses to back down from a combat of wits. When his master demands to know why he has run away, Brown reminds the white man that he himself had authorized the slave to seek out a "good master" to whom he could hire his time for wages. So, with uppity logic, the slave maintains that he had done just that. "I had acted according to his orders. He had told me to look for a master, and I had been to look for one." The master is so disarmed by his slave's nervy reply to his bullying question that he can only answer that "he did not tell me to go to Canada to look for a master."

In sparring matches like this one, where the slave uses his wits to assert that he is and must be his own master, Brown testifies to a key element of real-world, day-to-day master-slave relationships. Only rarely did a violent physical confrontation resolve the tensions that underlay the slave's and the master's perpetual struggle for authority and power on the plantation. Much more typically the slave used a kind of mental jujitsu, similar to the tactics of the slaves' folk hero, Brer Rabbit, to deceive or divert his oppressors, thereby seizing mastery of the moment and gaining a measure of opportunity and freedom. Thus it is often the ordinary, the representative, and the non-heroic—even the anti-heroic—that comes to the fore in Brown's *Narrative*. Yet in Brown's willingness to focus on himself as a slave trickster and to explore the contradictions between a slave's survival ethic and the dominant morality of his time, the reader discovers in him a striking brand of realism.

Brown's last autobiography, *My Southern Home*, appeared at the beginning of the 1880s, a decade that ushered in the literature of the New South riding a wave of popular nostalgia for romanticized images of life on the plantation before the Civil War. The title Brown chose for his last book is faintly redolent of the sentimentality lavished on New South idealizations of the Old South era. Calling the South his "home" seems incongruous for a former fugitive slave who, after escaping the South in 1834, never tried to return to live there again. In keeping with his unpredictable kind of realism, however, Brown's preface warns that he will not indulge his readers' emotions, nor will he transform the people of his past into "heroes or heroines." Instead Brown seems intent on treating the people of the plantation, whites and blacks alike, with a fairly democratic brand of comic caricature. In the opening chapters of *My Southern Home*, readers are introduced to a number of southern character types—the indulgent master, the pompous preacher, the witty slave, the beautiful quadroon, the hypocritical slave trader, and so forth—along with some of the more pic-

turesque elements of traditional southern local color such
as slave songs, corn-shucking verbal games, and voodoo
practices. With the exception of the speculators in slaves,
the antebellum whites are not pictured as inhuman or
depraved by their status as slave masters. What disqual-
ifies them from the authority that white New South writers accorded the plantation master and mistress is not so
much any moral blot as a comic predilection for self-
deception. Dr. Gaines and his wife, the master and mistress of Poplar Farm, the center of the action in the first
half of *My Southern Home,* are made ridiculous by the
ironic disparity between their actual behavior and the
myths that they appropriate from southern tradition to
help them aggrandize themselves in the eyes of a society
much less genteel than it makes itself out to be.

In *My Southern Home* the unmaking, or rather, the
unmasking of the pretentions of white mastery on the
antebellum plantation goes hand in hand with black attempts to become masters of their own fate, often at the
expense of their owners. In chapter after chapter of the
book, the narrator records instances of the witty guile-
fulness and resistance to masterly authority endemic
among Gaines's slaves. The narrator recalls that "most
of the negroes on 'Poplar Farm' . . . thought that to deceive the whites was a religious duty." The master and
mistress "were easily deceived by their servants." A
quick-witted slave like Cato, who appears repeatedly in
My Southern Home, plays a role in Gaines's household
similar to that of a court fool in one of Shakespeare's
plays. When called upon to toast his master, he does so
in a mocking bit of doggerel:

> "De big bee flies high,
> De little bee makes de honey,
> De black man raise de cotton,
> An' de white man gets de money."

That Cato only *plays* the fool becomes clear in his successful hoodwinking of slave-catchers and a treacherous
fellow slave, who vainly try to stop him from escaping
to freedom later in the narrative.

Dinkie, the resident conjurer on Poplar Farm, could
give lessons to his master in the art of the mystification

of authority. Dinkie alone among all the men on the plantation does no work, yet he commands universal respect from both whites and blacks because he knows how to turn their superstitious fear of the devil to his own advantage. Dinkie's only weapon is talk, but against his powers of suggestion even a hard-bitten overseer loses his nerve. The conjure man "was his own master" because he played the role better than Dr. Gaines did and enforced his authority more convincingly than either the doctor or his overseer.

Capping Brown's image of an antebellum South that recognizes no higher authority than self-preservation is Pompey, the servant of the Mississippi slave trader James Walker. Walker's practice is to cheat prospective buyers of his merchandise by advertising slaves as younger and healthier than they actually are. Pompey carries out his master's will by teaching the advertised slaves how to lie about their ages and conditions. Pompey assures the whites who deal with him that there is "no bogus" about him, but when his master decides to have him flogged in the New Orleans slave prison because of carelessness, Pompey proves himself a master practitioner, as well as teacher, of the art of self-misrepresentation. First he tricks a black freeman into taking his punishment; then he tricks his master into thinking that he received the beating that Walker intended for him.

My Southern Home recounts the struggles for power and prestige among whites and blacks in the slaveocracy in a deadpan, detached tone that seldom betrays the narrator's identification or sympathy with anyone, black or white, in his memories of the South. When compared to Brown's *Narrative,* written more than thirty years earlier, *My Southern Home* seems carefully designed to deindividualize the narrator, to distance his voice and his experience from that of William Wells Brown. Crucial aspects of Brown's life as a slave that were prominently featured in the *Narrative,* such as the whipping of his mother when Brown was only a child, go unmentioned in *My Southern Home.* Dr. and Mrs. Gaines appear to be modeled on Dr. John Young and his wife Martha, on whose farm just outside St. Louis, Missouri, Brown grew up. But the indulgent tone that the narrator takes in characterizing Dr. Gaines and his treatment of his slaves is

missing in Brown's antebellum autobiographies. Other
key episodes in the *Narrative,* such as the time Brown
spent working for Walker, the slave trader, or the incident in which he tricked a free Negro into taking a beating meant for himself, are reworked in *My Southern
Home* into the life of a semi-fictional character, Pompey,
who made his first appearance in Brown's 1853 novel,
Clotel. What the veiled narrator of *My Southern Home*
implies about himself in such comments as "we had three
or four trustworthy and faithful [black] servants" at Poplar Farm lets him pass fairly easily for a genial, elderly
white southerner, the house guest, rather than the former
slave, of Dr. Gaines and his wife. The narrator's tolerant,
even-handed attitude toward much of the antebellum past,
along with some of his condescending remarks about
blacks being "better adapted to follow than to lead,"
challenge William Wells Brown's blanket denunciations
of the slave system in the *Narrative,* as well as his de-
fense, particularly in the histories he wrote, of blacks as
founders and leaders of civilization.

These differences between the *Narrative* of 1848 and
the post-Reconstruction *My Southern Home* cannot be
easily explained. Brown left no clue as to how or whether
he intended the later book to be read as a revision of the
earlier autobiography. One might wonder if, compared to
the uncompromising attack on slavery in the *Narrative,*
Brown in 1880 was not trying to accommodate himself
to a new generation of white readers in a post-
Reconstruction era increasingly indifferent to the problems of slavery and racial justice over which the Civil
War had been fought. Yet if *My Southern Home* was written in a spirit of conciliation, especially with regard to
the book's image of the relationship of blacks and whites
in slavery, why does the narrator of *My Southern Home*
denounce the increasingly white supremacist governments of the post-Reconstruction South, attributing to
them a "cause of oppression scarcely second in hatefulness to that of chattel slavery" in the Old South? Are
African American rights in even greater danger in the so-
called New South than they were in the Old? Are the
relationships of antebellum slaves and masters pictured
less harshly in *My Southern Home* in order to call attention to just how totally the post-Reconstruction South has

perfected a system whereby "complete submission to the whites is the only way for the colored man to live in peace"?

Ultimately it seems as difficult to read into *My Southern Home* a consistent and verifiable sociopolitical message as it is to miss such a message in the 1848 *Narrative*. The narrator's identity and purposes are as hard to pin down in *My Southern Home* as they seem clear and easily fixed in the 1848 *Narrative*. It may be that Brown intended *My Southern Home* to present just such problems to his readers. Perhaps he wanted his last autobiography to show that he could not and would not be pigeonholed by the popular mind as a writer whose life's meaning had already been settled (in autobiographies then more than three decades old) and who therefore had nothing new to say for or about himself. Perhaps Brown adopted the masks and complex stance toward his own past in *My Southern Home* in order to remake himself for a new post-Reconstruction era, when a black writer could no longer expect to get a hearing simply by rehearsing the familiar horrors of antebellum southern life in the manner of abolitionist literature such as the *Narrative of William W. Brown*. In its use of a narrative mask, or persona, whose racial identity is often hard to determine, *My Southern Home* strains to escape the confines of the antebellum slave narrative form, epitomized in Douglass's 1845 *Narrative*, which demanded that the slave narrator authenticate himself and his experience as a former slave and conform to a strict standard of truth-telling in order to be believed. Thus it may be that one of the most significant features of *My Southern Home* is the fact that its narrator refuses to authenticate himself or establish a standard whereby the truthfulness of his view of the South, past or present, can readily be confirmed.

William Wells Brown proved much less adept at exploiting the literary possibilities of masking than later black southern writers, such as Charles Chesnutt in his turn-of-the-century "conjure stories," which are ostensibly narrated by a white man, and James Weldon Johnson, whose *The Autobiography of an Ex-Colored Man* (1912) would become a classic confession of a black man who had adopted the mask of whiteness. But as a transitional text that negotiates the space between the fact-orientation of the nineteenth-century slave narrative and the fictional art of early twentieth-century figures like Chesnutt and Johnson, *My Southern Home* occupies a signal position in the history of African American narrative literature. When paired with the *Narrative of William W. Brown,* these two autobiographies reveal where the African American narrative tradition was coming from and where it was heading, as it evolved out of the classic era of the fugitive slave narrative and moved into its first great period of fiction at the beginning of the twentieth century.

—*William L. Andrews*

A Note on the Text

The text of the *Narrative of William W. Brown, A Fugitive Slave* is reprinted from the second edition, which was published by the Boston office of the American Anti-Slavery Society in February 1848. A revised and expanded version of the original 1847 narrative, the second edition appends two essays by Brown that give the reader a good indication of the author's abilities as an expository writer. Although deleted in 1848, the dedication to Wells Brown, which begins the 1847 edition of the *Narrative*, has been included in this edition.

The text of *My Southern Home* is based on the third edition, which was published by Brown himself (under his wife's name) in Boston in 1882. The third edition of *My Southern Home* is an exact reprint of the first edition of that book, which Brown published in Boston in May 1880.

Inconsistencies in Brown's autobiographies in the italicizing of the names of boats and newspapers and in the capitalizing of the Bible and the Constitution have been regularized in this edition. All footnotes are those of Brown himself.

—*William L. Andrews*

NARRATIVE

OF

WILLIAM W. BROWN,

A

FUGITIVE SLAVE.

————

WRITTEN BY HIMSELF

————

> ———— Is there not some chosen curse,
> Some hidden thunder in the stores of heaven,
> Red with uncommon wrath, to blast the man
> Who gains his fortune from the blood of souls?
>
> Cowper.

SECOND EDITION, ENLARGED

BOSTON:
PUBLISHED AT THE ANTI-SLAVERY OFFICE,
No. 21 Cornhill
1848

Dedication to First Edition

Note to the Second Edition

The first edition, of three thousand copies, of this little work was sold in less than six months from the time of its publication. Encouraged by the rapid sale of the first, and by a demand for a second, edition, the author has been led to enlarge the work by the addition of matter which, he thinks, will add materially to its value.

And if it shall be instrumental in helping to undo the heavy burdens, and letting the oppressed go free, he will have accomplished the great desire of his heart in publishing this work.

Letter
From
Edmund Quincy, Esq.

Dedham, July 1, 1847.

To William W. Brown

My Dear Friend:—I heartily thank you for the privilege of reading the manuscript of your Narrative. I have read it with deep interest and strong emotion. I am much mistaken if it be not greatly successful and eminently useful. It presents a different phase of the infernal slave-system from that portrayed in the admirable story of Mr. Douglass, and gives us a glimpse of its hideous cruelties in other portions of its domain.

Your opportunities of observing the workings of this accursed system have been singularly great. Your experiences in the Field, in the House, and especially on the River in the service of the slave-trader, Walker, have been such as few individuals have had;—no one, certainly, who has been competent to describe them. What I have admired, and marvelled at, in your Narrative, is the simplicity and calmness with which you describe scenes and actions which might well "move the very stones to rise and mutiny" against the National Institution which makes them possible.

You will perceive that I have made very sparing use of your flattering permission to alter what you had written. To correct a few errors, which appeared to be merely clerical ones, committed in the hurry of composition under unfavorable circumstances, and to suggest a few curtailments, is all that I have ventured to do. I should be a bold man, as well as a vain one, if I should attempt to improve your descriptions of what you have seen and suffered. Some of the scenes are not unworthy of De Foe himself.

I trust and believe that your Narrative will have a wide circulation. I am sure it deserves it. At least, a man must be differently constituted from me, who can rise from the perusal of your Narrative without feeling that he understands slavery better, and hates it worse, than he ever did before.

I am, very faithfully and respectfully,

Your friend,

EDMUND QUINCY

fered. Some of the scenes are an eyewitness of the fact himself.

I trust and believe that your Narrative will have a wide circulation. I am sure it deserves it. At least a man must be differently constituted from me, who can read the thrilling narrative which it contains, without having his sympathies enlisted in behalf of the slave, and his indignation kindled against his oppressor.

PREFACE

The friends of freedom may well congratulate each other on the appearance of the following Narrative. It adds another volume to the rapidly increasing anti-slavery literature of the age. It has been remarked by a close observer of human nature, "Let me make the songs of a nation, and I care not who makes its laws"; and it may with equal truth be said, that, among a reading people like our own, their books will at least give character to their laws. It is an influence which goes forth noiselessly upon its mission, but fails not to find its way to many a warm heart, to kindle on the altar thereof the fires of freedom, which will one day break forth in a living flame to consume oppression.

This little book is a voice from the prison-house, unfolding the deeds of darkness which are there perpetrated. Our cause has received efficient aid from this source. The names of those who have come from thence, and battled manfully for the right, need not to be recorded here. The works of some of them are an enduring monument of praise, and their perpetual record shall be found in the grateful hearts of the redeemed bondman.

Few persons have had greater facilities for becoming acquainted with slavery, in all its horrible aspects, than WILLIAM W. BROWN. He has been behind the curtain. He has visited its secret chambers. Its iron has entered his own soul. The dearest ties of nature have been riven in his own person. A mother has been cruelly scourged before his own eyes. A father—alas! slaves have no father. A brother has been made the subject of its tender mercies. A sister has been given up to the irresponsible control of the pale-faced oppressor. This nation looks on approvingly. The American Union sanctions the deed. The Constitution shields the criminals. American religion sanctifies the crime. But the tide is turning. Already, a mighty under-current is sweeping onward. The voice of warning, of remonstrance, of rebuke, of entreaty, has gone forth. Hand is linked in hand, and heart mingles with heart, in this great work of the slave's deliverance.

The convulsive throes of the monster, even now, give evidence of deep wounds.

The writer of this Narrative was hired by his master to a *"soul-driver,"* and has witnessed all the horrors of the traffic, from the buying up of human cattle in the slave-breeding states, which produced a constant scene of separating the victims from all those whom they loved, to their final sale in the southern market, to be worked up in seven years, or given over to minister to the lust of southern *Christians*.

Many harrowing scenes are graphically portrayed; and yet with that simplicity and ingenuousness which carries with it a conviction of the truthfulness of the picture.

This book will do much to unmask those who have "clothed themselves in the livery of the court of heaven" to cover up the enormity of their deeds.

During the past three years, the author has devoted his entire energies to the anti-slavery cause. Laboring under all the disabilities and disadvantages growing out of his education in slavery—subjected, as he had been from his birth, to all the wrongs and deprivations incident to his condition—he yet went forth, impelled to the work by a love of liberty—stimulated by the remembrance of his own sufferings—urged on by the consideration that a mother, brothers, and sister, were still grinding in the prison-house of bondage, in common with three millions of our Father's children—sustained by an unfaltering faith in the omnipotence of truth and the final triumph of justice—to plead the cause of the slave; and by the eloquence of earnestness carried conviction to many minds, and enlisted the sympathy and secured the cooperation of many to the cause.

His labors have been chiefly confined to Western New York, where he has secured many warm friends, by his untiring zeal, persevering energy, continued fidelity, and universal kindness.

Reader, are you an Abolitionist? What have you done for the slave? What are you doing in his behalf? What do you purpose to do? There is a great work before us! Who will be an idler now? This is the great humanitary movement of the age, swallowing up, for the time being, all other questions, comparatively speaking. The course of human events, in obedience to the unchangeable laws of our being, is fast hastening the final crisis, and

"Have ye chosen, O my people, on whose party ye shall stand,
Ere the Doom from its worn sandal shakes the dust against our land?"

Are you a Christian? This is the carrying out of practical Christianity; and there is no other. Christianity is *practical* in its very nature and essence. It is a life, springing out of a soul imbued with its spirit. Are you a friend of the missionary cause? This is the greatest missionary enterprise of the day. Three millions of *Christian,* law-manufactured heathen are longing for the glad tidings of the gospel of freedom. Are you a friend of the Bible? Come, then, and help us to restore to these millions, whose eyes have been bored out by slavery, their sight, that they may see to read the Bible. Do you love God whom you have not seen? Then manifest that love, by restoring to your brother whom you have seen his rightful inheritance, of which he has been so long and so cruelly deprived.

It is not for a single generation alone, numbering three millions—sublime as would be that effort—that we are working. It is for Humanity, the wide world over, not only now, but for all coming time, and all future generations:—

"For he who settles Freedom's principles,
Writes the death-warrant of all tyranny."

It is a vast work—a glorious enterprise—worthy the unswerving devotion of the entire life-time of the great and the good.

Slaveholding and slaveholders must be rendered disreputable and odious. They must be stripped of their respectability and Christian reputation. They must be treated as "MEN-STEALERS—guilty of the highest kind of theft, and sinners of the first rank.'' Their more guilty accomplices in the persons of *northern apologists*, both in Church and State, must be placed in the same category. Honest men must be made to look upon their crimes with the same abhorrence and loathing with which they regard the less guilty robber and assassin, until

"The common damned shun their society,
And look upon themselves as fiends less foul."

When a just estimate is placed upon the crime of slaveholding, the work will have been accomplished, and the glorious day ushered in—

"When man nor woman in all our wide domain,
Shall buy, or sell, or hold, or be a slave."

—J. C. HATHAWAY

Farmington, N. Y., 1847.

NARRATIVE

CHAPTER I

I was born in Lexington, Ky. The man who stole me as soon as I was born, recorded the births of all the infants which he claimed to be born his property, in a book which he kept for that purpose. My mother's name was Elizabeth. She had seven children, viz.: Solomon, Leander, Benjamin, Joseph, Millford, Elizabeth, and myself. No two of us were children of the same father. My father's name, as I learned from my mother, was George Higgins. He was a white man, a relative of my master, and connected with some of the first families in Kentucky.

My master owned about forty slaves, twenty-five of whom were field hands. He removed from Kentucky to Missouri when I was quite young, and settled thirty or forty miles above St. Charles, on the Missouri, where, in addition to his practice as a physician, he carried on milling, merchandizing and farming. He had a large farm, the principal productions of which were tobacco and hemp. The slave cabins were situated on the back part of the farm, with the house of the overseer, whose name was Grove Cook, in their midst. He had the entire charge of the farm, and having no family, was allowed a woman to keep house for him, whose business it was to deal out the provisions for the hands.

A woman was also kept at the quarters to do the cooking for the field hands, who were summoned to their unrequited toil every morning at four o'clock, by the ringing of the bell, hung on a post near the house of the overseer. They were allowed half an hour to eat their breakfast, and get to the field. At half past four a horn was blown by the overseer, which was his signal to commence work; and every one that was not on the spot at the time, had to receive ten lashes from the negro-whip, with which the overseer always went armed. The handle was about three feet long, with the butt-end filled with lead, and the lash, six or seven feet in length, made of cow-hide, with platted wire on the end of it. This whip was put in requisition very frequently and freely, and a small offence on the part of a slave furnished an occasion for its use. During the time that Mr. Cook was overseer, I was a house servant—a situation preferable to that of a field hand, as I was better fed, better clothed, and not obliged to rise at the ringing of the bell, but about half an hour after. I have often laid and heard the crack of the whip, and the screams of the slave. My mother was a field hand, and one morning was ten or fifteen minutes behind the others in getting into the field. As soon as she reached the spot where they were at work, the overseer commenced whipping her. She cried, "Oh! pray—Oh! pray—Oh! pray"—these are generally the words of slaves, when imploring mercy at the hands of their oppressors. I heard her voice, and knew it, and jumped out of my bunk, and went to the door. Though the field was some distance from the house, I could hear every crack of the whip, and every groan and cry of my poor mother. I remained at the door, not daring to venture any further. The cold chills ran over me, and I wept aloud. After giving her ten lashes, the sound of the whip ceased, and I returned to my bed, and found no consolation but in my tears. Experience has taught me that nothing can be more heart-rending than for one to see a dear and beloved mother or sister tortured, and to hear their cries, and not be able to render them assistance. But such is the position which an American slave occupies.

My master, being a politician, soon found those who were ready to put him into office, for the favors he could render them; and a few years after his arrival in Missouri he was elected to a seat in the legislature. In his absence from home everything was left in charge of Mr. Cook, the overseer, and he soon became more tyrannical and cruel. Among the slaves on the plantation was one by the name of Randall. He was a man about six feet high, and well-proportioned, and known as a man of great strength and power. He was considered the most valuable and able-bodied slave on the plantation; but no matter how good or useful a slave may be, he seldom escapes the lash. But it was not so with Randall. He had been on the plantation since my earliest recollection, and I had never known of his being flogged. No thanks were due to the master or overseer for this. I have often heard him declare that no white man should ever whip him—that he would die first.

Cook, from the time that he came upon the plantation, had frequently declared that he could and would flog any nigger that was put into the field to work under him. My master had repeatedly told him not to attempt to whip Randall, but he was determined to try it. As soon as he was left sole dictator, he thought the time had come to put his threats into execution. He soon began to find fault with Randall, and threatened to whip him if he did not do better. One day he gave him a very hard task—more than he could possibly do; and at night, the task not being performed, he told Randall that he should remember him the next morning. On the following morning, after the hands had taken breakfast, Cook called out to Randall, and told him that he intended to whip him, and ordered him to cross his hands and be tied. Randall asked why he wished to whip him. He answered, because he had not finished his task the day before. Randall said that the task was too great, or he should have done it. Cook said it made no difference—he should whip him. Randall stood silent for a moment, and then said, "Mr. Cook, I have always tried to please you since you have been on the plantation, and I find you are determined not to be satisfied with my work, let me do as well as I may. No man has laid hands on me, to whip me, for the last ten years, and I have long since come to the conclusion not to be whipped by any man living." Cook, finding by Randall's determined look and gestures, that he would resist, called three of the hands from their work, and commanded them to seize Randall, and tie him. The hands stood still;—they knew Randall—and they also knew him to be a powerful man, and were afraid to grapple with him. As soon as Cook had ordered the men to seize him, Randall turned to them, and said—"Boys, you all know me; you know that I can handle any three of you, and the man that lays hands on me shall die. This white man can't whip me himself, and therefore he has called you to help him." The overseer was unable to prevail upon them to seize and secure Randall, and finally ordered them all to go to their work together.

Nothing was said to Randall by the overseer for more than a week. One morning, however, while the hands were at work in the field, he came into it, accompanied by three friends of his, Thompson, Woodbridge and Jones. They came up to where Randall was at work, and Cook ordered him to leave his work, and go with them to the barn. He refused to go; whereupon he was attacked by the overseer and his companions, when he turned upon them, and laid them, one after another, prostrate on the ground. Woodbridge drew out his pistol, and fired at him, and brought him to the ground by a pistol ball. The others rushed upon him with their clubs, and beat him over the head and face, until they succeeded in tying him. He was then taken to the barn, and tied to a beam. Cook gave him over one hundred lashes with a heavy cowhide, had him washed with salt and water, and left him tied during the day. The next day he was untied, and taken to a blacksmith's shop, and had a ball and chain attached to his leg. He was compelled to labor in the field, and perform the same amount of work that the other hands did. When his master returned home, he was much pleased to find that Randall had been subdued in his absence.

CHAPTER II

Soon afterwards, my master removed to the city of St. Louis, and purchased a farm four miles from there, which he placed under the charge of an overseer by the name of Friend Haskell. He was a regular Yankee from New England. The Yankees are noted for making the most cruel overseers.

My mother was hired out in the city, and I was also hired out there to Major Freeland, who kept a public house. He was formerly from Virginia, and was a horse-racer, cock-fighter, gambler, and withal an inveterate drunkard. There were ten or twelve servants in the house, and when he was present, it was cut and slash—knock down and drag out. In his fits of anger, he would take up a chair, and throw it at a servant; and in his more rational moments, when he wished to chastise one, he would tie them up in the smoke-house, and whip them; after which, he would cause a fire to be made of tobacco stems, and smoke them. This he called "*Virginia play.*"

I complained to my master of the treatment which I received from Major Freeland; but it made no difference. He cared nothing about it, so long as he received the money for my labor. After living with Major Freeland five or six months, I ran away, and went into the woods back of the city; and when night came on, I made my way to my master's farm, but was afraid to be seen, knowing that if Mr. Haskell, the overseer, should discover me, I should be again carried back to Major Freeland; so I kept in the woods. One day, while in the woods, I heard the barking and howling of dogs, and in a short time they came so near that I knew them to be the bloodhounds of Major Benjamin O'Fallon. He kept five or six, to hunt runaway slaves with.

As soon as I was convinced that it was them, I knew

there was no chance of escape. I took refuge in the top of a tree, and the hounds were soon at its base, and there remained until the hunters came up in a half or three quarters of an hour afterwards. There were two men with the dogs, who, as soon as they came up, ordered me to descend. I came down, was tied, and taken to St. Louis jail. Major Freeland soon made his appearance, and took me out, and ordered me to follow him, which I did. After we returned home, I was tied up in the smoke-house, and was very severely whipped. After the major had flogged me to his satisfaction, he sent out his son Robert, a young man eighteen or twenty years of age, to see that I was well smoked. He made a fire of tobacco stems, which soon set me to coughing and sneezing. This, Robert told me, was the way his father used to do to his slaves in Virginia. After giving me what they conceived to be a decent smoking, I was untied and again set to work.

Robert Freeland was a "chip of the old block." Though quite young, it was not unfrequently that he came home in a state of intoxication. He is now, I believe, a popular commander of a steamboat on the Mississippi River. Major Freeland soon after failed in business, and I was put on board the steamboat *Missouri*, which plied between St. Louis and Galena. The commander of the boat was William B. Culver. I remained on her during the sailing season, which was the most pleasant time for me that I had ever experienced. At the close of navigation I was hired to Mr. John Colburn, keeper of the Missouri Hotel. He was from one of the free states; but a more inveterate hater of the negro I do not believe ever walked God's green earth. This hotel was at that time one of the largest in the city, and there were employed in it twenty or thirty servants, mostly slaves.

Mr. Colburn was very abusive, not only to the servants, but to his wife also, who was an excellent woman, and one from whom I never knew a servant to receive a harsh word; but never did I know a kind one to a servant from her husband. Among the slaves employed in the hotel was one by the name of Aaron, who belonged to Mr. John F. Darby, a lawyer. Aaron was the knife-cleaner. One day, one of the knives was put on the table, not as clean as it might have been. Mr. Colburn, for this offence, tied Aaron up in the wood-house, and gave him over fifty lashes on the bare back with a cow-hide, after which, he made me wash him down with rum. This seemed to put him into more agony than the whipping. After being untied he went home to his master, and complained of the treatment which he had received. Mr. Darby would give no heed to anything he had to say, but sent him directly back. Colburn, learning that he had been to his master with complaints, tied him up again, and gave him a more severe whipping than before. The poor fellow's back was literally cut to pieces; so much so, that he was not able to work for ten or twelve days.

There was, also, among the servants, a girl whose master resided in the country. Her name was Patsey. Mr. Colburn tied her up one evening, and whipped her until several of the boarders came out and begged him to desist. The reason for whipping her was this. She was engaged to be married to a man belonging to Major William Christy, who resided four or five miles north of the city. Mr. Colburn had forbid her to see John Christy. The reason of this was said to be the regard which he himself had for Patsey. She went to meeting that evening, and John returned home with her. Mr. Colburn had intended to flog John, if he came within the inclosure; but John knew too well the temper of his rival, and kept at a safe distance:—so he took vengeance on the poor girl. If all the slave-drivers had been called together, I do not think a more cruel man than John Colburn—and he too a northern man—could have been found among them.

While living at the Missouri hotel, a circumstance occurred which caused me great unhappiness. My master sold my mother, and all her children, except myself. They were sold to different persons in the city of St. Louis.

CHAPTER III

I was soon after taken from Mr. Colburn's, and hired to Elijah P. Lovejoy, who was at that time publisher and editor of the St. Louis *Times*. My work, while with him, was mainly in the printing office, waiting on the hands, working the press, &c. Mr. Lovejoy was a very good man, and decidedly the best master that I had ever had. I am chiefly indebted to him, and to my employment in the printing office, for what little learning I obtained while in slavery.

Though slavery is thought, by some, to be mild in Missouri, when compared with the cotton, sugar and rice growing states, yet no part of our slaveholding country is more noted for the barbarity of its inhabitants than St. Louis. It was here that Col. Harney, a United States officer, whipped a slave woman to death. It was here that Francis McIntosh, a free colored man from Pittsburg, was taken from the steamboat Flora and burned at the stake. During a residence of eight years in this city, numerous cases of extreme cruelty came under my own observation; to record them all would occupy more space than could possibly be allowed in this little volume. I shall, therefore, give but a few more in addition to what I have already related.

Capt. J. B. Brant, who resided near my master, had a slave named John. He was his body servant, carriage driver, &c. On one occasion, while driving his master through the city—the streets being very muddy, and the horses going at a rapid rate—some mud spattered upon a gentleman by the name of Robert More. More was determined to be revenged. Some three or four months after this occurrence, he purchased John, for the express purpose, as he said, "to tame the d——d nigger." After the purchase he took him to a blacksmith's shop, and had a ball and chain fastened to his leg, and then put him to driving a yoke of oxen, and kept him at hard labor, until the iron around his leg was so worn into the flesh, that it was thought mortification would ensue. In addition to this, John told me that his master whipped him regularly three times a week for the first two months:—and all this to "*tame him.*" A more noble looking man than he was not to be found in all St. Louis, before he fell into the hands of More; and a more degraded and spirit-crushed looking being was never seen on a southern plantation, after he had been subjected to this "*taming*" process for three months. The last time that I saw him, he had nearly lost the entire use of his limbs.

While living with Mr. Lovejoy, I was often sent on errands to the office of the Missouri *Republican,* published by Mr. Edward Charles. Once, while returning to the office with type, I was attacked by several large boys, sons of slave-holders, who pelted me with snow-balls. Having the heavy form of type in my hands, I could not make my escape by running; so I laid down the type and gave them battle. They gathered around me, pelting me with stones and sticks, until they overpowered me, and would have captured me, if I had not resorted to my heels. Upon my retreat they took possession of the type; and what to do to regain it I could not devise. Knowing Mr. Lovejoy to be a very humane man, I went to the office and laid the case before him. He told me to remain in the office. He took one of the apprentices with him and went after the type, and soon returned with it; but on his return informed me that Samuel McKinney had told him he would whip me, because I had hurt his boy. Soon after, McKinney was seen making his way to the office by one of the printers, who informed me of the fact, and I made my escape through the back door.

McKinney not being able to find me on his arrival, left the office in a great rage, swearing that he would whip me to death. A few days after, as I was walking along Main street, he seized me by the collar, and struck me over the head five or six times with a large cane, which caused the blood to gush from my nose and ears in such a manner that my clothes were completely saturated with blood. After beating me to his satisfaction he let me go, and I returned to the office so weak from the loss of blood that Mr. Lovejoy sent me home to my master. It was five weeks before I was able to walk again. During this time it was necessary to have some one to supply my place at the office, and I lost the situation.

After my recovery, I was hired to Capt. Otis Reynolds, as a waiter on board the steamboat *Enterprise,* owned by Messrs. John and Edward Walsh, commission merchants at St. Louis. This boat was then running on the upper Mississippi. My employment on board was to wait on gentlemen, and the captain being a good man, the situation was a pleasant one to me:—but in passing from place to place, and seeing new faces every day, and knowing that they could go where they pleased, I soon became unhappy, and several times thought of leaving the boat at some landing place, and trying to make my escape to Canada, which I had heard much about as a place where the slave might live, be free, and be protected.

But whenever such thoughts would come into my mind, my resolution would soon be shaken by the remembrance that my dear mother was a slave in St. Louis, and I could not bear the idea of leaving her in that condition. She had often taken me upon her knee, and told me how she had carried me upon her back to the field when I was an infant—how often she had been whipped for leaving her work to nurse me—and how happy I would appear when she would take me into her arms. When these thoughts came over me, I would resolve never to leave the land of slavery without my mother. I thought that to leave her in slavery, after she had undergone and suffered so much for me, would be proving recreant to the duty which I owed to her. Besides this, I had three brothers and a sister there—two of my brothers having died.

My mother, my brothers Joseph and Millford, and my sister Elizabeth, belonged to Mr. Isaac Mansfield, formerly from one of the free states, (Massachusetts, I believe.) He was a tinner by trade, and carried on a large manufacturing establishment. Of all my relatives, mother was first, and sister next. One evening, while visiting them, I made some allusion to a proposed journey to Canada, and sister took her seat by my side, and taking my hand in hers, said, with tears in her eyes—

"Brother, you are not going to leave mother and your dear sister here without a friend, are you?"

I looked into her face, as the tears coursed swiftly down her cheeks, and bursting into tears myself, said—

"No, I will never desert you and mother!"

She clasped my hand in hers, and said—

"Brother, you have often declared that you would not end your days in slavery. I see no possible way in which you can escape with us; and now, brother, you are on a steamboat where there is some chance for you to escape to a land of liberty. I beseech you not to let us hinder you. If we cannot get our liberty, we do not wish to be the means of keeping you from a land of freedom."

I could restrain my feelings no longer, and an outburst of my own feelings caused her to cease speaking upon that subject. In opposition to their wishes, I pledged myself not to leave them in the hand of the oppressor. I took leave of them, and returned to the boat, and laid down in my bunk; but "sleep departed from mine eyes, and slumber from mine eyelids."

A few weeks after, on our downward passage, the boat took on board, at Hannibal, a drove of slaves, bound for the New Orleans market. They numbered from fifty to sixty, consisting of men and women from eighteen to forty years of age. A drove of slaves on a southern steamboat, bound for the cotton or sugar regions, is an occurrence so common, that no one, not even the passengers, appear to notice it, though they clank their chains at every step. There was, however, one in this gang that attracted the attention of the passengers and crew. It was a beautiful girl, apparently about twenty years of age, perfectly white, with straight light hair and blue eyes. But it was not the whiteness of her skin that created such sensation among those who gazed upon her—it was her almost unparalleled beauty. She had been on the boat but a short time, before the attention of all the passengers, including the ladies, had been called to her, and the common topic of conversation was about the beautiful slave-girl. She was not in chains. The man who claimed this article of human merchandise was a Mr. Walker—a well known slave-trader, residing in St. Louis. There was a general anxiety among the passengers and crew to learn the his-

tory of the girl. Her master kept close by her side, and
it would have been considered impudent for any of the
passengers to have spoken to her, and the crew were not
allowed to have any conversation with them. When we
reached St. Louis, the slaves were removed to a boat
bound for New Orleans, and the history of the beautiful
slave-girl remained a mystery.

I remained on the boat during the season, and it was
not an unfrequent occurrence to have on board gangs of
slaves on their way to the cotton, sugar and rice plantations of the south.

Toward the latter part of the summer Captain Reynolds
left the boat, and I was sent home. I was then placed on
the farm, under Mr. Haskell, the overseer. As I had been
some time out of the field, and not accustomed to work
in the burning sun, it was very hard; but I was compelled
to keep up with the best of the hands.

I found a great difference between the work in the
steamboat cabin and that in a corn-field.

My master, who was then living in the city, soon after
removed to the farm, when I was taken out of the field
to work in the house as a waiter. Though his wife was
very peevish, and hard to please, I much preferred to be
under her control than the overseer's. They brought with
them Mr. Sloane, a Presbyterian minister; Miss Martha
Tulley, a niece of theirs from Kentucky; and their nephew
William. The latter had been in the family a number of
years, but the others were all newcomers.

Mr. Sloane was a young minister, who had been at the
south but a short time, and it seemed as if his whole aim
was to please the slaveholders, especially my master and
mistress. He was intending to make a visit during the
winter, and he not only tried to please them, but I think
he succeeded admirably. When they wanted singing, he
sung; when they wanted praying, he prayed; when they
wanted a story told, he told a story. Instead of his teaching my master theology, my master taught theology to
him. While I was with Captain Reynolds my master "got
religion," and new laws were made on the plantation.
Formerly we had the privilege of hunting, fishing, making splint brooms, baskets, &c., on Sunday; but this

was all stopped. Every Sunday we were all compelled to attend meeting. Master was so religious that he induced some others to join him in hiring a preacher to preach to the slaves.

CHAPTER IV

My master had family worship, night and morning. At night the slaves were called in to attend; but in the mornings they had to be at their work, and master did all the praying. My master and mistress were great lovers of mint julep, and every morning, a pitcher-full was made, of which they all partook freely, not excepting little master William. After drinking freely all around, they would have family worship, and then breakfast. I cannot say but I loved the julep as well as any of them, and during prayer was always careful to seat myself close to the table where it stood, so as to help myself when they were all busily engaged in their devotions. By the time prayer was over, I was about as happy as any of them. A sad accident happened one morning. In helping myself, and at the same time keeping an eye on my old mistress, I accidentally let the pitcher fall upon the floor, breaking it in pieces, and spilling the contents. This was a bad affair for me; for as soon as prayer was over, I was taken and severely chastised.

My master's family consisted of himself, his wife, and their nephew, William Moore. He was taken into the family when only a few weeks of age. His name being that of my own, mine was changed for the purpose of giving precedence to his, though I was his senior by ten or twelve years. The plantation being four miles from the city, I had to drive the family to church. I always dreaded the approach of the Sabbath; for, during service, I was obliged to stand by the horses in the hot, broiling sun, or in the rain, just as it happened.

One Sabbath, as we were driving past the house of D. D. Page, a gentleman who owned a large baking establishment, as I was sitting upon the box of the carriage, which was very much elevated, I saw Mr. Page pursuing a slave around the yard with a long whip, cutting him at every jump. The man soon escaped from the yard, and was followed by Mr. Page. They came running past us, and the slave, perceiving that he would be overtaken, stopped suddenly, and Page stumbled over him, and falling on the stone pavement, fractured one of his legs, which crippled him for life. The same gentleman, but a short time previous, tied up a woman of his, by the name of Delphia, and whipped her nearly to death; yet he was a deacon in the Baptist church, in good and regular standing. Poor Delphia! I was well acquainted with her, and called to see her while upon her sick bed; and I shall never forget her appearance. She was a member of the same church with her master.

Soon after this, I was hired out to Mr. Walker, the same man whom I have mentioned as having carried a gang of slaves down the river on the steamboat *Enterprise*. Seeing me in the capacity of a steward on the boat, and thinking that I would make a good hand to take care of slaves, he determined to have me for that purpose; and finding that my master would not sell me, he hired me for the term of one year.

When I learned the fact of my having been hired to a negro speculator, or a "soul driver," as they are generally called among slaves, no one can tell my emotions. Mr. Walker had offered a high price for me, as I afterwards learned, but I suppose my master was restrained from selling me by the fact that I was a near relative of his. On entering the service of Mr. Walker, I found that my opportunity of getting to a land of liberty was gone, at least for the time being. He had a gang of slaves in readiness to start for New Orleans, and in a few days we were on our journey. I am at a loss for language to express my feelings on that occasion. Although my master had told me that he had not sold me, and Mr. Walker had told me that he had not purchased me, I did not believe them; and not until I had been to New Orleans, and was on my return, did I believe that I was not sold.

There was on the boat a large room on the lower deck, in which the slaves were kept, men and women, promiscuously—all chained two and two, and a strict watch kept that they did not get loose; for cases have occurred in which slaves have got off their chains, and made their escape at landing places, while the boats were taking in wood;—and with all our care, we lost one woman who had been taken from her husband and children, and having no desire to live without them, in the agony of her soul jumped overboard, and drowned herself. She was not chained.

It was almost impossible to keep that part of the boat clean.

On landing at Natchez, the slaves were all carried to the slave-pen, and there kept one week, during which time several of them were sold. Mr. Walker fed his slaves well. We took on board at St. Louis several hundred pounds of bacon (smoked meat) and corn-meal, and his slaves were better fed than slaves generally were in Natchez, so far as my observation extended.

At the end of a week, we left for New Orleans, the place of our final destination, which we reached in two days. Here the slaves were placed in a negro-pen, where those who wished to purchase could call and examine them. The negro-pen is a small yard, surrounded by buildings, from fifteen to twenty feet wide, with the exception of a large gate with iron bars. The slaves are kept in the building during the night, and turned out into the yard during the day. After the best of the stock was sold at private sale at the pen, the balance were taken to the Exchange Coffee-House Auction Rooms, kept by Isaac L. McCoy, and sold at public auction. After the sale of this lot of slaves, we left New Orleans for St. Louis.

CHAPTER V

On our arrival at St. Louis I went to Dr. Young, and told him that I did not wish to live with Mr. Walker any longer. I was heart-sick at seeing my fellow-creatures bought and sold. But the Dr. had hired me for the year, and stay I must. Mr. Walker again commenced purchasing another gang of slaves. He bought a man of Colonel John O'Fallon, who resided in the suburbs of the city. This man had a wife and three children. As soon as the purchase was made, he was put in jail for safe keeping, until we should be ready to start for New Orleans. His wife visited him while there, several times, and several times when she went for that purpose was refused admittance.

In the course of eight or nine weeks Mr. Walker had his cargo of human flesh made up. There was in this lot a number of old men and women, some of them with gray locks. We left St. Louis in the steamboat *Carlton,* Captain Swan, bound for New Orleans. On our way down, and before we reached Rodney, the place where we made our first stop, I had to prepare the old slaves for market. I was ordered to have the old men's whiskers shaved off, and the grey hairs plucked out where they were not too numerous, in which case he had a preparation of blacking to color it, and with a blacking brush we would put it on. This was new business to me, and was performed in a room where the passengers could not see us. These slaves were also taught how old they were by Mr. Walker, and after going through the blacking process they looked ten or fifteen years younger; and I am sure that some of those who purchased slaves of Mr. Walker were dreadfully cheated, especially in the ages of the slaves which they bought.

We landed at Rodney, and the slaves were driven to the pen in the back part of the village. Several were sold at this place, during our stay of four or five days, when we proceeded to Natchez. There we landed at night, and the gang were put in the warehouse until morning, when they were driven to the pen. As soon as the slaves are put in these pens, swarms of planters may be seen in and about them. They knew when Walker was expected, as he always had the time advertised beforehand when he would be in Rodney, Natchez, and New Orleans. These were the principal places where he offered his slaves for sale.

When at Natchez the second time, I saw a slave very cruelly whipped. He belonged to a Mr. Broadwell, a merchant who kept a store on the wharf. The slave's name was Lewis. I had known him several years, as he was formerly from St. Louis. We were expecting a steamboat down the river, in which we were to take passage for New Orleans. Mr. Walker sent me to the landing to watch for the boat, ordering me to inform him on its arrival. While there I went into the store to see Lewis. I saw a slave in the store, and asked him where Lewis was. Said he, "They have got Lewis hanging between the heavens and the earth." I asked him what he meant by that. He told me to go into the warehouse and see. I went in, and found Lewis there. He was tied up to a beam, with his toes just touching the floor. As there was no one in the warehouse but himself, I inquired the reason of his being in that situation. He said Mr. Broadwell had sold his wife to a planter six miles from the city, and that he had been to visit her—that he went in the night, expecting to return before daylight, and went without his master's permission. The patrol had taken him up before he reached his wife. He was put in jail, and his master had to pay for his catching and keeping, and that was what he was tied up for.

Just as he finished his story, Mr. Broadwell came in, and inquired what I was doing there. I knew not what to say, and while I was thinking what reply to make he struck me over the head with the cowhide, the end of which struck me over my right eye, sinking deep into the flesh, leaving a scar which I carry to this day. Before I visited Lewis he had received fifty lashes. Mr. Broadwell gave him fifty lashes more after I came out, as I was afterwards informed by Lewis himself.

The next day we proceeded to New Orleans, and put the gang in the same negro-pen which we occupied before. In a short time the planters came flocking to the pen to purchase slaves. Before the slaves were exhibited for sale, they were dressed and driven out into the yard. Some were set to dancing, some to jumping, some to singing, and some to playing cards. This was done to make them appear cheerful and happy. My business was to see that they were placed in those situations before the arrival of the purchasers, and I have often set them to dancing when their cheeks were wet with tears. As slaves were in good demand at that time, they were all soon disposed of, and we again set out for St. Louis.

On our arrival, Mr. Walker purchased a farm five or six miles from the city. He had no family, but made a housekeeper of one of his female slaves. Poor Cynthia! I knew her well. She was a quadroon, and one of the most beautiful women I ever saw. She was a native of St. Louis, and bore an irreproachable character for virtue and propriety of conduct. Mr. Walker bought her for the New Orleans market, and took her down with him on one of the trips that I made with him. Never shall I forget the circumstances of that voyage! On the first night that we were on board the steamboat, he directed me to put her into a state-room he had provided for her, apart from the other slaves. I had seen too much of the workings of slavery not to know what this meant. I accordingly watched him into the state-room, and listened to hear what passed between them. I heard him make his base offers, and her reject them. He told her that if she would accept his vile proposals, he would take her back with him to St. Louis, and establish her as his housekeeper on his farm. But if she persisted in rejecting them, he would sell her as a field hand on the worst plantation on the river. Neither threats nor bribes prevailed, however, and he retired, disappointed of his prey.

The next morning poor Cynthia told me what had passed, and bewailed her sad fate with floods of tears. I comforted and encouraged her all I could; but I foresaw but too well what the result must be. Without entering into any further particulars, suffice it to say that Walker performed his part of the contract at that time. He took her back to St. Louis, established her as his mistress and housekeeper at his farm, and before I left, he had two children by her. But, mark the end! Since I have been at the North, I have been credibly informed that Walker has been married, and, as a previous measure, sold poor Cynthia and her four children (she having had two more since I came away) into hopeless bondage!

He soon commenced purchasing to make up the third gang. We took steamboat, and went to Jefferson City, a town on the Missouri River. Here we landed, and took stage for the interior of the state. He bought a number of slaves as he passed the different farms and villages. After getting twenty-two or twenty-three men and women, we arrived at St. Charles, a village on the banks of the Missouri. Here he purchased a woman who had a child in her arms, appearing to be four or five weeks old.

We had been travelling by land for some days, and were in hopes to have found a boat at this place for St. Louis, but were disappointed. As no boat was expected for some days, we started for St. Louis by land. Mr. Walker had purchased two horses. He rode one, and I the other. The slaves were chained together, and we took up our line of march, Mr. Walker taking the lead, and I bringing up the rear. Though the distance was not more than twenty miles, we did not reach it the first day. The road was worse than any that I have ever travelled.

Soon after we left St. Charles the young child grew very cross, and kept up a noise during the greater part of the day. Mr. Walker complained of its crying several times, and told the mother to stop the child's d——d noise, or he would. The woman tried to keep the child from crying, but could not. We put up at night with an acquaintance of Mr. Walker, and in the morning, just as we were about to start, the child again commenced crying. Walker stepped up to her, and told her to give the child to him. The mother tremblingly obeyed. He took the child by one arm, as you would a cat by the leg, walked into the house, and said to the lady,

"Madam, I will make you a present of this little nigger; it keeps such a noise that I can't bear it."

"Thank you, sir," said the lady.

The mother, as soon as she saw that her child was to be left, ran up to Mr. Walker, and falling upon her knees, begged him to let her have her child; she clung around his legs, and cried, "Oh, my child! my child! master, do let me have my child! oh, do, do, do! I will stop its crying if you will only let me have it again." When I saw this woman crying for her child so piteously, a shudder—a feeling akin to horror—shot through my frame. I have often since in imagination heard her crying for her child:—

> "O, master, let me stay to catch
>   My baby's sobbing breath,
> His little glassy eye to watch,
>   And smooth his limbs in death,
>
> And cover him with grass and leaf,
>   Beneath the large oak tree:
> It is not sullenness, but grief—
>   O, master, pity me!
>
> The morn was chill—I spoke no word,
>   But feared my babe might die,
> And heard all day, or thought I heard,
>   My little baby cry.
>
> At noon, oh, how I ran and took
>   My baby to my breast!
> I lingered—and the long lash broke
>   My sleeping infant's rest.
>
> I worked till night—till darkest night,
>   In torture and disgrace;
> Went home and watched till morning light,
>   To see my baby's face.
>
> Then give me but one little hour—
>   O! do not lash me so!
> One little hour—one little hour—
>   And gratefully I'll go."

Mr. Walker commanded her to return into the ranks with the other slaves. Women who had children were not chained, but those that had none were. As soon as her child was disposed of she was chained in the gang.

The following song I have often heard the slaves sing,

when about to be carried to the far south. It is said to have been composed by a slave.

> "See these poor souls from Africa
> Transported to America;
> We are stolen, and sold to Georgia—
> Will you go along with me?
> We are stolen, and sold to Georgia—
> Come sound the jubilee!
>
> See wives and husbands sold apart,
> Their children's screams will break my heart;—
> There's a better day a coming—
> Will you go along with me?
> There's a better day a coming,
> Go sound the jubilee!
>
> O, gracious Lord! when shall it be,
> That we poor souls shall all be free?
> Lord, break them slavery powers—
> Will you go along with me?
> Lord, break them slavery powers,
> Go sound the jubilee!
>
> Dear Lord, dear Lord, when slavery 'll cease,
> Then we poor souls will have our peace;—
> There's a better day a coming—
> Will you go along with me?
> There's a better day a coming,
> Go sound the jubilee!"

We finally arrived at Mr. Walker's farm. He had a house built during our absence to put slaves in. It was a kind of domestic jail. The slaves were put in the jail at night, and worked on the farm during the day. They were kept here until the gang was completed, when we again started for New Orleans, on board the steamboat *North America,* Capt. Alexander Scott. We had a large number of slaves in this gang. One, by the name of Joe, Mr. Walker was training up to take my place, as my time was nearly out, and glad was I. We made our first stop at Vicksburg, where we remained one week and sold several slaves.

Mr. Walker, though not a good master, had not flogged a slave since I had been with him, though he had threatened me. The slaves were kept in the pen, and he always put up at the best hotel, and kept his wines in his room, for the accommodation of those who called to negotiate with him for the purchase of slaves. One day, while we were at Vicksburg, several gentlemen came to see him for that purpose, and as usual the wine was called for. I took the tray and started around with it, and having accidentally filled some of the glasses too full, the gentlemen spilled the wine on their clothes as they went to drink. Mr. Walker apologized to them for my carelessness, but looked at me as though he would see me again on this subject.

After the gentlemen had left the room, he asked me what I meant by my carelessness, and said that he would attend to me. The next morning he gave me a note to carry to the jailer, and a dollar in money to give to him. I suspected that all was not right, so I went down near the landing, where I met with a sailor, and, walking up to him, asked him if he would be so kind as to read the note for me. He read it over, and then looked at me. I asked him to tell me what was in it. Said he,

"They are going to give you hell."

"Why?" said I.

He said, "This is a note to have you whipped, and says that you have a dollar to pay for it."

He handed me back the note, and off I started. I knew not what to do, but was determined not to be whipped. I went up to the jail—took a look at it, and walked off again. As Mr. Walker was acquainted with the jailer, I feared that I should be found out if I did not go, and be treated in consequence of it still worse.

While I was meditating on the subject, I saw a colored man about my size walk up, and the thought struck me in a moment to send him with my note. I walked up to him, and asked him who he belonged to. He said he was a free man, and had been in the city but a short time. I told him I had a note to go into the jail, and get a trunk to carry to one of the steamboats; but was so busily engaged that I could not do it, although I had a dollar to pay for it. He asked me if I would not give him the job.

I handed him the note and the dollar, and off he started for the jail.

I watched to see that he went in, and as soon as I saw the door close behind him, I walked around the corner, and took my station, intending to see how my friend looked when he came out. I had been there but a short time, when a colored man came around the corner, and said to another colored man with whom he was acquainted—

"They are giving a nigger scissors in the jail."

"What for?" said the other. The man continued.

"A nigger came into the jail, and asked for the jailer. The jailer came out, and he handed him a note, and said he wanted to get a trunk. The jailer told him to go with him, and he would give him the trunk. So he took him into the room, and told the nigger to give up the dollar. He said a man had given him the dollar to pay for getting the trunk. But that lie would not answer. So they made him strip himself, and then they tied him down, and are now whipping him."

I stood by all the while listening to their talk, and soon found out that the person alluded to was my customer. I went into the street opposite the jail, and concealed myself in such a manner that I could not be seen by any one coming out. I had been there but a short time, when the young man made his appearance, and looked around for me. I, unobserved, came forth from my hiding place, behind a pile of brick, and he pretty soon saw me, and came up to me complaining bitterly, saying that I had played a trick upon him. I denied any knowledge of what the note contained, and asked him what they had done to him. He told me in substance what I heard the man tell who had come out of the jail.

"Yes," said he, "they whipped me and took my dollar, and gave me this note."

He showed me the note which the jailer had given him, telling him to give it to his master. I told him I would give him fifty cents for it—that being all the money I had. He gave it to me and took his money. He had received twenty lashes on his bare back, with the negro-whip.

I took the note and started for the hotel where I had left Mr. Walker. Upon reaching the hotel, I handed it to a stranger whom I had not seen before, and requested him to read it to me. As near as I can recollect, it was as follows:—

"Dear Sir:—By your direction, I have given your boy twenty lashes. He is a very saucy boy, and tried to make me believe that he did not belong to you, and I put it on to him well for lying to me.
"I remain
"Your obedient servant."

It is true that in most of the slave-holding cities, when a gentleman wishes his servants whipped, he can send him to the jail and have it done. Before I went in where Mr. Walker was, I wet my cheeks a little, as though I had been crying. He looked at me, and inquired what was the matter. I told him that I had never had such a whipping in my life, and handed him the note. He looked at it and laughed;—"And so you told him that you did not belong to me?" "Yes, sir," said I. "I did not know that there was any harm in that." He told me I must behave myself, if I did not want to be whipped again.

This incident shows how it is that slavery makes its victims lying and mean; for which vices it afterwards reproaches them, and uses them as arguments to prove that they deserve no better fate. Had I entertained the same views or right and wrong which I now do, I am sure I should never have practised the deception upon that poor fellow which I did. I know of no act committed by me while in slavery which I have regretted more than that; and I heartily desire that it may be at some time or other in my power to make him amends for his vicarious sufferings in my behalf.

CHAPTER VI

In a few days we reached New Orleans, and arriving there in the night, remained on board until morning. While at New Orleans this time, I saw a slave killed; an account of which has been published by Theodore D. Weld, in his book entitled "Slavery as it is." The circumstances were as follows. In the evening, between seven and eight o'clock, a slave came running down the levee, followed by several men and boys. The whites were crying out, "Stop that nigger! stop that nigger!" while the poor panting slave, in almost breathless accents, was repeating, "I did not steal the meat—I did not steal the meat." The poor man at last took refuge in the river. The whites who were in pursuit of him, run on board of one of the boats to see if they could discover him. They finally espied him under the bow of the steamboat *Trenton*. They got a pike-pole and tried to drive him from his hiding place. When they would strike at him he would dive under the water. The water was so cold, that it soon became evident that he must come out or be drowned.

While they were trying to drive him from under the bow of the boat or drown him, he would in broken and imploring accents say, "I did not steal the meat; I did not steal the meat. My master lives up the river. I want to see my master. I did not steal the meat. Do let me go home to master." After punching him, and striking him over the head for some time, he at last sunk in the water, to rise no more alive.

On the end of the pike-pole with which they were striking him was a hook, which caught in his clothing, and they hauled him up on the bow of the boat. Some said he was dead; others said he was "*playing possum*;" while others kicked him to make him get up; but it was of no use—he was dead.

As soon as they became satisfied of this, they commenced leaving, one after another. One of the hands on the boat informed the captain that they had killed the man, and that the dead body was lying on the deck. The captain came on deck, and said to those who were remaining, "You have killed this nigger; now take him off of my boat." The captain's name was Hart. The dead body was dragged on shore and left there. I went on board of the boat where our gang of slaves were, and during the whole night my mind was occupied with what I had seen. Early in the morning I went on shore to see if the dead body remained there. I found it in the same position that it was left the night before. I watched to see what they would do with it. It was left there until between eight and nine o'clock, when a cart, which takes up the trash out of the streets, came along, and the body was thrown in, and in a few minutes more was covered over with dirt which they were removing from the streets. During the whole time, I did not see more than six or seven persons around it, who, from their manner, evidently regarded it as no uncommon occurrence.

During our stay in the city I met with a young white man with whom I was well acquainted in St. Louis. He had been sold into slavery, under the following circumstances. His father was a drunkard, and very poor, with a family of five or six children. The father died, and left the mother to take care of and provide for the children as best she might. The eldest was a boy, named Burrill, about thirteen years of age, who did chores in a store kept by Mr. Riley, to assist his mother in procuring a living for the family. After working with him two years, Mr. Riley took him to New Orleans to wait on him while in that city on a visit, and when he returned to St. Louis, he told the mother of the boy that he had died with the yellow fever. Nothing more was heard from him, no one supposing him to be alive. I was much astonished when Burrill told me his story. Though I sympathized with him I could not assist him. We were both slaves. He was poor, uneducated, and without friends; and, if living, is, I presume, still held as a slave.

After selling out his cargo of human flesh, we returned to St. Louis, and my time was up with Mr. Walker. I had served him one year, and it was the longest year I ever lived.

CHAPTER VII

I was sent home, and was glad enough to leave the service of one who was tearing the husband from the wife, the child from the mother, and the sister from the brother—but a trial more severe and heart-rending than any which I had yet met with awaited me. My dear sister had been sold to a man who was going to Natchez, and was lying in jail awaiting the hour of his departure. She had expressed her determination to die, rather than go to the far south, and she was put in jail for safekeeping. I went to the jail the same day that I arrived, but as the jailer was not in I could not see her.

I went home to my master, in the country, and the first day after my return he came where I was at work, and spoke to me very politely. I knew from his appearance that something was the matter. After talking to me about my several journeys to New Orleans with Mr. Walker, he told me that he was hard pressed for money, and as he had sold my mother and all her children except me, he thought it would be better to sell me than any other one, and that as I had been used to living in the city, he thought it probable that I would prefer it to country life. I raised up my head, and looked him full in the face. When my eyes caught his he immediately looked to the ground. After a short pause, I said,

"Master, mother has often told me that you are a near relative of mine, and I have often heard you admit the fact; and after you have hired me out, and received, as I once heard you say, nine hundred dollars for my services—after receiving this large sum, will you sell me to be carried to New Orleans or some other place?"

"No," said he, "I do not intend to sell you to a negro trader. If I had wished to have done that, I might have sold you to Mr. Walker for a large sum, but I would not sell you to a negro trader. You may go to the city, and find you a good master.''

"But," said I, "I cannot find a good master in the whole city of St. Louis."

"Why?" said he.

"Because there are no good masters in the state."

"Do you not call me a good master?"

"If you were you would not sell me."

"Now I will give you one week to find a master in, and surely you can do it in that time."

The price set by my evangelical master upon my soul and body was the trifling sum of five hundred dollars. I tried to enter into some arrangement by which I might purchase my freedom; but he would enter into no such arrangement.

I set out for the city with the understanding that I was to return in a week with some one to become my new master. Soon after reaching the city, I went to the jail, to learn if I could once more see my sister; but could not gain admission. I then went to mother, and learned from her that the owner of my sister intended to start for Natchez in a few days.

I went to the jail again the next day, and Mr. Simonds, the keeper, allowed me to see my sister for the last time. I cannot give a just description of the scene at that parting interview. Never, never can be erased from my heart the occurrences of that day! When I entered the room where she was, she was seated in one corner, alone. There were four other women in the same room, belonging to the same man. He had purchased them, he said, for his own use. She was seated with her face towards the door where I entered, yet she did not look up until I walked up to her. As soon as she observed me she sprung up, threw her arms around my neck, leaned her head upon my breast, and, without uttering a word, burst into tears. As soon as she recovered herself sufficiently to speak, she advised me to take mother, and try to get out of slavery. She said there was no hope for herself—that she must live and die a slave. After giving her some advice, and taking from my finger a ring and placing it upon hers, I bade her farewell forever, and returned to my mother, and then and there made up my mind to leave for Canada as soon as possible.

I had been in the city nearly two days, and as I was to be absent only a week, I thought best to get on my journey as soon as possible. In conversing with mother, I found her unwilling to make the attempt to reach a land of liberty, but she counselled me to get my liberty if I could. She said, as all her children were in slavery, she did not wish to leave them. I could not bear the idea of leaving her among those pirates, when there was a prospect of being able to get away from them. After much persuasion I succeeded in inducing her to make the attempt to get away.

The time fixed for our departure was the next night. I had with me a little money that I had received, from time to time, from gentlemen for whom I had done errands. I took my scanty means and purchased some dried beef, crackers and cheese, which I carried to mother, who had provided herself with a bag to carry it in. I occasionally thought of my old master, and of my mission to the city to find a new one. I waited with the most intense anxiety for the appointed time to leave the land of slavery, in search of a land of liberty.

The time at length arrived, and we left the city just as the clock struck nine. We proceeded to the upper part of the city, where I had been two or three times during the day, and selected a skiff to carry us across the river. The boat was not mine, nor did I know to whom it did belong; neither did I care. The boat was fastened with a small pole, which, with the aid of a rail, I soon loosened from its moorings. After hunting round and finding a board to use as an oar, I turned to the city, and bidding it a long farewell, pushed off my boat. The current running very swift, we had not reached the middle of the stream before we were directly opposite the city.

We were soon upon the Illinois shore, and, leaping from the boat, turned it adrift, and the last I saw of it it was going down the river at good speed. We took the main road to Alton, and passed through just at daylight, when we made for the woods, where we remained during the day. Our reason for going into the woods was, that we expected that Mr. Mansfield (the man who owned my mother) would start in pursuit of her as soon as he discovered that she was missing. He also knew that I had been in the city looking for a new master, and we thought probably he would go out to my master's to see if he could find my mother, and in so doing, Dr. Young might be led to suspect that I had gone to Canada to find a purchaser.

We remained in the woods during the day, and as soon as darkness overshadowed the earth, we started again on our gloomy way, having no guide but the NORTH STAR. We continued to travel by night, and secrete ourselves in the woods by day; and every night, before emerging from our hidingplace, we would anxiously look for our friend and leader—the NORTH STAR. And in the language of Pierpont we might have exclaimed,

> "Star of the North! while blazing day
> Pours round me its full tide of light,
> And hides thy pale but faithful ray,
> I, too, lie hid, and long for night.
> For night;—I dare not walk at noon,
> Nor dare I trust the faithless moon,
> Nor faithless man, whose burning lust
> For gold hath riveted my chain;
> No other leader can I trust
> But thee, of even the starry train;
> For, all the host around thee burning,
> Like faithless man, keep turning, turning.
>
> In the dark top of southern pines
> I nestled, when the driver's horn
> Called to the field, in lengthening lines,
> My fellows, at the break of morn.
> And there I lay, till they sweet face
> Looked in upon my 'hiding place,'
> Star of the North!
> Thy light, that no poor slave deceiveth,
> Shall set me free."

CHAPTER VIII

As we travelled towards a land of liberty, my heart would at times leap for joy. At other times, being, as I was, almost constantly on my feet, I felt as though I could travel no further. But when I thought of slavery, with its democratic whips—its republican chains—its evangelical blood-hounds, and its religious slave-holders—when I thought of all this paraphernalia of American democracy and religion behind me, and the prospect of liberty before me, I was encouraged to press forward, my heart was strengthened, and I forgot that I was tired or hungry.

On the eighth day of our journey, we had a very heavy rain, and in a few hours after it commenced we had not a dry thread upon our bodies. This made our journey still more unpleasant. On the tenth day, we found ourselves entirely destitute of provisions, and how to obtain any we could not tell. We finally resolved to stop at some farmhouse, and try to get something to eat. We had no sooner determined to do this, than we went to a house, and asked them for some food. We were treated with great kindness, and they not only gave us something to eat, but gave us provisions to carry with us. They advised us to travel by day and lie by at night. Finding ourselves about one hundred and fifty miles from St. Louis, we concluded that it would be safe to travel by daylight, and did not leave the house until the next morning. We travelled on that day through a thickly settled country, and through one small village. Though we were fleeing from a land of oppression, our hearts were still there. My dear sister and two beloved brothers were behind us, and the idea of giving them up, and leaving them forever, made us feel sad. But with all this depression of heart, the thought that I should one day be free, and call my body

my own, buoyed me up and made my heart leap for joy.
I had just been telling my mother how I should try to get
employment as soon as we reached Canada, and how I
intended to purchase us a little farm, and how I would
earn money enough to buy sister and brothers, and how
happy we would be in our own FREE HOME—when
three men came up on horseback, and ordered us to
stop.

I turned to the one who appeared to be the principal
man, and asked him what he wanted. He said he had a
warrant to take us up. The three immediately dis-
mounted, and one took from his pocket a handbill, advertising us as runaways, and offering a reward of two
hundred dollars for our apprehension and delivery in the
city of St. Louis. The advertisement had been put out by
Isaac Mansfield and John Young.

While they were reading the advertisement, mother
looked me in the face, and burst into tears. A cold chill
ran over me, and such a sensation I never experienced
before, and I hope never to again. They took out a rope
and tied me, and we were taken back about six miles, to
the house of the individual who appeared to be the leader.
We reached there about seven o'clock in the evening, had
supper, and were separated for the night. Two men remained in the room during the night. Before the family
retired to rest, they were all called together to attend
prayers. The man who but a few hours before had bound
my hands together with a strong cord, read a chapter
from the Bible, and then offered up prayer, just as though
God had sanctioned the act he had just committed upon
a poor, panting, fugitive slave.

The next morning a blacksmith came in, and put a pair
of handcuffs on me, and we started on our journey back
to the land of whips, chains and Bibles. Mother was not
tied, but was closely watched at night. We were carried
back in a wagon, and after four days' travel, we came in
sight of St. Louis. I cannot describe my feelings upon
approaching the city.

As we were crossing the ferry, Mr. Wiggins, the
owner of the ferry, came up to me, and inquired
what I had been doing that I was in chains. He had not
heard that I had run away. In a few minutes we were
on the Missouri side, and were taken directly to the

jail. On the way thither, I saw several of my friends, who gave me a nod of recognition as I passed them. After reaching the jail, we were locked up in different apartments.

CHAPTER IX

I had been in jail but a short time when I heard that my master was sick, and nothing brought more joy to my heart than that intelligence. I prayed fervently for him— not for his recovery, but for his death. I knew he would be exasperated at having to pay for my apprehension, and knowing his cruelty, I feared him. While in jail, I learned that my sister Elizabeth, who was in prison when we left the city, had been carried off four days before our arrival.

I had been in jail but a few hours when three negro-traders, learning that I was secured thus for running away, came to my prison-house and looked at me, expecting that I would be offered for sale. Mr. Mansfield, the man who owned mother, came into the jail as soon as Mr. Jones, the man who arrested us, informed him that he had brought her back. He told her that he would not whip her, but would sell her to a negro-trader, or take her to New Orleans himself. After being in jail about one week, master sent a man to take me out of jail, and send me home. I was taken out and carried home, and the old man was well enough to sit up. He had me brought into the room where he was, and as I entered, he asked me where I had been? I told him I had acted according to his orders. He had told me to look for a master, and I had been to look for one. He answered that he did not tell me to go to Canada to look for a master. I told him that as I had served him faithfully, and had been the means of putting a number of hundreds of dollars into his pocket, I thought I had a right to my liberty. He said he had promised my father that I should not be sold to supply the New Orleans market, or he would sell me to a negro-trader.

I was ordered to go into the field to work, and was closely watched by the overseer during the day, and locked up at night. The overseer gave me a severe whipping on the second day that I was in the field. I had been at home but a short time, when master was able to ride to the city; and on his return he informed me that he had sold me to Samuel Willi, a merchant tailor. I knew Mr. Willi. I had lived with him three or four months some years before, when he hired me of my master.

Mr. Willi was not considered by his servants as a very bad man, nor was he the best of masters. I went to my new home, and found my new mistress was very glad to see me. Mr. Willi owned two servants before he purchased me—Robert and Charlotte. Robert was an excellent white-washer, and hired his time from his master, paying him one dollar per day, besides taking care of himself. He was known in the city by the name of Bob Music. Charlotte was an old woman, who attended to the cooking, washing, &c. Mr. Willi was not a wealthy man, and did not feel able to keep many servants around his house; so he soon decided to hire me out, and as I had been accustomed to service in steamboats, he gave me the privilege of finding such employment.

I soon secured a situation on board the steamer *Otto*, Capt. J. B. Hill, which sailed from St. Louis to Independence, Missouri. My former master, Dr. Young, did not let Mr. Willi know that I had run away, or he would not have permitted me to go on board a steamboat. The boat was not quite ready to commence running, and therefore I had to remain with Mr. Willi. But during this time, I had to undergo a trial for which I was entirely unprepared. My mother, who had been in jail since her return until the present time, was now about being carried to New Orleans, to die on a cotton, sugar, or rice plantation!

I had been several times to the jail, but could obtain no interview with her. I ascertained, however, the time the boat in which she was to embark would sail, and as I had not seen mother since her being thrown into prison, I felt anxious for the hour of sailing to come. At last, the day arrived when I was to see her for the first time after our painful separation, and, for aught that I knew, for the last time in this world!

At about ten o'clock in the morning I went on board of the boat, and found her there in company with fifty or sixty other slaves. She was chained to another woman. On seeing me, she immediately dropped her head upon her heaving bosom. She moved not, neither did she weep. Her emotions were too deep for tears. I approached, threw my arms around her neck, kissed her, and fell upon my knees, begging her forgiveness, for I thought myself to blame for her sad condition; for if I had not persuaded her to accompany me, she would not then have been in chains.

She finally raised her head, looked me in the face, (and such a look none but an angel can give!) and said, *"My dear son, you are not to blame for my being here. You have done nothing more nor less than your duty. Do not, I pray you, weep for me. I cannot last long upon a cotton plantation. I feel that my heavenly Master will soon call me home, and then I shall be out of the hands of the slave-holders!"*

I could bear no more—my heart struggled to free itself from the human form. In a moment she saw Mr. Mansfield coming toward that part of the boat, and she whispered into my ear, *"My child, we must soon part to meet no more this side of the grave. You have ever said that you would not die a slave; that you would be a freeman. Now try to get your liberty! You will soon have no one to look after but yourself!"* and just as she whispered the last sentence into my ear, Mansfield came up to me, and with an oath, said, "Leave here this instant; you have been the means of my losing one hundred dollars to get this wench back"—and at the same time kicking me with a heavy pair of boots. As I left her, she gave one shriek, saying, "God be with you!" It was the last time that I saw her, and the last word I heard her utter.

I walked on shore. The bell was tolling. The boat was about to start. I stood with a heavy heart, waiting to see her leave the wharf. As I thought of my mother, I could but feel that I had lost

> "——the glory of my life,
> My blessing and my pride!
> I half forgot the name of slave,
> When she was by my side."

The love of liberty that had been burning in my bosom had well-nigh gone out. I felt as though I was ready to

die. The boat moved gently from the wharf, and while
she glided down the river, I realized that my mother was
indeed

"Gone—gone—sold and gone,
To the rice swamp, dank and lone!"

After the boat was out of sight I returned home; but
my thoughts were so absorbed in what I had witnessed,
that I knew not what I was about half of the time. Night
came, but it brought no sleep to my eyes.

In a few days, the boat upon which I was to work being
ready, I went on board to commence. This employment
suited me better than living in the city, and I remained
until the close of navigation; though it proved anything
but pleasant. The captain was a drunken, profligate, hard-
hearted creature, not knowing how to treat himself, or
any other person.

The boat, on its second trip, brought down Mr. Walker,
the man of whom I have spoken in a previous chapter,
as hiring my time. He had between one and two hundred
slaves, chained and manacled. Among them was a man
that formerly belonged to my old master's brother, Aaron
Young. His name was Solomon. He was a preacher, and
belonged to the same church with his master. I was glad
to see the old man. He wept like a child when he told
me how he had been sold from his wife and children.

The boat carried down, while I remained on board,
four or five gangs of slaves. Missouri, though a comparatively new state, is very much engaged in raising slaves
to supply the southern market. In a former chapter, I have
mentioned that I was once in the employ of a slave-trader,
or driver, as he is called at the south. For fear that some
may think that I have misrepresented a slave-driver, I will
here give an extract from a paper published in a slave-
holding state, Tennessee, called *The "Millennial Trum-
peter."*

"Droves of negroes, chained together in dozens and
scores, and hand-cuffed, have been driven through our
country in numbers far surpassing any previous year, and
these vile slave-drivers and dealers are swarming like
buzzards around a carrion. Through this county, you cannot pass a few miles in the great roads without having

every feeling of humanity insulted and lacerated by this spectacle, nor can you go into any county or any neighborhood, scarcely, without seeing or hearing of some of these despicable creatures, called negro-drivers.

"Who is a negro-driver? One whose eyes dwell with delight on lacerated bodies of helpless men, women and children; whose soul feels diabolical raptures at the chains, and hand-cuffs, and cart-whips, for inflicting tortures on weeping mothers torn from helpless babes, and on husbands and wives torn asunder forever!"

Dark and revolting as is the picture here drawn, it is from the pen of one living in the midst of slavery. But though these men may cant about negro-drivers, and tell what despicable creatures they are, who is it, I ask, that supplies them with the human beings that they are tearing asunder? I answer, as far as I have any knowledge of the state where I came from, that those who raise slaves for the market are to be found among all classes, from Thomas H. Benton down to the lowest political demagogue who may be able to purchase a woman for the purpose of raising stock, and from the doctor of divinity down to the most humble lay member in the church.

It was not uncommon in St. Louis to pass by an auction-stand, and behold a woman upon the auction-block, and hear the seller crying out, *"How much is offered for this woman? She is a good cook, good washer, a good obedient servant. She has got religion!"* Why should this man tell the purchasers that she has religion? I answer, because in Missouri, and as far as I have any knowledge of slavery in the other states, the religious teaching consists in teaching the slave that he must never strike a white man; that God made him for a slave; and that, when whipped, he must not find fault—for the Bible says, "He that knoweth his master's will and doeth it not, shall be beaten with many stripes!" And slave-holders find such religion very profitable to them.

After leaving the steamer *Otto*, I resided at home, in Mr. Willi's family, and again began to lay my plans for making my escape from slavery. The anxiety to be a freeman would not let me rest day or night. I would think of the northern cities that I had heard so much about;—of Canada, where so many of my acquaintances had found a refuge. I would dream at night that I was in Canada, a

freeman, and on waking in the morning, weep to find
myself so sadly mistaken.

> "I would think of Victoria's domain,
>   And in a moment I seemed to be there!
> But the fear of being taken again,
>   Soon hurried me back to despair.

Mr. Willi treated me better than Dr. Young ever had;
but instead of making me contented and happy, it only
rendered me the more miserable, for it enabled me better
to appreciate liberty. Mr. Willi was a man who loved
money as most men do, and without looking for an opportunity to sell me, he found one in the offer of Captain
Enoch Price, a steamboat owner and commission merchant, living in the city of St. Louis. Captain Price ten-
dered seven hundred dollars, which was two hundred
more than Mr. Willi had paid. He therefore thought best
to accept the offer. I was wanted for a carriage driver,
and Mrs. Price was very much pleased with the captain's
bargain. His family consisted besides of one child. He
had three servants besides myself—one man and two
women.

Mrs. Price was very proud of her servants, always
keeping them well dressed, and as soon as I had been
purchased, she resolved to have a new carriage. And soon
one was procured, and all preparations were made for a
turn-out in grand style, I being the driver.

One of the female servants was a girl some eighteen
or twenty years of age, named Maria. Mrs. Price was
very soon determined to have us united, if she could so
arrange matters. She would often urge upon me the necessity of having a wife, saying that it would be so pleasant for me to take one in the same family! But getting
married, while in slavery, was the last of my thoughts;
and had I been ever so inclined, I should not have married Maria, as my love had already gone in another quarter. Mrs. Price soon found out that her efforts at this
match-making between Maria and myself would not prove
successful. She also discovered (or thought she had) that
I was rather partial to a girl named Eliza, who was owned
by Dr. Mills. This induced her at once to endeavor the

purchase of Eliza, so great was her desire to get me a wife!

Before making the attempt, however, she deemed it best to talk to me a little upon the subject of love, courtship, and marriage. Accordingly, one afternoon she called me into her room—telling me to take a chair and sit down. I did so, thinking it rather strange, for servants are not very often asked thus to sit down in the same room with the master or mistress. She said that she had found out that I did not care enough about Maria to marry her. I told her that was true. She then asked me if there was not a girl in the city that I loved. Well, now, this was coming into too close quarters with me! People, generally, don't like to tell their love stories to everybody that may think fit to ask about them, and it was so with me. But, after blushing a while and recovering myself, I told her that I did not want a wife. She then asked me if I did not think something of Eliza. I told her that I did. She then said that if I wished to marry Eliza, she would purchase her if she could.

I gave but little encouragement to this proposition, as I was determined to make another trial to get my liberty, and I knew that if I should have a wife, I should not be willing to leave her behind; and if I should attempt to bring her with me, the chances would be difficult for success. However, Eliza was purchased, and brought into the family.

CHAPTER X

But the more I thought of the trap laid by Mrs. Price to make me satisfied with my new home, by getting me a wife, the more I determined never to marry any woman on earth until I should get my liberty. But this secret I was compelled to keep to myself, which placed me in a very critical position. I must keep upon good terms with Mrs. Price and Eliza. I therefore promised Mrs. Price that I would marry Eliza; but said that I was not then ready. And I had to keep upon good terms with Eliza, for fear that Mrs. Price would find out that I did not intend to get married.

I have here spoken of marriage, and it is very common among slaves themselves to talk of it. And it is common for slaves to be married; or at least to have the marriage ceremony performed. But there is no such thing as slaves being lawfully married. There has never yet a case occurred where a slave has been tried for bigamy. The man may have as many women as he wishes, and the women as many men; and the law takes no cognizance of such acts among slaves. And in fact some masters, when they have sold the husband from the wife, compel her to take another.

There lived opposite Captain Price's, Dr. Farrar, well known in St. Louis. He sold a man named Ben to one of the traders. He also owned Ben's wife, and in a few days he compelled Sally (that was her name) to marry Peter, another man belonging to him. I asked Sally "why she married Peter so soon after Ben was sold." She said, "because master made her do it."

Mr. John Calvert, who resided near our place, had a woman named Lavinia. She was quite young, and a man to whom she was about to be married was sold, and carried into the country near St. Charles, about twenty miles from St. Louis. Mr. Calvert wanted her to get a husband; but she had resolved not to marry any other man, and she refused. Mr. Calvert whipped her in such a manner that it was thought she would die. Some of the citizens had him arrested, but it was soon hushed up. And that was the last of it. The woman did not die, but it would have been the same if she had.

Captain Price purchased me in the month of October, and I remained with him until December, when the family made a voyage to New Orleans, in a boat owned by himself, and named the *Chester*. I served on board as one of the stewards. On arriving at New Orleans, about the middle of the month, the boat took in freight for Cincinnati; and it was decided that the family should go up the river in her, and what was of more interest to me, I was to accompany them.

The long looked for opportunity to make my escape from slavery was near at hand.

Captain Price had some fears as to the propriety of taking me near a free state, or a place where it was likely I could run away, with a prospect of liberty. He asked me if I had ever been in a free state. "Oh yes," said I, "I have been in Ohio; my master carried me into that state once, but I never liked a free state."

It was soon decided that it would be safe to take me with them, and what made it more safe, Eliza was on the boat with us, and Mrs. Price, to try me, asked if I thought as much as ever of Eliza. I told her that Eliza was very dear to me indeed, and that nothing but death should part us. It was the same as if we were married. This had the desired effect. The boat left New Orleans, and proceeded up the river.

I had at different times obtained little sums of money, which I had reserved for a "rainy day." I procured some cotton cloth, and made me a bag to carry provisions in. The trials of the past were all lost in hopes for the future. The love of liberty, that had been burning in my bosom for years, and had been well-nigh extinguished, was now resuscitated. At night, when all around was peaceful, I would walk the decks, meditating upon my happy prospects.

I should have stated, that, before leaving St. Louis, I went to an old man named Frank, a slave, owned by a

Mr. Sarpee. This old man was very distinguished (not only among the slave population, but also the whites) as a fortune-teller. He was about seventy years of age, something over six feet high, and very slender. Indeed, he was so small around his body, that it looked as though it was not strong enough to hold up his head.

Uncle Frank was a very great favorite with the young ladies, who would go to him in great numbers to get their fortunes told. And it was generally believed that he could really penetrate into the mysteries of futurity. Whether true or not, he had the *name,* and that is about half of what one needs in this gullible age. I found Uncle Frank seated in the chimney corner, about ten o'clock at night. As soon as I entered, the old man left his seat. I watched his movement as well as I could by the dim light of the fire. He soon lit a lamp, and coming up, looked me full in the face, saying, "Well, my son, you have come to get uncle to tell your fortune, have you?" "Yes," said I. But how the old man should know what I came for, I could not tell. However, I paid the fee of twenty-five cents, and he commenced by looking into a gourd, filled with water. Whether the old man was a prophet, or the son of a prophet, I cannot say; but there is one thing certain, many of his predictions were verified.

I am no believer in soothsaying; yet I am sometimes at a loss to know how Uncle Frank could tell so accurately what would occur in the future. Among the many things he told was one which was enough to pay me for all the trouble of hunting him up. It was that I *should be free*! He further said, that in trying to get my liberty I would meet with many severe trials. I thought to myself any fool could tell me that!

The first place in which we landed in a free state was Cairo, a small village at the mouth of the Ohio river. We remained here but a few hours, when we proceeded to Louisville. After unloading some of the cargo, the boat started on her upward trip. The next day was the first of January. I had looked forward to New Year's day as the commencement of a new era in the history of my life. I had decided upon leaving the peculiar institution that day.

During the last night that I served in slavery I did not close my eyes a single moment. When not thinking of the future, my mind dwelt on the past. The love of a dear mother, a dear sister, and three dear brothers, yet living, caused me to shed many tears. If I could only have been assured of their being dead, I should have felt satisfied; but I imagined I saw my dear mother in the cotton-field, followed by a merciless taskmaster, and no one to speak a consoling word to her! I beheld my dear sister in the hands of a slave-driver, and compelled to submit to his cruelty! None but one placed in such a situation can for a moment imagine the intense agony to which these reflections subjected me.

CHAPTER XI

At last the time for action arrived. The boat landed at a point which appeared to me the place of all others to start from. I found that it would be impossible to carry anything with me but what was upon my person. I had some provisions, and a single suit of clothes, about half worn. When the boat was discharging her cargo, and the passengers engaged carrying their baggage on and off shore, I improved the opportunity to convey myself with my little effects on land. Taking up a trunk, I went up the wharf, and was soon out of the crowd. I made directly for the woods, where I remained until night, knowing well that I could not travel, even in the state of Ohio, during the day, without danger of being arrested.

I had long since made up my mind that I would not trust myself in the hands of any man, white or colored. The slave is brought up to look upon every white man as an enemy to him and his race; and twenty-one years in slavery had taught me that there were traitors, even among colored people. After dark, I emerged from the woods into a narrow path, which led me into the main travelled road. But I knew not which way to go. I did not know north from south, east from west. I looked in vain for the North Star; a heavy cloud hid it from my view. I walked up and down the road until near midnight, when the clouds disappeared, and I welcomed the sight of my friend—truly the slave's friend—the North Star!

As soon as I saw it, I knew my course, and before daylight I travelled twenty or twenty-five miles. It being in the winter, I suffered intensely from the cold; being without an overcoat, and my other clothes rather thin for the season. I was provided with a tinder-box, so that I could make up a fire when necessary. And but for this, I should certainly have frozen to death; for I was deter-

mined not to go to any house for shelter. I knew of a
man belonging to Gen. Ashly, of St. Louis, who had run
away near Cincinnati, on the way to Washington, but had
been caught and carried back into slavery; and I felt that
a similar fate awaited me, should I be seen by any one.
I travelled at night, and lay by during the day.

On the fourth day my provisions gave out, and then
what to do I could not tell. Have something to eat I must;
but how to get it was the question! On the first night after
my food was gone, I went to a barn on the road-side and
there found some ears of corn. I took ten or twelve of
them, and kept on my journey. During the next day, while
in the woods, I roasted my corn and feasted upon it,
thanking God that I was so well provided for.

My escape to a land of freedom now appeared certain,
and the prospects of the future occupied a great part of
my thoughts. What should be my occupation, was a subject of much anxiety to me; and the next thing what
should be my name? I have before stated that my old
master, Dr. Young, had no children of his own, but had
with him a nephew, the son of his brother, Benjamin
Young. When this boy was brought to Dr. Young, his
name being William, the same as mine, my mother was
ordered to change mine to something else. This, at the
time, I thought to be one of the most cruel acts that could
be committed upon my rights; and I received several very
severe whippings for telling people that my name was
William, after orders were given to change it. Though
young, I was old enough to place a high appreciation
upon my name. It was decided, however, to call me
"Sandford," and this name I was known by, not only
upon my master's plantation, but up to the time that I
made my escape. I was sold under the name of Sandford.

But as soon as the subject came to my mind, I resolved
on adopting my old name of William, and let Sandford
go by the board, for I always hated it. Not because there
was anything peculiar in the name; but because it had
been forced upon me. It is sometimes common, at the
south, for slaves to take the name of their masters. Some
have a legitimate right to do so. But I always detested the
idea of being called by the name of either of my masters.
And as for my father, I would rather have adopted the
name of "Friday," and been known as the servant of

some Robinson Crusoe, than to have taken his name. So I was not only hunting for my liberty, but also hunting for a name; though I regarded the latter as of little consequence, if I could but gain the former. Travelling along the road, I would sometimes speak to myself, sounding my name over, by way of getting used to it, before I should arrive among civilized human beings. On the fifth or sixth day, it rained very fast, and froze about as fast as it fell, so that my clothes were one glare of ice. I travelled on at night until I became so chilled and benumbed—the wind blowing into my face—that I found it impossible to go any further, and accordingly took shelter in a barn, where I was obliged to walk about to keep from freezing.

I have ever looked upon that night as the most eventful part of my escape from slavery. Nothing but the providence of God, and that old barn, saved me from freezing to death. I received a very severe cold, which settled upon my lungs, and from time to time my feet had been frostbitten, so that it was with difficulty I could walk. In this situation, I travelled two days, when I found that I must seek shelter somewhere, or die.

The thought of death was nothing frightful to me, compared with that of being caught, and again carried back into slavery. Nothing but the prospect of enjoying liberty could have induced me to undergo such trials, for

"Behind I left the whips and chains,
Before me were sweet Freedom's plains!"

This, and this alone, cheered me onward. But I at last resolved to seek protection from the inclemency of the weather, and therefore I secured myself behind some logs and brush intending to wait there until some one should pass by; for I thought it probable that I might see some colored person, or, if not, some one who was not a slaveholder; for I had an idea that I should know a slave-holder as far as I could see him.

The first person that passed was a man in a buggy-wagon. He looked too genteel for me to hail him. Very soon another passed by on horseback. I attempted to speak to him, but fear made my voice fail me. As he passed, I left my hidingplace and was approaching the road, when I observed an old man walking towards me, leading a white horse. He had on a broad-brimmed hat and a very long coat, and was evidently walking for exercise. As soon as I saw him, and observed his dress, I thought to myself, "You are the man that I have been looking for!" Nor was I mistaken. He was the very man!

On approaching me, he asked me, "if I was not a slave." I looked at him some time, and then asked him, "if he knew of any one who would help me, as I was sick." He answered that he would; but again asked, if I was not a slave. I told him I was. He then said that I was in a very pro-slavery neighborhood, and if I would wait until he went home, he would get a covered wagon for me. I promised to remain. He mounted his horse, and was soon out of sight.

After he was gone, I meditated whether to wait or not; being apprehensive that he had gone for some one to arrest me. But I finally concluded to remain until he should return; removing some few rods to watch his movements. After a suspense of an hour and a half or more, he returned with a two-horse covered wagon, such as are usually seen under the shed of a Quaker meeting-house on Sundays and Thursdays; for the old man proved to be a Quaker of the George Fox stamp.

He took me to his house, but it was some time before I could be induced to enter it; not until the old lady came out, did I venture into the house. I thought I saw something in the old lady's cap that told me I was not only safe, but welcome, in her house. I was not, however, prepared to receive their hospitalities. The only fault I found with them was their being too kind. I had never had a white man treat me as an equal, and the idea of a white lady waiting on me at the table was still worse! Though the table was loaded with the good things of his life, I could not eat. I thought if I could only be allowed the privilege of eating in the kitchen I should be more than satisfied!

Finding that I could not eat, the old lady, who was a "Thompsonian," [a believer in the herbal remedies of Samuel Thomson] made me a cup of "composition," or "number six;" but it was so strong and hot, that I called it *"number seven!"* However, I soon found myself at home in this family. On different occasions, when telling these facts, I have been asked how I felt upon finding myself regarded as a man by a white family; especially just having run away from one. I cannot say that I have ever answered the question yet.

The fact that I was in all probability a freeman, sounded in my ears like a charm. I am satisfied that none but a slave could place such an appreciation upon liberty as I did at that time. I wanted to see my mother and sister, that I might tell them "I was free!" I wanted to see my fellow-slaves in St. Louis, and let them know that the chains were no longer upon my limbs. I wanted to see Captain Price, and let him learn from my own lips that I was no more a chattel, but a man! I was anxious, too, thus to inform Mrs. Price that she must get another coachman. And I wanted to see Eliza more than I did either Mr. or Mrs. Price!

The fact that I was a freeman—could walk, talk, eat and sleep, as a man, and no one to stand over me with the blood-clotted cow-hide—all this made me feel that I was not myself.

The kind friend that had taken me in was named Wells Brown. He was a devoted friend of the slave; but was very old, and not in the enjoyment of good health. After being by the fire awhile, I found that my feet had been very much frozen. I was seized with a fever, which threatened to confine me to my bed. But my Thompsonian friends soon raised me, treating me as kindly as if I had been one of their own children. I remained with them twelve or fifteen days, during which time they made me some clothing, and the old gentleman purchased me a pair of boots.

I found that I was about fifty or sixty miles from Dayton, in the State of Ohio, and between one and two hundred miles from Cleaveland, on Lake Erie, a place I was desirous of reaching on my way to Canada. This I know will sound strangely to the ears of people in foreign lands, but it is nevertheless true. An American citizen was fleeing from a democratic, republican, Christian government, to receive protection under the monarchy of Great Britain. While the people of the United States boast of their freedom, they at the same time keep three millions of their own citizens in chains; and while I am seated here in sight of Bunker Hill Monument, writing this narrative, I am a slave, and no law, not even in Massachusetts, can protect me from the hands of the slave-holder!

Before leaving this good Quaker friend, he inquired what my name was besides William. I told him that I had no other name. "Well," said he, "thee must have another name. Since thee has got out of slavery, thee has become a man, and men always have two names."

I told him that he was the first man to extend the hand of friendship to me, and I would give him the privilege of naming me.

"If I name thee," said he, "I shall call thee Wells Brown, after myself."

"But," said I, "I am not willing to lose my name of William. As it was taken from me once against my will, I am not willing to part with it again upon any terms."

"Then," said he, "I will call thee William Wells Brown."

"So be it," said I; and I have been known by that name ever since I left the house of my first white friend, Wells Brown.

After giving me some little change, I again started for Canada. In four days I reached a public house, and went in to warm myself. I there learned that some fugitive slaves had just passed through the place. The men in the bar-room were talking about it, and I thought that it must have been myself they referred to, and I was therefore afraid to start, fearing they would seize me; but I finally mustered courage enough, and took my leave. As soon as I was out of sight, I went into the woods, and remained there until night, when I again regained the road, and travelled on until next day.

Not having had any food for nearly two days, I was faint with hunger, and was in a dilemma what to do, as the little cash supplied me by my adopted father, and which had contributed to my comfort, was now all gone. I however concluded to go to a farm-house, and ask for something to eat. On approaching the door of the first one presenting itself, I knocked, and was soon met by a man who asked me what I wanted. I told him that I would like something to eat. He asked me where I was from, and where I was going. I replied that I had come some way, and was going to Cleaveland.

After hesitating a moment or two, he told me that he

could give me nothing to eat, adding, "that if I would work, I could get something to eat."

I felt bad, being thus refused something to sustain nature, but did not dare tell him that I was a slave.

Just as I was leaving the door, with a heavy heart, a woman, who proved to be the wife of this gentleman, came to the door, and asked her husband what I wanted. He did not seem inclined to inform her. She therefore asked me herself. I told her that I had asked for something to eat. After a few other questions, she told me to come in, and that she would give me something to eat.

I walked up to the door, but the husband remained in the passage, as if unwilling to let me enter.

She asked him two or three times to get out of the way, and let me in. But as he did not move, she pushed him on one side, bidding me walk in! I was never before so glad to see a woman push a man aside! Ever since that act, I have been in favor of "woman's rights"!

After giving me as much food as I could eat, she presented me with ten cents, all the money then at her disposal, accompanied with a note to a friend, a few miles further on the road. Thanking this angel of mercy from an overflowing heart, I pushed on my way, and in three days arrived at Cleaveland, Ohio.

Being an entire stranger in this place, it was difficult for me to find where to stop. I had no money, and the lake being frozen, I saw that I must remain until the opening of the navigation, or go to Canada by way of Buffalo. But believing myself to be somewhat out of danger, I secured an engagement at the Mansion House, as a table waiter, in payment for my board. The proprietor, however, whose name was E. M. Segur, in a short time, hired me for twelve dollars a month; on which terms I remained until spring, when I found good employment on board a lake steamboat.

I purchased some books, and at leisure moments perused them with considerable advantage to myself. While at Cleaveland, I saw, for the first time, an anti-slavery newspaper. It was the *"Genius of Universal Emancipation,"* published by Benjamin Lundy; and though I had no home, I subscribed for the paper. It was my great desire, being out of slavery myself, to do what I could for the emancipation of my brethren yet in chains, and

while on Lake Erie, I found many opportunities of
"helping their cause along."

It is well known that a great number of fugitives make
their escape to Canada, by way of Cleaveland; and while
on the lakes, I always made arrangement to carry them
on the boat to Buffalo or Detroit, and thus effect their
escape to the "promised land." The friends of the slave,
knowing that I would transport them without charge,
never failed to have a delegation when the boat arrived
at Cleaveland. I have sometimes had four or five on board
at one time.

In the year 1842, I conveyed, from the first of May to
the first of December, sixty-nine fugitives over Lake Erie
to Canada. In 1843, I visited Malden, in Upper Canada,
and counted seventeen in that small village, whom I had
assisted in reaching Canada. Soon after coming north I
subscribed for *The Liberator,* edited by that champion of
freedom, William Lloyd Garrison. I had heard nothing
of the anti-slavery movement while in slavery, and as
soon as I found that my enslaved countrymen had friends
who were laboring for their liberation, I felt anxious to
join them, and give what aid I could to the cause.

I early embraced the temperance cause, and found that
a temperance reformation was needed among my colored
brethren. In company with a few friends, I commenced
a temperance reformation among the colored people in
the city of Buffalo, and labored three years, in which
time a society was built up, numbering over five hundred
out of a population of less than seven hundred.

In the autumn, 1843, impressed with the importance
of spreading anti-slavery truth, as a means to bring about
the abolition of slavery, I commenced lecturing as an
agent of the western New York Anti-Slavery Society, and
have ever since devoted my time to the cause of my enslaved countrymen.

From *The Liberty Bell* of 1848

THE AMERICAN SLAVE-TRADE

BY WILLIAM WELLS BROWN

Of the many features which American slavery presents, the most cruel is that of the slave-trade. A traffic in the bodies and souls of native-born Americans is carried on in the slave-holding states to an extent little dreamed of by the great mass of the people in the non-slave-holding states. The precise number of slaves carried from the slave-raising to the slave-consuming states we have no means of knowing. But it must be very great, as forty thousand were sold and carried out of the State of Virginia in one single year!

This heart-rending and cruel traffic is not confined to any particular class of persons. No person forfeits his or her character or standing in society by being engaged in raising and selling slaves to supply the cotton, sugar, and rice plantations of the south. Few persons who have visited the slave states have not, on their return, told of the gangs of slaves they had seen on their way to the southern market. This trade presents some of the most revolting and atrocious scenes which can be imagined. Slave-prisons, slave-auctions, handcuffs, whips, chains, blood-hounds, and other instruments of cruelty, are part of the furniture which belongs to the American slave-trade. It is enough to make humanity bleed at every pore, to see these implements of torture.

Known to God only is the amount of human agony and suffering which sends its cry from these slave-prisons, unheard or unheeded by man, up to His ear; mothers weeping for their children—breaking the night-silence with the shrieks of their breaking hearts. We wish no human being to experience emotions of needless pain, but we do wish that every man, woman, and child in New England, could visit a southern slave-prison and auction-stand.

I shall never forget a scene which took place in the city of St. Louis, while I was in slavery. A man and his wife, both slaves, were brought from the country to the city, for sale. They were taken to the rooms of Austin & Savage, auctioneers. Several slave-speculators, who are always to be found at auctions where slaves are to be sold, were present. The man was first put up, and sold to the highest bidder. The wife was next ordered to ascend the platform. I was present. She slowly obeyed the order. The auctioneer commenced, and soon several hundred dollars were bid. My eyes were intensely fixed on the face of the woman, whose cheeks were wet with tears. But a conversation between the slave and his new master attracted my attention. I drew near them to listen. The slave was begging his new master to purchase his wife. Said he, "Master, if you will only buy Fanny, I know you will get the worth of your money. She is a good cook, a good washer, and her last mistress liked her very much. If you will only buy her how happy I shall be." The new master replied that he did not want her, but if she sold cheap he would purchase her. I watched the countenance of the man while the different persons were bidding on his wife. When his master bid on his wife you could see the smile upon his countenance, and the tears stop; but as soon as another would bid, you could see the countenance change and the tears start afresh. From this change of countenance one could see the workings of the inmost soul. But this suspense did not last long; the wife was struck off to the highest bidder, who proved not to be the owner of her husband. As soon as they became aware that they were to be separated, they both burst into tears; and as she descended from the auction-stand, the husband, walking up to her and taking her by the hand, said, "Well, Fanny, we are to part forever, on earth; you have been a good wife to me, I did all that I could to get my new master to buy you; but he did not want you, and all I have to say is, I hope you will try to meet me in heaven. I shall try to meet you there." The wife made no reply, but her sobs and cries told, too well, her own feelings. I saw the countenances of a number of whites who were present, and whose eyes were dim with tears at hearing the man bid his wife farewell.

Such are but common occurrences in the slave states.

At these auction-stands, bones, muscles, sinews, blood and nerves, of human beings, are sold with as much indifference as a farmer in the north sells a horse or sheep. And this great American nation is, at the present time, engaged in the slave-trade. I have before me now the Washington *Union*, the organ of the government, in which I find an advertisement of several slaves to be sold for the benefit of the government. They will, in all human probability, find homes among the rice-swamps of Georgia, or the cane-brakes of Mississippi.

With every disposition on the part of those who are engaged in it to veil the truth, certain facts have, from time to time, transpired, sufficient to show, if not the full amount of the evil, at least that it is one of prodigious magnitude. And what is more to be wondered at, is the fact that the greatest slave-market is to be found at the capital of the country! The American slave-trader marches by the capitol with his "coffle-gang,"—the stars and stripes waving over their heads, and the Constitution of the United States in his pocket!

The Alexandria *Gazette,* speaking of the slave-trade at the capital, says, "Here you may behold fathers and brothers leaving behind them the dearest objects of affection, and moving slowly along in the mute agony of despair; there, the young mother, sobbing over the infant whose innocent smile seems but to increase her misery. From some you will hear the burst of bitter lamentation, while from others, the loud hysteric laugh breaks forth, denoting still deeper agony. Such is but a faint picture of the American slave-trade."

Boston, Massachusetts.

THE BLIND SLAVE BOY

BY MRS. BAILEY

Come back to me mother! why linger away
From thy poor little blind boy the long weary day!
I mark every footstep, I list to each tone,
And wonder my mother should leave me alone!
There are voices of sorrow, and voices of glee,
But there's no one to joy or to sorrow with me;
For each hath of pleasure and trouble his share,
And none for the poor little blind boy will care.

My mother, come back to me! close to thy breast
Once more let thy poor little blind boy be pressed;
Once more let me feel thy warm breath on my
      cheek,
And hear thee in accents of tenderness speak.
O mother! I've no one to love me—no heart
Can bear like thine own in my sorrows a part,
No hand is so gentle, no voice is so kind,
Oh! none like a mother can cherish the blind!

Poor blind one! No mother thy wailing can hear,
No mother can hasten to banish thy fear;
For the slave-owner drives her o'er mountain and
      wild,
And for one paltry dollar hath sold thee, poor child;
Ah, who can in language of mortals reveal
The anguish that none but a mother can feel.
When man in his vile lust of mammon hath trod
On her child, who is stricken or smitten of God!

Blind, helpless, forsaken, with strangers alone,
She hears in her anguish his piteous moan;
As he eagerly listens—but listens in vain—
To catch the loved tones of his mother again!
The curse of the broken in spirit shall fall
On the wretch who hath mingled this wormwood
      and gall,
And his gain like a mildew shall blight and destroy,
Who hath torn from his mother the little blind boy!

APPENDIX

In giving a history of my own sufferings in slavery, as well as the sufferings of others with which I was acquainted, or which came under my immediate observation, I have spoken harshly of slaveholders, in church and state.

Nor am I inclined to apologize for anything which I have said. There are exceptions among slaveholders, as well as among other sinners; and the fact that a slaveholder feeds his slaves better, clothes them better, than another, does not alter the case; he is a slaveholder. I do not ask the slaveholder to feed, clothe, or to treat his victim better as a slave. I am not waging a warfare against the collateral evils, or what are sometimes called the abuses, of slavery. I wage a war against slavery itself, because it takes man down from the lofty position which God intended he should occupy, and places him upon a level with the beasts of the field. It decrees that the slave shall not worship God according to the dictates of his own conscience; it denies him the word of God; it makes him a chattel, and sells him in the market to the highest bidder; it decrees that he shall not protect the wife of his bosom; it takes from him every right which God gave him. Clothing and food are as nothing compared with liberty. What care I for clothing or food, while I am the slave of another? You may take me and put cloth upon my back, boots upon my feet, a hat upon my head, and cram a beef-steak down my throat, and all of this will not satisfy me as long as I know that you have the power to tear me from my dearest relatives. All I ask of the slaveholder is to give the slave his liberty. It is freedom I ask for the *slave*. And that the American slave will eventually get his freedom, no one can doubt. You cannot keep the human mind forever locked up in darkness.

A ray of light, a spark from freedom's altar, the idea of inherent right, each, all, will become fixed in the soul; and that moment his "limbs swell beyond the measure of his chains," that moment he is free; then it is that the slave dies to become a freeman; then it is felt that one hour of virtuous liberty is worth an eternity of bondage; then it is, in the madness and fury of his blood, that the excited soul exclaims,

> "From life without freedom, oh! who would not fly;
> For one day of freedom, oh! who would not die?"

The rising of the slaves in Southampton, Virginia, in 1831, has not been forgotten by the American people. Nat Turner, a slave for life,—a Baptist minister,—entertained the idea that he was another Moses, whose duty it was to lead his people out of bondage. His soul was fired with the love of liberty, and he declared to his fellow-slaves that the time had arrived, and that "They who would be free, themselves must strike the blow." He knew that it would be "liberty or death" with his little band of patriots, numbering less than three hundred. He commenced the struggle for liberty; he knew his cause was just, and he loved liberty more than he feared death. He did not wish to take the lives of the whites; he only demanded that himself and brethren might be free. The slaveholders found that men whose souls were burning for liberty, however small their numbers, could not be put down at their pleasure; that something more than water was wanted to extinguish the flame. They trembled at the idea of meeting men in open combat, whose backs they had lacerated, whose wives and daughters they had torn from their bosoms, whose hearts were bleeding from the wounds inflicted by them. They appealed to the United States government for assistance. A company of United States troops was sent into Virginia to put down men whose only offence was, that they wanted to be free. Yes! northern men, men born and brought up in the free states, at the demand of slavery, marched to its rescue. They succeeded in reducing the poor slave again to his chains; but they did not succeed in crushing his spirit.

Not the combined powers of the American Union, not the slaveholders, with all their northern allies, can extin-

guish that burning desire of freedom in the slave's soul!
Northern men may stand by as the body-guard of slaveholders. They may succeed for the time being in keeping
the slave in his chains; but unless the slaveholders lib-
erate their victims, and that, too, speedily, some modern
Hannibal will make his appearance in the southern states,
who will trouble the slaveholders as the noble Cartha-
ginian did the Romans. Abolitionists deprecate the shedding of blood; they have warned the slaveholders again
and again. Yet they will not give heed, but still persist
in robbing the slave of liberty.

"But for the fear of northern bayonets, pledged for the
master's protection, the slaves would long since have
wrung a peaceful emancipation from the fears of their
oppressors, or sealed their own redemption in blood."
To the shame of the northern people, the slaveholders
confess that to them they are "indebted for a permanent
safe-guard against insurrection;" that "a million of their
slaves stand ready to strike for liberty at the first tap of
the drum;" and but for the aid of the north they would
be too weak to keep them in their chains, I ask in the
language of the slave's poet,

> "What! shall ye guard your neighbor still,
> While woman shrieks beneath his rod,
> And while he tramples down at will
> The image of a common God?
> Shall watch and ward be 'round him set,
> Of northern nerve and bayonet?"

The countenance of the people at the north has quieted
the fears of the slaveholders, especially the countenance
which they receive from northern churches. "But for the
countenance of the northern church, the southern conscience would have long since awakened to its guilt: and
the impious sight of a church made up of slaveholders,
and called the church of Christ, been scouted from the
world." So says a distinguished writer.

Slaveholders hide themselves behind the church. A
more praying, preaching, psalm-singing people cannot
be found than the slaveholders at the south. The religion
of the south is referred to every day, to prove that slaveholders are good, pious men. But with all their preten-

sions, and all the aid which they get from the northern
church, they cannot succeed in deceiving the Christian portion of the world. Their child-robbing, man-stealing,
woman-whipping, chain-forging, marriage-destroying,
slave-manufacturing, man-slaying religion, will not be received as genuine; and the people of the free states cannot
expect to live in union with slaveholders, without becoming contaminated with slavery. They are looked upon as
one people; they *are* one people; the people in the free and
slave states form the "American Union." Slavery is a national institution. The nation licenses men to traffic in the
bodies and souls of men; it supplies them with public
buildings at the capital of the country to keep their victims
in. For a paltry sum it gives the auctioneer a license to sell
American men, women, and children, upon the auction-
stand. The American slave-trader, with the Constitution in
his hat and his license in his pocket, marches his gang of
chained men and women under the very eaves of the nation's capitol. And this, too, in a country professing to be
the freest nation in the world. They profess to be democrats, republicans, and to believe in the natural equality of
men; that they are "all created with certain inalienable
rights, among which are life, liberty, and the pursuit of
happiness." They call themselves a Christian nation; they
rob three millions of their countrymen of their liberties,
and then talk of their piety, their democracy and their love
of liberty; and in the language of Shakspeare, say,

> "And thus I clothe my naked villany,
> And seem a saint when most I play the devil."

The people of the United States, with all their high
professions, are forging chains for unborn millions, in
their wars for slavery. With all their democracy, there is
not a foot of land over which the "stars and stripes" fly,
upon which the American slave can stand and claim protection. Wherever the United States Constitution has jurisdiction, and the American flag is seen flying, they point
out the slave as a chattel, a thing, a piece of property.
But I thank God there is one spot in America upon which
the slave can stand and be a man. No matter whether the
claimant be a United States president, or a doctor of divinity; no matter with what solemnities some American

court may have pronounced him a slave; the moment he makes his escape from under the "stars and stripes," and sets foot upon the soil of CANADA, "the altar and the god sink together in the dust; his soul walks abroad in his own majesty; his body swells beyond the measure of his chains, that burst from around him; and he stands redeemed, regenerated, and disenthralled, by the irresistible genius of universal emancipation."

But slavery must and will be banished from the United States soil:

"Let tyrants scorn, while tyrants dare,
The shrieks and writhings of despair;
The end will come, it will not wait,
Bonds, yokes, and scourges have their date;
Slavery itself must pass away,
And be a tale of yesterday."

But I will now stop, and let the slaveholders speak for themselves. I shall here present some evidences of the treatment which slaves receive from their masters; after which I will present a few of the slave-laws. And it has been said, and I believe truly, that no people were ever found to be better than their laws. And, as an American slave,—as one who is identified with the slaves of the south by the scars which I carry on my back,—as one identified with them by the tenderest ties of nature,—as one whose highest aspirations are to serve the cause of truth and freedom,—I beg of the reader not to lay this book down until he or she has read every page it contains. I ask it not for my own sake, but for the sake of three millions who cannot speak for themselves.

From the Livingston County (Alabama) *Whig* of Nov. 16, 1845:

"Negro Dogs.—The undersigned having brought the entire pack of Negro Dogs, (of the Hayes & Allen stock,) he now proposes to catch runaway Negroes. His charge will be three dollars per day for hunting, and fifteen dollars for catching a runaway. He resides three and a half miles north of Livingston, near the lower Jones' Bluff road.

"William Gambrel.
"Nov. 6, 1845."

The Wilmington [North Carolina] *Advertiser* of July 13, 1838, contains the following advertisement:

"Ranaway, my Negro man Richard. A reward of $25 will be paid for his apprehension, DEAD or ALIVE. Satisfactory proof will only be required of his being killed. He has with him, in all probability, his wife Eliza, who ran away from Col. Thompson, now a resident of Alabama, about the time he commenced his journey to that state.

"D.H. Rhodes."

The St. Louis *Gazette* says—

"A wealthy man here had a boy named Reuben, almost white, whom he caused to be branded in the face with the words 'A slave for life.' "

From the N.C. *Standard*, July 28, 1838:

"Twenty Dollars Reward.—Ranaway from the subscriber, a negro woman and two children; the woman is tall and black, and *a few days before she went off* I burnt her on the left side of her face: I tried to make the letter M, *and she kept a cloth over her head and face, and a fly bonnet over her head, so as to cover the burn;* her children are both boys, the oldest is in his seventh year; he is a *mulatto* and has blue eyes; the youngest is a black, and is in his fifth year.

"Micajah Ricks, Nash County."

"One of my neighbors sold to a speculator a negro boy, about 14 years old. It was more than his poor mother could bear. Her reason fled, and she became a perfect *maniac,* and had to be kept in close confinement. She would occasionally get out and run off to the neighbors. On one of these occasions she came to my house. With tears rolling down her cheeks, and her frame shaking with agony, she would cry out, *'Don't you hear him— they are whipping him now, and he is calling for me!'* This neighbor of mine, who tore the boy away from his poor mother, and thus broke her heart, was a *member of the Presbyterian church.*"—*Rev. Francis Hawley, Baptist minister, Colebrook, Ct.*

A colored man in the city of St. Louis was taken by a mob, and burnt alive at the stake. A bystander gives the following account of the scene:—

"After the flames had surrounded their prey, and when his clothes were in a blaze all over him, his eyes burnt out of his head, and his mouth seemingly parched to a cinder, some one in the *crowd*, more compassionate than the rest, proposed to put an end to his misery by shooting him, when it was replied, that it would be of no use, since he was already out of his pain. 'No,' said the wretch, 'I am not, I am suffering as much as ever,—shoot me, shoot me.' 'No, no,' said one of the fiends, who was standing about the sacrifice they were roasting, 'he shall not be shot; I would sooner slacken the fire, if that would increase his misery;' and the man who said this was, we understand, an *officer of justice.*"—*Alton Telegraph*.

"We have been informed that the slave William, who murdered his master (Huskey) some weeks since, was taken by a party a few days since from the sheriff of Hot Spring, and *burned alive!* yes, tied up to the limb of a tree and a fire built under him, and consumed in a slow lingering torture."—*Arkansas Gazette*, Oct. 29, 1836.

The Natchez *Free Trader*, 16th June, 1842, gives a horrible account of the execution of the negro Joseph on the 5th of that month for murder:

"The body," says the paper, "was taken and chained to a tree immediately on the bank of the Mississippi, on what is called Union Point. The torches were lighted and placed in the pile. He watched unmoved the curling flame as it grew, until it began to entwine itself around and feed upon his body; then he sent forth cries of agony painful to the ear, begging some one to blow his brains out; at the same time surging with almost superhuman strength, until the staple with which the chain was fastened to the tree, not being well secured, drew out, and he leaped from the burning pile. At that moment the sharp ring of several rifles was heard, and the body of the negro fell a corpse to the ground. He was picked up by two or three, and again thrown into the fire and consumed."

"Another Negro burned.—We learn from the clerk of the Highlander, that, while wooding a short distance below the mouth of Red river, they were *invited to stop a short time and see another negro burned.*"—*New Orleans Bulletin*.

We can assure the Bostonians, one and all, who have embarked in the nefarious scheme of abolishing slavery at the south, that lashes will hereafter be spared the backs of their emissaries. Let them send out their men to Louisiana; they will never return to tell their sufferings, but they shall expiate the crime of interfering in our domestic institutions by being burned at the stake.''—*New Orleans True American*.

''The cry of the whole south should be death, instant death, to the abolitionist, wherever he is caught.'' —*Augusta (Geo.) Chronicle*.

''Let us declare through the public journals of our country, that the question of slavery is not and shall not be open for discussion: that the system is too deep-rooted among us, and must remain forever; that the very moment any private individual attempts to lecture us upon its evils and immorality, and the necessity of putting means in operation to secure us from them, in the same moment his tongue shall be cut out and cast upon the dunghill.''—*Columbia (S. C.) Telescope*.

From the St. Louis *Republican:*
''On Friday last the coroner held an inquest at the house of Judge Dunica, a few miles south of the city, over the body of a negro girl, about 8 years of age, belonging to Mr. Cordell. The body exhibited evidence of the most cruel whipping and beating we have ever heard of. The flesh on the back and limbs were beaten to a jelly—one shoulder-bone was laid bare—there were several cuts, apparently from a club, on the head—and around the neck was the indentation of a cord, by which it is supposed she had been confined to a tree. She had been hired by a man by the name of Tanner, residing in the neighborhood, and was sent home in this condition. After coming home, her constant request, until her death, was for bread, by which it would seem that she had been starved as well as unmercifully whipped. The jury returned a verdict that she came to her death by the blows inflicted by some persons unknown whilst she was in the employ of Mr. Tanner. Mrs. Tanner has been tried and acquitted.''

A correspondent of the N. Y. *Herald* writes from St. Louis, Oct. 19:

"I yesterday visited the cell of Cornelia, the slave charged with being the accomplice of Mrs. Ann Tanner (recently acquitted) in the murder of a little negro girl, by whipping and starvation. She admits her participancy, but says she was compelled to take the part she did in the affair. On one occasion she says the child was tied to a tree from Monday morning till Friday night, exposed by day to the scorching rays of the sun, and by night to the stinging of myriads of musquitoes; and that during all this time the child had nothing to eat, but was whipped daily. The child told the same story to Dr. McDowell."

From the Carroll County *Mississippian*, May 4th, 1844:

"Committed to jail in this place, on the 29th of April last, a runaway slave named Creesy, and says she belongs to William Barrow, of Carroll county, Mississippi. Said woman is stout built, five feet four inches high, and appears to be about twenty years of age; she has a band of iron on each ankle, and a trace chain around her neck, fastened with a common padlock.

"J. N. Spencer, Jailer.
"May 15, 1844."

The Savannah, Ga., *Republican* of the 13th of March, 1845, contains an advertisement, one item of which is as follows:—

"Also, at the same time and place, the following negro slaves, to wit: Charles, Peggy, Antonnett, Davy, September, Maria, Jenny, and Isaac—levied on as the property of Henry T. Hall, to satisfy a mortgage fi. fia. issued out of McIntosh Superior Court, in favor of the board of directors of the *Theological Seminary of the Synod of South Carolina and Georgia*, vs. said Henry T. Hall. Conditions, cash.

"C. O'Neal, Deputy Sheriff, M.C."

In the Macon (Georgia) *Telegraph*, May 28, is the following:

"About the first of March last, the negro man Ransom left me, without the least provocation whatever. I will give a reward of $20 dollars for said negro, if taken dead or alive,—and if killed in any attempt an advance of $5 will be paid.

"Bryant Johnson.
"Crawford Co., Ga."

From the Apalachicola *Gazette*, May 9:
"One Hundred and Fifty Dollars Reward.—Ranaway from my plantation on the 6th inst., three negro men, all of dark complexion.

"Bill is about five feet four inches high, aged about twenty-six, *a scar on his upper lip,* also *one on his shoulder,* and has been *badly cut on his arm;* speaks quick and broken, and a venomous look.

"Daniel is about the same height, chunky and well set, broad, flat mouth, with a pleasing countenance, rather inclined to show his teeth when talking, no particular marks recollected, aged about twenty-three.

"Noah is about six feet three or four inches high, twenty-eight years old, with rather a down, impudent look, insolent in his discourse, with a large mark on his breast, *a good many large scars,* caused by the whip, on his back—*has been shot in the back of his arm* with small shot. The above reward will be paid to any one who will kill the three, or fifty for each one, or twenty dollars apiece for them delivered to me at my plantation alive, on Chattahoochie, Early county.

"J. McDonald."

From the Alabama *Beacon*, June 14, 1845:
"Ranaway, on the 15th of May, from me, a negro woman named Fanny. Said woman is twenty years old; is rather tall, can read and write, and so forge passes for herself. Carried away with her a pair of ear-rings, a Bible with a red cover, is very pious. She prays a great deal, and was, as supposed, contented and happy. She is as white as most white women, with straight light hair, and blue eyes, and can pass herself for a white woman. I will give five hundred dollars for her apprehension and delivery to me. She is very intelligent.

"John Balch.
"Tuscaloosa, May, 29, 1845."

From the N. O. *Commercial Bulletin*, Sept. 30:
"Ten Dollars Reward.—Ranaway from the subscribers, on the 15th of last month, the negro man Charles, about 45 years of age, 5 feet 6 inches high; red com-

plexion, has had the *upper lid of his right eye torn, and a scar on his forehead;* speaks English only, and stutters when spoken to; he had on when he left, *an iron collar, the prongs of which he broke off before absconding.* The above reward will be paid for the arrest of said slave.

"W. E. & R. Murphy,
"132 Old Raisin."

From the N.O. *Bee,* Oct. 5:
"Ranaway from the residence of Messrs. F. Duncom & Co., the negro Francois, aged from 25 to 30 years, about 5 feet 1 inch in height; the *upper front teeth are missing;* he had *chains on both of his legs,* dressed with a kind of blouse made of sackcloth. A proportionate reward will be given to whoever will bring him back to the bakery, No. 74, Bourbon Street."

From the N. O. *Picayune* of Sunday, Dec. 17:
"Cock-Pit.—*Benefit of Fire Company No. 1, Lafayette.*—A cock-fight will take place on Sunday, the 17th inst., at the well-known house of the subscriber. As the entire proceeds are for the benefit of the fire company, a full attendance is respectfully solicited.
"Corner of Josephine and Tchoupitolas streets, Lafayette."

From the N. O. *Picayune:*
"Turkey Shooting.—This day, Dec. 17, from 10 o'clock, A. M., until 6 o'clock, P.M., and the following Sundays at M'Donoughville, opposite the Second Municipality Ferry."

The next is an advertisement from the New Orleans *Bee,* an equally popular paper:
"A Bull Fight, between a ferocious bull and a number of dogs, will take place on Sunday next, at 4¼ o'clock, P.M., on the other side of the river, at Algiers, opposite Canal street. After the bull fight, a fight will take place between a bear and some dogs. The whole to conclude by a combat between an ass and several dogs.
"Amateurs bringing dogs to participate in the fight will be admitted gratis. Admittance—Boxes, 50 cts.; Pit, 30 cts. The spectacle will be repeated every Sunday, weather permitting.

"Pepe Llulla."

Extracts from
the American Slave Code.

The following are mostly abridged selections from the statutes of the slave states and of the United States. They give but a faint view of the cruel oppression to which the slaves are subject, but a strong one enough, it is thought, to fill every honest heart with a deep abhorrence of the atrocious system. Most of the important provisions here cited, though placed under the name of only one state, prevail in nearly all the states, with slight variations in language, and some diversity in the penalties. The extracts have been made in part from Stroud's Sketch of the Slave Laws but chiefly from authorized editions of the statute books referred to, found in the Philadelphia Law Library. As the compiler has not had access to many of the later enactments of the several states, nearly all he has cited are acts of an earlier date than that of the present anti-slavery movement, so that their severity cannot be ascribed to its influence.

The cardinal principal of slavery, that the slave is not to be ranked among *sentient beings*, but among things— is an article of property, a chattel personal—obtains as undoubted law in all the slave states.*—*Stroud's Sketch,* p. 22.

The dominion of the master is as unlimited as is that which is tolerated by the laws of any civilized country in relation to brute animals—to *quadrupeds;* to use the words of the civil law.—*Ib.* 24.

---

*In accordance with this doctrine, an act of Maryland, 1798, enumerates among articles of property, *"slaves, working beasts, animals of any kind, stock, furniture, plate, and so forth."*—*Ib* 23.

Slaves cannot even contract matrimony.†—*Ib.* 61.

LOUISIANA.—A slave is one who is in the power of his master, to whom he belongs. The master may sell him, dispose of his person, his industry and his labor; he can do nothing, possess nothing, nor acquire anything, but what must belong to his master.—*Civil Code*, Art. 35.

Slaves are incapable of inheriting or transmitting property.—*Civil Code,* Art. 945; also Art. 175, and *Code of Practice,* Art. 103.

Martin's Digest, Act of June 7, 1806—Slaves shall always be reputed and considered real estate; shall be as such subject to be mortgaged, according to the rules prescribed by law, and they shall be seized and sold as real estate.—*Vol. I.,* p. 612.

Dig. Stat. Sec. 13—No owner of slaves shall hire his slaves to themselves, under a penalty of twenty-five dollars for each offence.—*Vol. 1.,* p. 102.

Sec. 15.—No slave can possess anything in his own right, or dispose of the produce of his own industry, without the consent of his master.—p. 103.

Sec. 16.—No slave can be party in a civil suit, or witness in a civil or criminal matter, against any white person.—p. 103. *See also Civil Code,* Art. 117, p. 28.

Sec. 18.—A slave's subordination to his master is susceptible of no restriction, (except in what incites to crime,) and he owes to him and all his family, respect without bounds, and absolute obedience.—p. 103.

Sec. 25.—Every slave found on horseback, without a written permission from his master, shall receive twenty-five lashes.—p. 105.

Sec. 32.—Any freeholder may seize and correct any slave found absent from his usual place of work or residence, without some white person, and if the slave resist or try to escape, he may use arms, and if the slave *assault** and strike him, he may *kill* the slave—p. 109., p. 115.

Sec. 35.—It is lawful to fire upon runaway negroes

†A slave is not admonished for incontinence, punished for adultery, nor prosecuted for bigamy.—*Attorney General of Maryland, Md. Rep. Vol. I.* 561.

*The legal meaning of assault is to *offer* to do personal violence.

who are armed, and upon those who, when pursued, refuse to surrender.—p. 109.

Sec. 38.—No slave may buy, sell, or exchange any kind of goods, or hold any boat, or bring up for his own use any horses or cattle, under a penalty of forfeiting the whole.—p. 110.

Sec. 7.—Slaves or free colored persons are punished with *death* for wilfully burning or destroying any stack of produce or any building.

Sec. 15.—The punishment of a slave for striking a white person, shall be for the first and second offences at the discretion of the court,* but not extending to life or limb, and for the third offence *death;* but for grievously wounding or multilating a white person, *death* for the first offence; provided, if the blow or wound is given in defence of the person or *property of his master,* or the person having charge of him, he is entirely justified.

Act of Feb. 22, 1824, Sec. 2.—A slave for wilfully striking his master or mistress, or the child of either, or his white overseer, so as to cause a bruise or shedding of blood, *shall be punished with death.*—p. 125.

Act of March 6, 1819.—Any person cutting or breaking any iron chain or collar used to prevent the escape of slaves, shall be fined not less than two hundred dollars, nor more than one thousand dollars, and be imprisoned not more than two years nor less than six months.—p. 64 of the session.

Law of January 8, 1813, Sec. 71.—All slaves sentenced to death or perpetual imprisonment, in virtue of existing laws, shall be paid for out of the public treasury, provided the sum paid shall not exceed $300 for each slave.

Law of March 16, 1830, Sec. 93.—The state treasurer shall pay the owners the value of all slaves whose punishment has been commuted from that of death to that of imprisonment for life, &c.

If any slave shall *happen* to be slain for refusing to surrender him or herself, contrary to law, or in unlawfully resisting any officer or *other person,* who shall apprehend,

---

*A court for the trial of slaves consists of one justice of the peace, and three freeholders, and the justice and one freeholder, i.e., *one half the court, may convict, though the other two are for acquittal.*—Martin's Dig., I. 646.

or endeavor to apprehend, such slave or slaves, &c., such officer or *other person so killing such slave as aforesaid*, making resistance, shall be, and he is by this act, *indemnified*, from any prosecution for such killing aforesaid, &c.—*Maryland Laws, act of* 1751, *chap xiv.*, §9.

And by the negro act of 1740 of South Carolina, it is declared:

If any slave who shall be out of the house or plantation where such slave shall live, or shall be usually employed, or without some white person in company with such slave, shall *refuse to submit* to undergo the examination of *any white* person, it shall be lawful for such white person to pursue, apprehend, and moderately correct such slave; and if such slave shall assault and strike such white person, such slave may be *lawfully killed!!*—2 *Brevard's Digest*, 231.

MISSISSIPPI. *Chapt.* 92, Sec. 110.—Penalty for any slave or free colored person exercising the functions of a minister of the gospel, thirty-nine lashes; but any master may permit his slave to preach on his own premises, no slaves but his own being permitted to assemble.—*Digest of Stat.*, p. 770.

Act of June 18, 1822, Sec. 21.—No negro or mulatto can be a witness in any case, except against negroes or mulattoes.—p. 749. *New Code*, 372.

Sec. 25.—Any master licensing his slave to go at large and trade as a freeman, shall forfeit fifty dollars to the state for the literary fund.

Penalty for teaching a slave to read, imprisonment one year. For using language having a *tendency* to promote discontent among free colored people, or insubordination among slaves, imprisonment at *hard labor*, not less than three, nor more than twenty-one years, or death, at the discretion of the court.—*L. M. Child's Appeal*, p. 70.

Sec. 26.—It is *lawful* for *any* person, and the duty of every sheriff, deputy-sheriff, coroner and constable to apprehend any slave going at large, or hired out by him, or herself, and take him or her before a justice of the peace, who shall impose a penalty of not less than twenty dollars, nor more than fifty dollars, on the owner, who has permitted such slave to do so.

Sec. 32.—Any negro or mulatto, for using abusive language, or lifting his hand in opposition to any white person (except in self-defence against a wanton assault), shall, on proof of the offence by oath of such person, receive such punishment as a justice of the peace may order, not exceeding thirty-nine lashes.

Sec. 41.—Forbids the holding of cattle, sheep or hogs by slaves, even with consent of the master, under penalty of forfeiture, half to the county and half to the *informer*.

Sec. 42.—Forbids a slave keeping a dog, under a penalty of twenty-five stripes; and requires any master who permits it to pay a fine of five dollars, and make good all damages done by such dog.

Sec. 43.—Forbids slaves cultivating cotton for his own use, and imposes a fine of fifty dollars on the master or overseer who permits it.

Revised Code.—Every negro or mulatto found in the state, not able to show himself entitled to freedom, may be sold as a slave—p. 389. The owner of any plantation, on which a slave comes without written leave from his master, and not on lawful business, may inflict ten lashes for every such offence.—p. 371.

ALABAMA.—*Aiken's Digest*. Tit. *Slaves, &c.*, Sec. 31.—For *attempting* to teach any free colored person, or slave, to spell, read or write, a fine of not less than two hundred and fifty dollars, nor more than five hundred dollars!—p. 397.

Sec. 35 and 36.—Any free colored person found with slaves in a kitchen, outhouse or negro quarter, without a written permission from the master or overseer of said slaves, and any slave found without such permission with a free negro on his premises, shall receive fifteen lashes for the first offence, and thirty-nine for each subsequent offence; to be inflicted by master, overseer, or member of any patrol company.—p. 397.

Toulmin's Digest.—No slave can be emancipated but by a *special* act of the Legislature.—p. 623.

Act Jan. 1st, 1823—Authorizes an agent to be appointed by the governor of the state, *to sell for the benefit of the state* all persons of color brought into the United States and within the jurisdiction of Alabama, *contrary to the laws of congress prohibiting the slave trade.*—p. 643.

georgia.—*Prince's Digest*. Act Dec. 19, 1818.—Penalty for any free person of color (except regularly articled seamen) coming into the state, a fine of one hundred dollars on failure of payment to be sold as a slave.—p.465.

Penalty for permitting a slave to labor or do business

for himself, except on his master's premises, thirty dollars per week.—p. 457.

No slave can be a party to any suit against a white man, except on claim of his freedom, *and every colored person is presumed to be a slave, unless he can prove himself free.*—p. 446.

Act Dec. 13, 1792—Forbids the assembling of negroes under pretence of divine worship, contrary to the act regulating patrols, p. 342. This act provides that any justice of the peace may disperse any assembly of slaves which *may* endanger the peace; and every slave found at such meeting shall receive, *without trial,* twenty-five stripes!—p. 447.

Any person who sees more than seven men slaves without any white person, in a high road, may whip each slave *twenty* lashes.—p. 454.

Any slave who harbors a runaway, may suffer punishment *to any extent,* not affecting life or limb.—p. 452.

SOUTH CAROLINA.—*Brevard's Digest.*—Slaves shall be deemed sold, taken, reputed, and adjudged in law to be *chattels personal* in the hands of their owners and possessors, and their executors, administrators, and assigns, *to all intents, constructions and purposes whatever.*— Vol. ii., p. 229.

Act of 1740, in the preamble, states that "*many* owners of slaves and others that have the management of them do confine them *so closely to hard labor,* that they have *not sufficient time for natural rest,*" and enacts that no slave shall be compelled to labor more than *fifteen* hours in the twenty-four from March 25th to Sept. 25th, or *fourteen* in the twenty-four for the rest of the year. Penalty from £5 to £20.—Vol. ii., p. 243.

[Yet, in several of the slave states, the time of work for *criminals* whose *punishment* is hard labor, is eight hours a day for three months, nine hours for two months, and ten for the rest of the year.]

A slave endeavoring to entice another slave to run away, if provision be prepared for the purpose of aiding or abetting such endeavor, shall suffer *death.*—pp. 233 and 244.

Penalty for cruelly scalding or burning a slave, cutting out his tongue, putting out his eye, or depriving him of any limb, a fine of £100. For beating with a *horse*-whip, cow-skin, switch or small stick, or putting irons on, or imprisoning a slave, *no penalty or prohibition.*—p. 241.

Any person who, not having lawful authority to do so, shall beat a slave, so as to disable him from *working*, shall pay fifteen shillings a day *to the owner*, for the slave's lost time, and the charge of his cure.—p. 231 and 232.

A slave claiming his freedom may sue for it by some friend who will act as guardian, but if the action be judged groundless, said guardian shall pay *double* costs of suit, and such damages to the owner as the court may decide.—p. 260.

Any assembly of slaves or free colored persons, in a secret or confined place, for mental instruction, (even if white persons *are* present,) is an unlawful meeting, and magistrates must disperse it, breaking doors if necessary, and may inflict *twenty lashes* upon each slave or colored person present.—pp. 254 and 255.

Meetings for religious worship, before sunrise, or after 9 o'clock, P. M., unless a majority are white persons, are forbidden; and magistrates are required to disperse them.—p. 261.

A slave who lets loose any boat from the place where the owner has fastened it, for the first *offence shall receive thirty-nine lashes, and for the second shall have one ear cut off.*—p. 228.

James' Digest.—Penalty for *killing* a slave, on *sudden heat of passion*, or by *undue correction*, a fine of $500 and imprisonment not over six months.—p. 392.

NORTH CAROLINA.—*Haywood's Manual.*—Act of 1798, Sec. 3, enacts, that the killing of a slave shall be punished like that of a free man; *except* in the case of a slave *out-lawed*,* or a slave *offering to resist* his master or a slave *dying under moderate correction.*—p. 530.

Act of 1799.—Any slave set free, except for meritorious services, to be adjudged of by the county court, may be seized by any freeholder, committed to jail, *and sold to the highest bidder.*†—p. 525.

Patrols are not liable to the master for punishing his

---

*A slave may be out-lawed when he runs away, conceals himself, and, to sustain life, kills a hog, or any animal of the cattle kind.—*Haywood's Manual*, p. 521.

†In South Carolina, *any* person may seize such freed man and keep him as his property.

slave, unless their conduct clearly shows malice *against the master.—Hawk's Reps.*, vol. i., p. 418.

TENNESSEE.—*Stat. Law,* Chap. 57, Sec. 1.—Penalty on master for hiring to any slave his own time, a fine of not less than one dollar nor more than two dollars a day, *half* to the informer.—p. 679.

Chap. 2, Sec. 102.—No slave can be emancipated but on condition of immediately removing from the state, and the person emancipating shall give bond, in a sum equal to the slave's value, to have him removed.—p. 279.

Laws of 1813. Chap. 35.—In the trial of slaves, the sheriff chooses the court, which must consist of three justices and twelve *slaveholders* to serve as jurors.

ARKANSAS.—*Rev. Stat.*, Sec. 4, requires the patrol to visit all places suspected of unlawful assemblages of slaves; and sec. 5 provides that any slave found at such assembly, or strolling about without a pass, *shall receive* any number of *lashes*, at the discretion of the patrol, not exceeding twenty.—p. 604.

MISSOURI.—*Laws, I.*—Any master may commit to jail, there to remain, at *his pleasure*, any slave who refuses to obey him or his overseer.—p. 309.

Whether a slave claiming freedom may even commence a suit for it, may depend on the decision of a single judge.—*Stroud's Sketch*, p. 78, note which refers to Missouri laws, I., 404.

KENTUCKY.—*Dig. of Stat.*, Act Feb. 8, 1798, Sec. 5—No colored person may *keep* or *carry* gun, powder, shot, *club* or *other weapon*, on penalty of *thirty-nine lashes*, and forfeiting the weapon, which any person is authorized to take.

VIRGINIA.—*Rev. Code.*—Any emancipated slave remaining in the state more than a year, may be sold by the overseers of the *poor*, for the benefit of the *literary fund*!—Vol. i., p. 436.

Any slave or free colored person found at any school for teaching reading or writing, by day or night, may be whipped, at the discretion of a justice, not exceeding twenty lashes.—p. 424.

Supp. Rev. Code.—Any person assembling with slaves, for the *purpose* of teaching them to read or write, shall be fined, not less than 10 dollars, nor more than 100 dollars; or with free colored persons, shall be fined not more than fifty dollars, and imprisoned not more than two months.—p. 245.

By the revised code, *seventy-one* offences are punished with *death* when committed by slaves, and by nothing more than imprisonment when by the whites.—*Stroud's Sketch*, p. 107.

Rev. Code.—In the trial of slaves, the court consists of five justices without juries, even in capital cases.— I., p. 420.

MARYLAND.—*Stat. Law*, Sec. 8.—Any slave, for rambling in the night, or riding horses by day without leave, or running away may be punished by whipping, cropping, or branding in the cheek, or otherwise, not rendering him unfit for labor.—p. 237.

Any slave convicted of petty treason, murder, or *wilful burning of dwelling houses*, may be sentenced *to have the right hand cut off, to be hanged in the usual manner, the head severed from the body, the body divided into four quarters, and the head and quarters set up in the most public place in the country where such fact was committed!!*—p. 190.

Act 1717, Chap. 13, Sec. 5—Provides that any free colored person marrying a slave, becomes a slave for life, except mulattoes born of white women.

DELAWARE.—*Laws.*—More than six men slaves, meeting together, not belonging to one master, unless on lawful business of their owners, may be whipped to the extent of twenty-one lashes each.—p. 104.

UNITED STATES.—*Constitution.*—The chief proslavery provisions of the constitution, as is generally known, are, 1st, that by virtue of which the slave states are represented in congress for three-fifths of their slaves;* 2nd, that requiring the giving up of any runaway slaves to their masters: 3rd, that pledging the physical force of the whole country to suppress insurrections, i.e., attempts to gain freedom by such means as the framers of the instrument themselves used.

Act of Feb. 12, 1793—Provides that any master or his

---

*By the operation of this provision, twelve slaveholding states, whose white population only equals that of New York and Ohio, send to congress 24 senators and 102 representatives, while these two states only send 4 senators and 59 representatives.

agent may seize any person whom he claims as a "fugitive from service," and take him before a judge of the U.S. court, or magistrate of the city or county where he is taken, and the magistrate, on proof, in support of the claim, to his satisfaction, must give the claimant a certificate authorizing the removal of such fugitive to the state he fled from.*

DISTRICT OF COLUMBIA.—The act of congress incorporating Washington city, gives the corporation power to prescribe the terms and conditions on which free negroes and mulattoes may reside in the city. *City Laws,* 6 and 11. By this authority, the city in 1827 enacted that any free colored person coming there to reside, should give the mayor satisfactory evidence of his freedom, and enter into bond with two freehold sureties, in the sum of five hundred dollars, for his good conduct, to be renewed each year for three years; or failing to do so, must leave the city, or be committed to the workhouse, for not more than one year, and if he still refuse to go, may be again committed for the same period, and so on.—*Ib.* 198.

Colored persons residing in the city, who cannot prove their title to freedom, shall be imprisoned as absconding slaves.—*Ib.* 198.

Colored persons found without free papers may be arrested as runaway slaves, and after two months' notice, if no claimant appears, must be advertised ten days, and sold to pay their jail fees.†—*Stroud,* 85, note.

The city of Washington grants a license to *trade in slaves,* for profit, as agent, or otherwise, for four hundred dollars.—*City Laws,* p. 249.

Reader, you uphold these laws *while you do nothing for their repeal.* You *can do* much. You can take and read

---

*Thus it may be seen that a *man* may be doomed to slavery by an authority not considered sufficient to settle a claim of *twenty dollars.*

†The prisons of the district, built with the money of the nation, are used as store-houses of the slaveholder's human merchandize. "From the statement of the keeper of a jail at Washington, it appears that in five years, upwards of 450 colored persons were committed to the national prison in that city, for safekeeping, i.e., until they could be disposed of in the course of the *slave trade,* besides nearly 300 who had been taken up as runaways." —*Miner's Speech in H. Rep.,* 1829.

the antislavery journals. They will give you an impartial history of the cause, and arguments with which to convert its enemies. You can countenance and aid those who are laboring for its promotion. You can petition against slavery; you can refuse to vote for slaveholders or proslavery men, constitutions and compacts; can abstain from products of slave labor; and can use your social influence to spread right principles and awaken a right feeling. Be as earnest for freedom as its foes are for slavery, and you can diffuse an anti-slavery sentiment through your whole neighborhood, and merit "the blessing of them that are ready to perish."

The following is from the old colonial law of North Carolina:

Notice of the commitment of runaways—viz., 1741, c. 24, §29. "An act concerning servants and slaves."

Copy of notice containing a full description of such runaway and his clothing—The sheriff is to "cause a copy of such notice to be sent to the clerk or reader of each church or chapel within his county, who are hereby required to make publication thereof by setting up the same in some open and convenient place, near the said church or chapel, on every Lord's day, during the space of two months from the date thereof."

1741, c. 24, §45.—"Which proclamation shall be published on a Sabbath day at the door of every church or chapel, or, for want of such, at the place where divine service shall be performed in the said county, by the parish clerk or reader, immediately after divine service; and if any slave or slaves, against whom proclamation hath been thus issued, stay out and do not immediately return home, it shall be lawful for any person or persons whatsoever to kill and destroy such slave or slaves by such way or means as he or she shall think fit, without accusation or impeachment of any crime for the same."

It is well known that slavery makes labor disreputable in the slave states. Laboring men of the north, hear how contemptibly slaveholders speak of you.

Mr. Robert Wickliffe of Kentucky, in a speech published in the Louisville *Advertiser,* in opposition to those who were averse to the importation of slaves from the states, thus discourseth:

"Gentlemen wanted to drive out the black population that they may obtain WHITE NEGROES in their place. WHITE NEGROES have this advantage over black negroes, they can be converted into voters; and the men who live upon the sweat of their brow, and pay them but a dependent and scanty subsistence, can, if able to keep then thousand of them in employment, come up to the polls and change the destiny of the country.

"How improved will be our condition when we have such white negroes as perform the servile labors of Europe, of old England, and he would add now of *New England,* when our body servants and our cart drivers, and our street sweepers, are *white negroes* instead of black. Where will be the independence, the proud spirit, and chivalry of the Kentuckians then?"

We believe the servitude which prevails in the south far preferable to that of the *north,* or in Europe. Slavery will exist in all communities. There is a class which may be nominally free, but they will be virtually *slaves."*
—*Mississippian, July 6th, 1838.*

"Those who depend on their daily labor for their daily subsistence can never enter into political affairs, they never do, never will, never can."—*B. W. Leigh, in Virginia Convention,* 1829.

"All society settles down into a classification of capitalists and laborers. The former will *own* the latter, either collectively through the government, or individually in a state of domestic servitude as exists in the southern states of this confederacy. If LABORERS ever obtain the political power of a country, it is in fact in a state of REVOLUTION. The capitalists north of Mason and Dixon's line have precisely the same interest in the labor of the country that the capitalists of England have in their labor. Hence it is, that they must have a strong federal government [!] *to control* the labor of the nation. But it is precisely the reverse with us. We have already not only a right to the proceeds of our laborers, but we own a *class of laborers* themselves. But let me say to gentlemen who represent the great class of capitalists in the north, beware that you do not drive us into a separate system, for if you do, as certain as the decrees of heaven, you will be compelled to *appeal to the sword to maintain yourselves at home*. It may not come in your day; but your children's children will be covered with the blood of domestic factions, and a *plundering mob contending for power and conquest*."—*Mr. Pickens, of South Carolina, in Congress, 21st Jan., 1836*.

"In the very nature of things there must be classes of persons to discharge all the different offices of society from the highest to the lowest. Some of these offices are regarded as *degraded*, although they must and will be performed. Hence those manifest forms of dependent servitude which produce a sense of superiority in the masters or employers, and of inferiority on the part of the servants. Where these offices are performed by *members of the political community*, a dangerous element is obviously introduced into the body politic. Hence the alarming tendency to violate the rights of property by agrarian legislation which is beginning to be manifest in the older states where universal suffrage *prevails without* domestic slavery.

"In a word, the institution of domestic slavery supersedes the *necessity* of An Order of Nobility and All the Other Appendages of a Hereditary System of Government."—*Gov. M'Duffie's Message to the South Carolina Legislature, 1836.*

"We of the south have cause now, and shall soon have greater, to congratulate ourselves on the existence of a population among us which excludes the populace which in effect rules some of our northern neighbors, and is rapidly gaining strength wherever slavery does not exist— a populace made up of the dregs of Europe, and the most worthless portion of the native population."—*Richmond Whig, 1837.*

"Would you do a benefit to the horse or the ox by giving him a cultivated understanding, a fine feeling! So far as the mere laborer has the pride, the knowledge or the aspiration of a freeman, he is unfitted for his situation. If there are sordid, servile, *laborious* offices to be performed, is it not better that there should be sordid, servile, laborious beings to perform them?

"Odium has been cast upon our legislation on account of its forbidding the elements of education being communicated to slaves. But in truth what injury is done them by this? *He who works during the day with his hands,* does not read in the intervals of leisure for his amusement or the improvement of his mind, or the exception is so very rare as scarcely to need the being provided for."—*Chancellor Harper, of South Carolina.*—*Southern Lit. Messenger.*

"Our slave population is decidedly preferable, as an orderly and laboring class, to a northern laboring class, that have just learning enough to make them wondrous wise, and make them the most dangerous class to well regulated liberty under the sun."—*Richmond (Virginia) Enquirer.*

William Wells Brown

My Southern Home:

OR,

THE SOUTH AND ITS PEOPLE.

BY

WM. WELLS BROWN, M.D.

AUTHOR OF
"SKETCHES OF PLACES AND PEOPLE ABROAD,"
"CLOTELLE," "THE BLACK MAN," "THE NEGRO IN
THE REBELLION," "THE RISING SON," ETC.

"Go, little book, from this thy solitude!
 I cast thee on the waters—go thy ways!
And if, as I believe, thy vein be good,
 The world will find thee after many days."
                                        —*Southey.*

PREFACE.

No attempt has been made to create heroes or heroines, or to appeal to the imagination or the heart.

The earlier incidents were written out from the author's recollections. The later sketches here given, are the results of recent visits to the South, where the incidents were jotted down at the time of their occurrence, or as they fell from the lips of the narrators, and in their own unadorned dialect.

Boston, May, 1880.

CONTENTS.

X.

The mysterious, veiled Lady. The white Slave Child. The beautiful Quadroon,—her heroic death. The Slave Trader and his Victim. Lola, the white Slave,—the Law's Victim.

XI.

The introduction of the Cotton Gin, and its influence on the Price of Slaves. Great rise in Slave property. The great Southern Slave Trader. How a man got flogged when intended for another.

XII.

New Orleans in the olden time. A Congo Dance. Visiting the Angels, and chased by the Devil. A live Ghost.

XIII.

The Slave's Escape. He is Captured, and again Escapes. How he outwitted the Slave-Catchers. Quaker Wit and Humor.

XIV.

The Free colored people of the South before the Rebellion. Their hard lot. Attempt to Enslave them. Reopening of the African Slave Trade. Sentiments of distinguished Southern Fire-Eaters.

XV.

Southern Control of the National Government. Their contempt for Northerners. Insult to Northern Statesmen.

XVI.

Proclamation of Emancipation. The last night of Slavery. Waiting for the Hour. Music from the Banjo on the Wall. Great rejoicing. Hunting friends. A Son known, Twenty Years after separation, by the Mark on the bottom of his Foot.

XVII.

Negro equality. Blacks must Paddle their own Canoe. The War of Races.

XVIII.

Blacks enjoying a Life of Freedom. Alabama negro Cotton-Growers. Negro street Peddlers; their music and their humors. A man with One Hundred Children. His experience.

XIX.

The whites of Tennessee,—their hatred to the negro,—their antecedents. Blacks in Southern Legislatures,—

cessity. Should follow the Example of other Races. Professions and Trades needed.

XXIX.

Mixture of Races. The Anglo-Saxon. Isolated Races: The Negro—the Irish—the Coptic—the Jews—the Gypsies—the Romans, Mexicans, and Peruvians. Progressive Negroes,—Artists and Painters. Pride of Race.

MY SOUTHERN HOME.

CHAPTER I.

Ten miles north of the city of St. Louis, in the State of Missouri, forty years ago, on a pleasant plain, sloping off toward a murmuring stream, stood a large frame-house, two stories high; in front was a beautiful lake, and, in the rear, an old orchard filled with apple, peach, pear, and plum trees, with boughs untrimmed, all bearing indifferent fruit. The mansion was surrounded with piazzas, covered with grape-vines, clematis, and passion flowers; the Pride of China mixed its oriental-looking foliage with the majestic magnolia, and the air was redolent with the fragrance of buds peeping out of every nook, and nodding upon you with a most unexpected welcome.

The tasteful hand of art, which shows itself in the grounds of European and New-England villas, was not seen there, but the lavish beauty and harmonious disorder of nature was permitted to take its own course, and exhibited a want of taste so commonly witnessed in the sunny South.

The killing effects of the tobacco plant upon the lands of "Poplar Farm," was to be seen in the rank growth of the brier, the thistle, the burdock, and the jimpson weed, showing themselves wherever the strong arm of the bondman had not kept them down.

Dr. Gaines, the proprietor of "Poplar Farm," was a good-humored, sunny-sided old gentleman, who, always feeling happy himself, wanted everybody to enjoy the same blessing. Unfortunately for him, the Doctor had been born and brought up in Virginia, raised in a family claiming to be of the "F. F. V.'s," but, in reality, was comparatively poor. Marrying Mrs. Sarah Scott Pepper, an accomplished widow lady of medium fortune, Dr.

Gaines emigrated to Missouri, where he became a leading man in his locality.

Deeply imbued with religious feeling of the Calvanistic school, well-versed in the Scriptures, and having an abiding faith in the power of the Gospel to regenerate the world, the Doctor took great pleasure in presenting his views wherever his duties called him.

As a physician, he did not rank very high, for it was currently reported, and generally believed, that the father, finding his son unfit for mercantile business, or the law, determined to make him either a clergyman or a physician. Mr. Gaines, Senior, being somewhat superstitious, resolved not to settle the question too rashly in regard to the son's profession, therefore, it is said, flipped a cent, feeling that "heads or tails" would be a better omen than his own judgment in the matter. Fortunately for the cause of religion, the head turned up in favor of the medical profession. Nevertheless, the son often said that he believed God had destined him for the *sacred calling*, and devoted much of his time in exhorting his neighbors to seek repentance.

Most planters in our section cared but little about the religious training of their slaves, regarding them as they did their cattle,—an investment, the return of which was only to be considered in dollars and cents. Not so, however, with Dr. John Gaines, for he took special pride in looking after the spiritual welfare of his slaves, having them all in the "great house," at family worship, night and morning.

On Sabbath mornings, reading of the Scriptures, and explaining the same, generally occupied from one to two hours, and often till half of the negroes present were fast asleep. The white members of the family did not take as kindly to the religious teaching of the doctor, as did the blacks.

For his Christian zeal, I had the greatest respect, for I always regarded him as a truly pious and conscientious man, willing at all times to give of his means the needful in spreading the Gospel.

Mrs. Sarah Gaines was a lady of considerable merit, well-educated, and of undoubted piety. If she did not join heartily in her husband's religious enthusiasm, it was not for want of deep and genuine Christian feeling, but from the idea that he was of more humble origin than herself, and, therefore, was not a capable instructor.

This difference in birth, this difference in antecedents does much in the South to disturb family relations wherever it exists, and Mrs. Gaines, when wishing to show her contempt for the Doctor's opinions, would allude to her own parentage and birth in comparison to her husband's. Thus, once, when they were having a "family jar," she, with tears streaming down her cheeks, and wringing her hands, said,—

"My mother told me that I was a fool to marry a man so much beneath me,—one so much my inferior in society. And now you show it by hectoring and aggravating me all you can. But, never mind; I thank the Lord that He has given me religion and grace to stand it. Never mind, one of these days the Lord will make up His jewels,—take me home to glory, out of your sight,—and then I'll be devilish glad of it!"

These scenes of unpleasantness, however, were not of everyday occurrence, and, therefore, the great house at the "Poplar Farm," may be considered as having a happy family.

Slave children, with almost an alabaster complexion, straight hair, and blue eyes, whose mothers were jet black, or brown, were often a great source of annoyance in the Southern household, and especially to the mistress of the mansion.

Billy, a quadroon of eight or nine years, was amongst the young slaves, in the Doctor's house, then being trained up for a servant. Any one taking a hasty glance at the lad would never suspect that a drop of negro blood coursed through his blue veins. A gentleman, whose acquaintance Dr. Gaines had made, but who knew nothing of the latter's family relations, called at the house in the Doctor's absence. Mrs. Gaines received the stranger, and asked him to be seated, and remain till the host's return. While thus waiting, the boy, Billy, had occasion to pass through the room. The stranger, presuming the lad to be a son of the Doctor, exclaimed, "How do you do?" and turning to the lady, said, "how much he looks like his father; I should have known it was the Doctor's son, if I had met him in Mexico!"

With flushed countenance and excited voice, Mrs.

Gaines informed the gentleman that the little fellow was
"only a slave and nothing more." After the stranger's
departure, Billy was seen pulling up grass in the garden,
with bare head, neck and shoulders, while the rays of the
burning sun appeared to melt the child.

This process was repeated every few days for the purpose of giving the slave the color that nature had refused
it. And yet, Mrs. Gaines was not considered a cruel
woman,—indeed she was regarded as a kind-feeling mistress. Billy, however, a few days later, experienced a
roasting far more severe than the one he had got in the
sun.

The morning was cool, and the breakfast table was
spread near the fireplace, where a newly-built fire was
blazing up. Mrs. Gaines, being seated near enough to
feel very sensibly the increasing flames, ordered Billy to
stand before her.

The lad at once complied. His thin clothing giving him
but little protection from the fire, the boy soon began to
make up faces and to twist and move about, showing
evident signs of suffering.

"What are you riggling about for?" asked the mistress. "It burns me," replied the lad; "turn round,
then," said the mistress; and the slave commenced turning around, keeping it up till the lady arose from the
table.

Billy, however, was not entirely without his crumbs of
comfort. It was his duty to bring the hot biscuit from the
kitchen to the great house table while the whites were at
meal. The boy would often watch his opportunity, take
a "cake" from the plate, and conceal it in his pocket till
breakfast was over, and then enjoy his stolen gain. One
morning Mrs. Gaines, observing that the boy kept moving about the room, after bringing in the "cakes," and
also seeing the little fellow's pocket sticking out rather
largely, and presuming that there was something hot
there, said, "Come here." The lad came up; she pressed
her hand against the hot pocket, which caused the boy to
jump back. Again the mistress repeated, "Come here,"
and with the same result.

This, of course, set the whole room, servants and all,
in a roar. Again and again the boy was ordered to "come
up," which he did, each time jumping back, until the

heat of the biscuit was exhausted, and then he was made to take it out and throw it into the yard, where the geese seized it and held a carnival over it. Billy was heartily laughed at by his companions in the kitchen and the quarters, and the large blister, caused by the hot biscuit, created merriment among the slaves, rather than sympathy for the lad.

Mrs. Gaines, being absent from home one day, and the rest of the family out of the house, Billy commenced playing with the shot-gun, which stood in the corner of the room, and which the boy supposed was unloaded; upon a corner shelf, just above the gun, stood a band-box, in which was neatly laid away all of Mrs. Gaines' caps and cuffs, which, in those days, were in great use.

The gun having the flint lock, the boy amused himself with bringing down the hammer and striking fire. By this action powder was jarred into the pan, and the gun, which was heavily charged with shot, was discharged, the contents passing through the band-box of caps, cutting them literally to pieces and scattering them over the floor.

Billy gathered up the fragments, put them in the box and placed it upon the shelf,—he alone aware of the accident.

A few days later, and Mrs. Gaines was expecting company; she called to Hannah to get her a clean cap. The servant, in attempting to take down the box, exclaimed: "Lor, misses, ef de rats ain't bin at dees caps an' cut 'em all to pieces, jes look here." With a degree of amazement not easily described the mistress beheld the fragments as they were emptied out upon the floor.

Just then a new idea struck Hannah, and she said: "I lay anything dat gun has been shootin' off."

"Where is Billy? Where is Billy?" exclaimed the mistress; "Where is Billy?" echoed Hannah; fearing that the lady would go into convulsions, I hastened out to look for the boy, but he was nowhere to be found; I returned only to find her weeping and wringing her hands, exclaiming, "O, I am ruined, I am ruined; the company's coming and not a clean cap about the house; O, what shall I do, what shall I do?"

I tried to comfort her by suggesting that the servants might get one ready in time; Billy soon made his appearance, and looked on with wonderment; and, when asked how he came to shoot off the gun, declared that he knew nothing about it: and "ef de gun went off, it was of its own accord." However, the boy admitted the snapping of the lock or trigger. A light whipping was all that he got, and for which he was well repaid by having an opportunity of telling how the "caps flew about the room when de gun went off."

Relating the event some time after in the quarters he said: "I golly, you had aughty seen dem caps fly, and de dust and smok'in de room. I thought de judgment day had come, sure nuff." On the arrival of the company, Mrs. Gaines made a very presentable appearance, although the caps and laces had been destroyed. One of the visitors on this occasion was a young Mr. Sarpee, of St. Louis, who, although above twenty-one years of age, had never seen anything of country life, and, therefore, was very anxious to remain over night, and go on a coon hunt. Dr. Gaines, being lame, could not accompany the gentleman, but sent Ike, Cato, and Sam; three of the most expert coon-hunters on the farm. Night came, and off went the young man and the boys on the coon hunt. The dogs scented game, after being about half an hour in the woods, to the great delight of Mr. Sarpee, who was armed with a double barrel pistol, which, he said, he carried both to "protect himself, and to shoot the coon."

The halting of the boys and the quick, sharp bark of the dogs announced that the game was "treed," and the gentleman from the city pressed forward with fond expectation of seeing the coon, and using his pistol. However, the boys soon raised the cry of "polecat, polecat; get out de way"; and at the same time, retreating as if they were afraid of an attack from the animal. Not so with Mr. Sarpee; he stood his ground, with pistol in hand, waiting to get a sight of the game. He was not long in suspense, for the white and black spotted creature soon made its appearance, at which the city gentleman opened fire upon the skunk, which attack was immediately answered by the animal, and in a manner that caused the young man to wish that he, too, had retreated with the boys. Such an odor, he had never before inhaled; and, what was worse, his face, head, hands and clothing was covered with the cause of the smell, and the gentleman, at once, said: "Come, let's go home; I've got enough of coon-hunting." But, didn't the boys enjoy the fun.

The return of the party home was the signal for a hearty laugh, and all at the expense of the city gentleman. So great and disagreeable was the smell, that the young man had to go to the barn, where his clothing was removed, and he submitted to the process of washing by the servants. Soap, scrubbing brushes, towels, indeed, everything was brought into requisition, but all to no purpose. The skunk smell was there, and was likely to remain. Both family and visitors were at the breakfast table, the next morning, except Mr. Sarpee. He was still in the barn, where he had slept the previous night. Nor did there seem to be any hope that he would be able to visit the house, for the smell was intolerable. The substitution of a suit of the Doctor's clothes for his own failed to remedy the odor.

Dinkie, the conjurer, was called in. He looked the young man over, shook his head in a knowing manner, and said it was a big job. Mr. Sarpee took out a Mexican silver dollar, handed it to the old negro, and told him to do his best. Dinkie smiled, and he thought that he could remove the smell.

His remedy was to dig a pit in the ground large enough to hold the man, put him in it, and cover him over with fresh earth; consequently, Mr. Sarpee was, after removing his entire clothing, buried, all except his head, while his clothing was served in the same manner. A servant held an umbrella over the unhappy man, and fanned him during the eight hours that he was there.

Taken out of the pit at six o'clock in the evening, all joined with Dinkie in the belief that Mr. Sarpee "smelt sweeter" than when interred in the morning; still the smell of the "polecat" was there. Five hours longer in the pit, the following day, with a rub down by Dinkie, with his "Goopher," fitted the young man for a return home to the city.

I never heard that Mr. Sarpee ever again joined in a "coon hunt."

No description of mine, however, can give anything like a correct idea of the great merriment of the entire slave population on "Poplar Farm," caused by the "coon hunt." Even Uncle Ned, the old superannuated slave, who seldom went beyond the confines of his own cabin, hobbled out, on this occasion, to take a look at "de gentleman fum de city," while buried in the pit.

At night, in the quarters, the slaves had a merry time over the "coon hunt."

"I golly, but didn't de polecat give him a big dose?" said Ike.

"But how Mr. Sarpee did talk French to hissef when de old coon peppered him," remarked Cato.

"He won't go coon huntin' agin, soon, I bet you," said Sam.

"De coon hunt," and "de gemmen fum de city," was the talk for many days.

CHAPTER II.

I have already said that Dr. Gaines was a man of deep religious feeling, and this interest was not confined to the whites, for he felt that it was the Christian duty to help to save all mankind, white and black. He would often say, "I regard our negroes as given to us by an All Wise Providence, for their especial benefit, and we should impart to them Christian civilization." And to this end, he labored most faithfully.

No matter how driving the work on the plantation, whether seed-time or harvest, whether threatened with rain or frost, nothing could prevent his having the slaves all in at family prayers, night and morning. Moreover, the older servants were often invited to take part in the exercises. They always led the singing, and, on Sabbath mornings, were permitted to ask questions eliciting Scriptural explanations. Of course, some of the questions and some of the prayers were rather crude, and the effect, to an educated person, was rather to call forth laughter than solemnity.

Leaving home one morning, for a visit to the city, the Doctor ordered Jim, an old servant, to do some mowing in the rye-field; on his return, finding the rye-field as he had left it in the morning, he called Jim up, and severely flogged him without giving the man an opportunity of telling why the work had been neglected. On relating the circumstance at the supper-table, the wife said,—

"I am very sorry that you whipped Jim, for I took him to do some work in the garden, amongst my flower-beds."

To this the Doctor replied, "Never mind, I'll make it all right with Jim."

And sure enough he did, for that night, at prayers, he said, "I am sorry, Jim, that I corrected you, to-day, as your mistress tells me that she set you to work in the flower-garden. Now, Jim," continued he, in a most feeling manner, "I always want to do justice to my servants, and you know that I never abuse any of you intentionally, and now, tonight, I will let you lead in prayer."

Jim thankfully acknowledged the apology, and, with grateful tears, and an overflowing heart, accepted the situation; for Jim aspired to be a preacher, like most colored men, and highly appreciated an opportunity to show his persuasive powers; and that night the old man made splendid use of the liberty granted to him. After praying for everything generally, and telling the Lord what a great sinner he himself was, he said,—

"Now, Lord, I would specially ax you to try to save marster. You knows dat marster thinks he's mighty good; you knows dat marster says he's gwine to heaven; but Lord, I have my doubts; an' yet I want marster saved. Please to convert him over agin; take him, dear Lord, by de nap of de neck, and shake him over hell and show him his condition. But, Lord, don't let him fall into hell, jes let him see whar he ought to go to, but don't let him go dar. An' now, Lord, ef you jes save marster, I will give you de glory."

The indignation expressed by the doctor, at the close of Jim's prayer, told the old negro that for once he had overstepped the mark. "What do you mean, Jim, by insulting me in that manner? Asking the Lord to convert me over again. And praying that I might be shaken over hell. I have a great mind to tie you up, and give you a good correcting. If you ever make another such a prayer, I'll whip you well, that I will."

Dr. Gaines felt so intensely the duty of masters to their slaves that he, with some of his neighbors, inaugurated a religious movement, whereby the blacks at the Corners could have preaching once a fortnight, and that, too, by an educated white man. Rev. John Mason, the man selected for this work, was a heavy-set, fleshy, lazy man who, when entering a house, sought the nearest chair, taking possession of it, and holding it to the last.

He had been employed many years as a colporteur or missionary, sometimes preaching to the poor whites, and, at other times, to the slaves, for which service he was compensated either by planters, or by the dominant religious denomination in the section where he labored. Mr. Mason had carefully studied the character of the people to whom he was called to preach, and took every opportunity to shirk his duties, and to throw them upon some of the slaves, a large number of whom were always ready and willing to exhort when called upon.

We shall never forget his first sermon, and the profound sensation that it created both amongst masters and slaves, and especially the latter. After taking for his text, "He that knoweth his master's will, and doeth it not, shall be beaten with many stripes," he spoke substantially as follows:—

"Now when *correction* is given you, you either deserve it, or you do not deserve it. But whether you really deserve it or not, it is your duty, and Almighty God requires that you bear it patiently. You may, perhaps, think that this is hard doctrine, but if you consider it right you must needs think otherwise of it. Suppose then, that you deserve correction, you cannot but say that it is just and right you should meet with it. Suppose you do not, or at least you do not deserve so much, or so severe a correction for the fault you have committed, you, perhaps, have escaped a great many more, and are at last paid for all. Or suppose you are quite innocent of what is laid to your charge, and suffer wrongfully in that particular thing, is it not possible you may have done some other bad thing which was never discovered, and that Almighty God, who saw you doing it, would not let you escape without punishment one time or another? And ought you not, in such a case, to give glory to Him, and be thankful that he would rather punish you in this life for your wickedness, than destroy your souls for it in the next life? But suppose that even this was not the case (a case hardly to be imagined), and that you have by no means, known or unknown, deserved the correction you suffered, there is this great comfort in it, that if you bear it patiently, and leave your cause in the hands of God, he will reward you for it in heaven, and the punishment you suffer unjustly here, shall turn to your exceeding great glory, hereafter."

At this point, the preacher hesitated a moment, and then continued, "I am now going to give you a description of hell, that awful place, that you will surely go to, if you don't be good and faithful servants.

"Hell is a great pit, more than two hundred feet deep, and is walled up with stone, having a strong, iron grating at the top. The fire is built of pitch pine knots, tar barrels, lard kegs, and butter firkins. One of the devil's imps appears twice a day, and throws about half a bushel of brimstone on the fire, which is never allowed to cease burning. As sinners die they are pitched headlong into the pit, and are at once taken up upon the pitchforks by the devil's imps, who stand, with glaring eyes and smiling countenances, ready to do their master's work."

Here the speaker was disturbed by the "Amens," "Bless God, I'll keep out of hell," "Dat's my sentiments," which plainly told him that he had struck the right key.

"Now," continued the preacher, "I will tell you where heaven is, and how you are to obtain a place there. Heaven is above the skies; its streets are paved with gold; seraphs and angels will furnish you with music which never ceases. You will all be permitted to join in the singing and you will be fed on manna and honey, and you will drink from fountains, and will ride in golden chariots."

"I am bound for hebben," ejaculated one.

"Yes, blessed God, hebben will be my happy home," said another.

These outbursts of feeling were followed, while the man of God stood with folded arms, enjoying the sensation that his eloquence had created.

After pausing a moment or two, the reverend man continued, "Are there any of you here who would rather burn in hell than rest in heaven? Remember that once in hell you can never get out. If you attempt to escape little devils are stationed at the top of the pit, who will, with their pitchforks, toss you back into the pit, *curchunk,* where you must remain forever. But once in heaven, you will be free the balance of your days." Here the wildest enthusiasm showed itself, amidst which the preacher took his seat.

A rather humorous incident now occurred which created no little merriment amongst the blacks, and to the somewhat discomfiture of Dr. Gaines,—who occupied a seat with the whites who were present.

Looking about the room, being unacquainted with the

negroes, and presuming that all or nearly so were experimentally interested in religion, Mr. Mason called on Ike to close with prayer. The very announcement of Ike's name in such a connection called forth a broad grin from the larger portion of the audience.

Now, it so happened that Ike not only made no profession of religion, but was in reality the farthest off from the church of any of the servants at "Poplar Farm"; yet Ike was equal to the occasion, and at once responded, to the great amazement of his fellow slaves.

Ike had been, from early boyhood, an attendant upon whites, and he had learned to speak correctly for an uneducated person. He was pretty well versed in Scripture and had learned the principal prayer that his master was accustomed to make, and would often get his fellowservants together at the barn on a rainy day and give them the prayer, with such additions and improvements as the occasion might suggest. Therefore, when called upon by Mr. Mason, Ike at once said, "Let us pray."

After floundering about for a while, as if feeling his way, the new beginner struck out on the well-committed prayer, and soon elicited a loud "amen," and "bless God for that," from Mr. Mason, and to the great amusement of the blacks. In his eagerness, however, to make a grand impression, Ike attempted to weave into his prayer some poetry on "Cock Robin," which he had learned, and which nearly spoiled his maiden prayer.

After the close of the meeting, the Doctor invited the preacher to remain over night, and accepting the invitation, we in the great house had an opportunity of learning more of the reverend man's religious views.

When comfortably seated in the parlor, the Doctor said, "I was well pleased with your discourse, I think the tendency will be good upon the servants."

"Yes," responded the minister, "The negro is eminently a religious being, more so, I think, than the white race. He is emotional, loves music, is wonderfully gifted with gab; the organ of alimentativeness largely developed, and is fond of approbation. I therefore try always to satisfy their vanity; call upon them to speak, sing, and pray, and sometimes to preach. That suits for this world. Then I give them a heaven with music in it, and with something to eat. Heaven without singing and food would be no place for the negro. In the cities, where many of them are free, and have control of their own time, they are always late to church meetings, lectures, or almost anything else. But let there be a festival or supper announced and they are all there on time.''

"But did you know," said Dr. Gaines, "that the prayer that Ike made to-day he learned from me?''

"Indeed?'' responded the minister.

"Yes, that boy has the imitative power of his race in a larger degree than most negroes that I have seen. He remembers nearly everything that he hears, is full of wit, and has most excellent judgment. However his dovetailing the Cock Robin poetry into my prayer was too much, and I had to laugh at his adroitness.''

The Doctor was much pleased with the minister, but Mrs. Gaines was not. She had great contempt for professional men who sprung from the lower class, and she regarded Mr. Mason as one to be endured but not encouraged. The Rev. Henry Pinchen was her highest idea of a clergyman. This gentleman was then expected in the neighborhood, and she made special reference to the fact, to her husband, when speaking of the ''negro missionary,'' as she was wont to call the new-comer.

The preparation made, a few days later, for the reception of Mrs. Gaines' favorite spiritual adviser, showed plainly that a religious feast was near at hand, and in which the lady was to play a conspicuous part; and whether her husband was prepared to enter into the enjoyment or not, he would have to tolerate considerable noise and bustle for a week.

"Go, Hannah,'' said Mrs. Gaines, "and tell Dolly to kill a couple of fat pullets, and to put the biscuit to rise. I expect Brother Pinchen here this afternoon, and I want everything in order. Hannah, Hannah, tell Melinda to come here. We mistresses do have a hard time in this world; I don't see why the Lord should have imposed such heavy duties on us poor mortals. Well, it can't last always. I long to leave this wicked world, and go home to glory.''

At the hurried appearance of the waiting maid the mistress said: "I am to have company this afternoon, Melinda. I expect Brother Pinchen here, and I want everything in order. Go and get one of my new caps, with the lace border, and get out my scolloped-bottomed dimity petticoat, and when you go out, tell Hannah to clean the white-handled knives, and see that not a speck is on them; for I want everything as it should be while Brother Pinchen is here.''

Mr. Pinchen was possessed with a large share of the superstition that prevails throughout the South, not only with the ignorant negro, who brought it with him from his native land, but also by a great number of well educated and influential whites.

On the first afternoon of the reverend gentleman's visit, I listened with great interest to the following conversation between Mrs. Gaines and her ministerial friend.

"Now, Brother Pinchen, do give me some of your experience since you were last here. It always does my soul good to hear religious experience. It draws me nearer and nearer to the Lord's side. I do love to hear good news from God's people.''

"Well, Sister Gaines," said the preacher, "I've had great opportunities in my time to study the heart of man. I've attended a great many camp-meetings, revival meetings, protracted meetings, and death-bed scenes, and I am satisfied, Sister Gaines, that the heart of man is full of sin, and desperately wicked. This is a wicked world, Sister Gaines, a wicked world.''

"Were you ever in Arkansas, Brother Pinchen?" inquired Mrs. Gaines; "I've been told that the people out there are very ungodly.''

Mr. P. "Oh, yes, Sister Gaines. I once spent a year at Little Rock, and preached in all the towns round about there; and I found some hard cases out there, I can tell you. I was once spending a week in a district where there were a great many horse thieves, and, one night, somebody stole my pony. Well, I knowed it was no use to make a fuss, so I told Brother Tarbox to say nothing about it, and I'd get my horse by preaching God's everlasting gospel; for I had faith in the truth, and knowed that my Saviour would not let me lose my pony. So the next Sunday I preached on horse-stealing, and told the brethren to come up in the evenin' with their hearts filled with the grace of God. So that night the house was crammed brimfull with anxious souls, panting for the bread of life. Brother Bingham opened with prayer, and

Brother Tarbox followed, and I saw right off that we were gwine to have a blessed time. After I got 'em pretty well warmed up, I jumped on to one of the seats, stretched out my hands' and said: "I know who stole my pony; I've found out; and you are in here tryin' to make people believe that you've got religion; but you ain't got it. And if you don't take my horse back to Brother Tarbox's pasture this very night, I'll tell your name right out in meetin' to-morrow night. Take my pony back, you vile and wretched sinner, and come up here and give your heart to God.' So the next mornin', I went out to Brother Tarbox's pasture, and sure enough, there was my bob-tail pony. Yes, Sister Gaines, there he was, safe and sound. Ha, ha, ha!''

Mrs. G. "Oh, how interesting, and how fortunate for you to get your pony! And what power there is in the gospel! God's children are very lucky. Oh, it is so sweet to sit here and listen to such good news from God's people! [*Aside.*] 'You Hannah, what are you standing there listening for, and neglecting your work? Never mind, my lady, I'll whip you well when I am done here. Go at your work this moment, you lazy huzzy! Never mind, I'll whip you well.' Come, do go on, Brother Pinchen, with your godly conversation. It is so sweet! It draws me nearer and nearer to the Lord's side.''

Mr. P. "Well, Sister Gaines, I've had some mighty queer dreams in my time, that I have. You see, one night I dreamed that I was dead and in heaven, and such a place I never saw before. As soon as I entered the gates of the celestial empire, I saw many old and familiar faces that I had seen before. The first person that I saw was good old Elder Pike, the preacher that first called my attention to religion. The next person I saw was Deacon Billings, my first wife's father, and then I saw a host of godly faces. Why, Sister Gaines, you knowed Elder Goosbee, didn't you?''

Mrs. G. "Why, yes; did you see him there? He married me to my first husband.''

Mr. P. "Oh, yes, Sister Gaines, I saw the old Elder, and he looked for all the world as if he had just come out of a revival meetin'.''

Mrs. G. "Did you see my first husband there, Brother Pinchen?''

Mr. P. "No, Sister Gaines, I didn't see Brother Pepper there; but I've no doubt but that Brother Pepper was there."

Mrs. G. "Well, I don't know; I have my doubts. He was not the happiest man in the world. He was always borrowing trouble about something or another. Still, I saw some happy moments with Mr. Pepper. I was happy when I made his acquaintance, happy during our courtship, happy a while after our marriage, and happy when he died." *[Weeps.]*

Hannah. "Massa Pinchen, did you see my ole man Ben up dar in hebben?"

Mr. P. "No, Hannah, I didn't go amongst the niggers."

Mrs. G. "No, of course Brother Pinchen didn't go among the blacks. What are you asking questions for? *[Aside.]* 'Never mind, my lady, I'll whip you well when I'm done here. I'll skin you from head to foot.' Do go on with your heavenly conversation, Brother Pinchen; it does my very soul good. This is indeed a precious moment for me. I do love to hear of Christ and Him crucified."

Mr. P. "Well, Sister Gaines, I promised Sister Daniels that I'd come over and see her a few moments this evening, and have a little season of prayer with her, and I suppose I must go."

Mrs. G. "If you must go, then I'll have to let you; but before you do, I wish to get your advice upon a little matter that concerns Hannah. Last week Hannah stole a goose, killed it, cooked it, and she and her man Sam had a fine time eating the goose; and her master and I would never have known anything about it if it had not been for Cato, a faithful servant, who told his master all about it. And then, you see, Hannah had to be severely whipped before she'd confess that she stole the goose. Next Sabbath is sacrament day, and I want to know if you think that Hannah is fit to go to the Lord's Supper, after stealing the goose."

"Well, Sister Gaines," responded the minister, "that depends on circumstances. If Hannah has confessed that she stole the goose, and has been sufficiently whipped, and has begged her master's pardon, and begged your pardon, and thinks she will not do the like again, why then I suppose she can go to the Lord's Supper; for—

   'While the lamp holds out to burn,
   The vilest sinner may return.'

But she must be sure that she has repented, and won't steal any more.''

"Do you hear that, Hannah?" said the mistress. "For my part," continued she, "I don't think she's fit to go to the Lord's Supper; for she had no cause to steal the goose. We give our servants plenty of good food. They have a full run to the meal-tub, meat once a fortnight, and all the sour milk on the place, and I am sure that's enough for any one. I do think that our negroes are the most ungrateful creatures in the world. They aggravate my life out of me.''

During this talk on the part of the mistress, the servant stood listening with careful attention, and at its close Hannah said:—

"I know, missis, dat I stole de goose, an' massa whip me for it, an' I confess it, an' I is sorry for it. But, missis, I is gwine to de Lord's Supper, next Sunday, kase I ain't agwine to turn my back on my bressed Lord an' Massa for no old tough goose, dat I ain't.'' And here the servant wept as if she would break her heart.

Mr. Pinchen, who seemed moved by Hannah's words, gave a sympathizing look at the negress, and said, "Well, Sister Gaines, I suppose I must go over and see Sister Daniels; she'll be waiting for me.''

After seeing the divine out, Mrs. Gaines said, "Now, Hannah, Brother Pinchen is gone, do you get the cowhide and follow me to the cellar, and I'll whip you well for aggravating me as you have to-day. It seems as if I can never sit down to take a little comfort with the Lord, without you crossing me. The devil always puts it into your head to disturb me, just when I am trying to serve the Lord. I've no doubt but that I'll miss going to heaven on your account. But I'll whip you well before I leave this world, that I will. Get the cowhide and follow me to the cellar.''

In a few minutes the lady returned to the parlor, followed by the servant whom she had been correcting, and she was in a high state of perspiration, and, on taking a seat, said, "Get the fan, Hannah, and fan me; you ought to be ashamed of yourself to put me into such a passion, and cause me to heat myself up in this way, whipping you. You know that it is a great deal harder for me than it is for you. I have to exert myself, and it puts me all in a fever; while you have only to stand and take it."

On the following Sabbath,—it being Communion,—Mr. Pinchen officiated. The church being at the Corners, a mile or so from "Poplar Farm," the Communion wine, which was kept at the Doctor's, was sent over by the boy, Billy. It happened to be in the month of April, when the maple trees had been tapped, and the sap freely running.

Billy, while passing through the "sugar camp," or sap bush, stopped to take a drink of the sap, which looked inviting in the newly-made troughs. All at once it occurred to the lad that he could take a drink of the wine, and fill it up with sap. So, acting upon this thought, the youngster put the decanter to his mouth, and drank freely, lowering the beverage considerably in the bottle.

But filling the bottle with the sap was much more easily contemplated than done. For, at every attempt, the water would fall over the sides, none going in. However, the boy, with the fertile imagination of his race, soon conceived the idea of sucking his mouth full of the sap, and then squirting it into the bottle. This plan succeeded admirably, and the slave boy sat in the church gallery that day, and wondered if the communicants would have partaken so freely of the wine, if they had known that his mouth had been the funnel through which a portion of it had passed.

Slavery has had the effect of brightening the mental powers of the negro to a certain extent, especially those brought into close contact with the whites.

It is also a fact, that these blacks felt that when they could get the advantage of their owners, they had a perfect right to do so; and the boy, Billy, no doubt, entertained a consciousness that he had done a very cunning thing in thus drinking the wine entrusted to his care.

CHAPTER III.

Dr. Gaines' practice being confined to the planters and their negroes, in the neighborhood of "Poplar Farm," caused his income to be very limited from that source, and consequently he looked more to the products of his plantation for support. True, the new store at the Corners, together with McWilliams' Tannery and Simpson's Distillery, promised an increase of population, and, therefore, more work for the physician. This was demonstrated very clearly by the Doctor's coming in one morning somewhat elated, and exclaiming: "Well, my dear, my practice is steadily increasing. I forgot to tell you that neighbor Wyman engaged me yesterday as his family physician; and I hope that the fever and ague, which is now taking hold of the people, will give me more patients. I see by the New Orleans papers that the yellow fever is raging there to a fearful extent. Men of my profession are reaping a harvest in that section this year. I would that we could have a touch of the yellow fever here, for I think I could invent a medicine that would cure it. But the yellow fever is a luxury that we medical men in this climate can't expect to enjoy; yet we may hope for the cholera."

"Yes," replied Mrs. Gaines, "I would be glad to see it more sickly, so that your business might prosper. But we are always unfortunate. Everybody here seems to be in good health, and I am afraid they'll keep so. However, we must hope for the best. We must trust in the Lord. Providence may possibly send some disease amongst us for our benefit."

On going to the office the Doctor found the faithful servant hard at work, and saluting him in his usual kind and indulgent manner, asked, "Well, Cato, have you made the batch of ointment that I ordered?"

Cato. "Yes, massa; I dun made de intment, an' now I is making the bread pills. De tater pills is up on the top shelf."

Dr. G. "I am going out to see some patients. If any gentlemen call, tell them I shall be in this afternoon. If any servants come, you attend to them. I expect two of Mr. Campbell's boys over. You see to them. Feel their pulse, look at their tongues, bleed them, and give them each a dose of calomel. Tell them to drink no cold water, and to take nothing but water gruel."

Cato. "Yes, massa; I'll tend to 'em."

The negro now said, "I allers knowed I was a doctor, an' now de ole boss has put me at it; I muss change my coat. Ef any niggers comes in, I wants to look suspectable. Dis jacket don't suit a doctor; I'll change it."

Cato's vanity seemed at this point to be at its height, and having changed his coat, he walked up and down before the mirror, and viewed himself to his heart's content, and saying to himself, "Ah! now I looks like a doctor. Now I can bleed, pull teef, or cut off a leg. Oh, well, well! ef I ain't put de pill stuff an' de intment stuff togedder. By golly, dat ole cuss will be mad when he finds it out, won't he? Nebber mind, I'll make it up in pills, and when de flour is on dem, he won't know what's in' em; an'I'll make some new intment. Ah! yonder comes Mr. Campbell's Pete an' Ned; dem's de ones massa sed was comin'. I'll see ef I looks right. [*Goes to the looking-glass and views himself.*] I 'em some punkins, ain't I? [*Knock at the door.*] Come in." *Enter* Pete *and* Ned.

Pete. "Whar is de Doctor?"

Cato. "Here I is; don't you see me?"

Pete. "But whar is de ole boss?"

Cato. "Dat's none you business. I dun tole you dat I is de doctor, an' dat's enuff."

Ned. "Oh, do tell us whar de Doctor is. I is almos' dead. Oh, me! oh, dear me! I is so sick." [*Horrible faces.*]

Pete. "Yes, do tell us; we don't want to stan' here foolin."

Cato. "I tells you again dat I is de doctor. I larn de trade under massa."

Ned. "Oh! well den; give me somethin' to stop dis pain. Oh, dear me! I shall die."

Cato. "Let me feel your pulse. Now, put out your tongue. You is berry sick. Ef you don't mine, you'll die. Come out in de shed, an' I'll bleed you. [*Taking them out and bleeding them.*] "Dar, now, take dese pills, two in de mornin', and two at night, and ef you don't feel better, double de dose. Now, Mr. Pete, what's de matter wid you?"

Pete. "I is got de cole chills, an' has a fever in de night."

"Come out in de shed, an' I'll bleed you," said Cato, at the same time viewing himself in the mirror, as he passed out. After taking a quart of blood, which caused the patient to faint, they returned, the black doctor saying, "Now, take dese pills, two in de mornin', and two at night, an' ef dey don't help you, double de dose. Ah! I like to forget to feel your pulse, and look at your tongue. Put out your tongue. [*Feels his pulse.*] Yes, I tells by de feel ob your pulse dat I is gib you de right pills?"

Just then, Mr. Parker's negro boy Bill, with his hand up to his mouth, and evidently in great pain, entered the office without giving the usual knock at the door, and which gave great offence to the new physician.

"What you come in dat door widout knockin' for?" exclaimed Cato.

Bill. "My toof ache so, I didn't tink to knock. Oh, my toof! my toof! Whar is de Doctor?"

Cato. "Here I is; don't you see me?"

Bill. "What! you de Doctor, you brack cuss! You looks like a doctor! Oh, my toof! my toof! Whar is de Doctor?"

Cato. "I tells you I is de doctor. Ef you don't believe me, ax dese men. I can pull your toof in a minnit."

Bill. "Well, den, pull it out. Oh, my toof! how it aches! Oh, my toof!" [*Cato gets the rusty turnkeys.*]

Cato. "Now lay down on your back."

Bill. "What for?"

Cato. "Dat's de way massa does."

Bill. "Oh, my toof! Well, den come on." [*Lies down. Cato gets astraddle of Bill's breast, puts the turnkeys on the wrong tooth, and pulls—Bill kicks, and cries out*]—Oh, do stop! Oh, oh, oh! [*Cato pulls the wrong tooth—Bill jumps up.*]

Cato. "Dar, now, I told you I could pull your toof for you."

Bill. "Oh, dear me! Oh, it aches yet! Oh, me! Oh, Lor-e-massy! You dun pull de wrong toof. Drat your skin! ef I don't pay you for this, you brack cuss! [*They fight, and turn over table, chairs, and bench—Pete and Ned look on.*]

During the *melée,* Dr. Gaines entered the office, and unceremoniously went at them with his cane, giving both a sound drubbing before any explanation could be offered. As soon as he could get an opportunity, Cato said, "Oh, massa! he's to blame, sir, he's to blame. He struck me fuss."

Bill. "No, sir; he's to blame; he pull de wrong toof. Oh, my toof! oh, my toof!"

Dr. G. "Let me see your tooth. Open your mouth. As I live, you've taken out the wrong tooth. I am amazed. I'll whip you for this; I'll whip you well. You're a pretty doctor. Now, lie down, Bill, and let him take out the right tooth; and if he makes a mistake this time, I'll cowhide him well. Lie down, Bill." [*Bill lies down, and Cato pulls the tooth.*] "There, now, why didn't you do that in the first place?"

Cato. "He wouldn't hole still, sir."

Bill. "I did hole still."

Dr. G. "Now go home, boys; go home."

"You've made a pretty muss of it, in my absence," said the Doctor. "Look at the table! Never mind, Cato; I'll whip you well for this conduct of yours to-day. Go to work now, and clear up the office."

As the office door closed behind the master, the irritated negro, once more left to himself, exclaimed, "Confound dat nigger! I wish he was in Ginny. He bite my finger, and scratch my face. But didn't I give it to him? Well, den, I reckon I did. [*He goes to the mirror, and discovers that his coat is torn—weeps.*] Oh, dear me! Oh, my coat—my coat is tore! Dat nigger has tore my coat. [*He gets angry, and rushes about the room frantic.*] Cuss dat nigger! Ef I could lay my hands on him, I'd tare him all to pieces,—dat I would. An' de old boss hit me wid his cane after dat nigger tore my coat. By golly, I wants

to fight somebody. Ef ole massa should come in now, I'd
fight him. [*Rolls up his sleeves.*] Let 'em come now, ef
dey dare—ole massa, or anybody else; I'm ready for
'em.''

Just then the Doctor returned and asked, ''What's all
this noise here?''

Cato. ''Nuffin', sir; only jess I is puttin' things to
rights, as you tole me. I didn't hear any noise, except de
rats.''

Dr. G. ''Make haste, and come in; I want you to go
to town.''

Once more left alone, the witty black said, ''By golly,
de ole boss like to cotch me dat time, didn't he? But
wasn't I mad? When I is mad, nobody can do nuffin' wid
me. But here's my coat tore to pieces. Cuss dat nigger!
[*Weeps.*] Oh, my coat! oh, my coat! I rudder he had broke
my head, den to tore my coat. Drat dat nigger! Ef he ever
comes here agin, I'll pull out every toof he's got in his
head—dat I will.''

CHAPTER IV.

During the palmy days of the South, forty years ago, if there was one class more thoroughly despised than another, by the high-born, well-educated Southerner, it was the slave-trader who made his money by dealing in human cattle. A large number of the slave-traders were men of the North or free States, generally from the lower order, who, getting a little money by their own hard toil, invested it in slaves purchased in Virginia, Maryland, or Kentucky, and sold them in the cotton, sugar, or rice-growing States. And yet the high-bred planter, through mismanagement, or other causes, was compelled to sell his slaves, or some of them, at auction, or to let the "soul-buyer" have them.

Dr. Gaines' financial affairs being in an unfavorable condition, he yielded to the offers of a noted St. Louis trader by the name of Walker. This man was the terror of the whole South-west amongst the black population, bond and free,—for it was not unfrequently that even free colored persons were kidnapped and carried to the far South and sold. Walker had no conscientious scruples, for money was his God, and he worshipped at no other altar.

An uncouth, ill-bred, hard-hearted man, with no education, Walker had started at St. Louis as a dray-driver, and ended as a wealthy slave-trader. The day was set for this man to come and purchase his stock, on which occasion, Mrs. Gaines absented herself from the place; and even the Doctor, although alone, felt deeply the humiliation. For myself, I sat and bit my lips with anger, as the vulgar trader said to the faithful man,—

"Well, my boy, what's your name?"

Sam. "Sam, sir, is my name.

Walk. "How old are you, Sam?"

Sam. ''Ef I live to see next corn plantin' time I'll be twenty-seven, or thirty, or thirty-five—I don't know which, sir.''

Walk. ''Ha, ha, ha! Well, Doctor, this is rather a green boy. Well, mer feller, are you sound?''

Sam. ''Yes, sir, I spec I is.''

Walk. ''Open your mouth and let me see your teeth. I allers judge a nigger's age by his teeth, same as I dose a hoss. Ah! pretty good set of grinders. Have you got a good appetite?''

Sam. ''Yes, sir.''

Walk. ''Can you eat your allowance?''

Sam. ''Yes, sir, when I can get it.''

Walk. ''Get out on the floor and dance; I want to see if you are supple.''

Sam. ''I don't like to dance; I is got religion.''

Walk. ''Oh, ho! you've got religion, have you? That's so much the better. I likes to deal in the gospel. I think he'll suit me. Now, mer gal, what's your name?''

Sally. ''I is Big Sally, sir.''

Walk. ''How old are you, Sally?''

Sally. ''I don't know, sir; but I heard once dat I was born at sweet pertater diggin' time.''

Walk. ''Ha, ha, ha! Don't you know how old you are? Do you know who made you?''

Sally. ''I hev heard who it was in de Bible dat made me, but I dun forget de gentman's name.''

Walk. ''Ha, ha, ha! Well, Doctor, this is the greenest lot of niggers I've seen for some time.''

The last remark struck the Doctor deeply, for he had just taken Sally for debt, and, therefore, he was not responsible for her ignorance. And he frankly told him so.

''This is an unpleasant business for me, Mr. Walker,'' said the Doctor, ''but you may have Sam for $1,000, and Sally for $900. They are worth all I ask for them. I never banter, Mr. Walker. There they are; you can take them at that price, or let them alone, just as you please.''

Walk. ''Well, Doctor, I reckon I'll take 'em; but it's all they are worth. I'll put the handcuffs on 'em, and then I'll pay you. I likes to go accordin' to Scripter. Scripter says ef eatin' meat will offend your brother, you must quit it; and I say ef leavin' your slaves without the handcuffs will make 'em run away, you must put the handcuffs on 'em. Now, Sam, don't you and Sally cry. I am of a tender heart, and it allers makes me feel bad to see people cryin'. Don't cry, and the first place I get to, I'll buy each of you a great big *ginger cake*,—that I will.''

And with the last remark the trader took from a small satchel two pairs of handcuffs, putting them on, and with a laugh said: "Now, you look better with the ornaments on.''

Just then, the Doctor remarked, "There comes Mr. Pinchen.'' Walker, looking out and seeing the man of God, said: "It is Mr. Pinchen, as I live; jest the very man I wants to see.'' And as the reverend gentleman entered, the trader grasped his hand, saying: "Why, how do you do, Mr. Pinchen? What in the name of Jehu brings you down here to Muddy Creek? Any camp-meetins, revival meetins, death-bed scenes, or anything else in your line going on down here? How is religion prosperin' now, Mr. Pinchen? I always like to hear about religion.''

Mr. Pin. "Well, Mr. Walker, the Lord's work is in good condition everywhere now. I tell you, Mr. Walker, I've been in the gospel ministry these thirteen years, and I am satisfied that the heart of man is full of sin and desperately wicked. This is a wicked world, Mr. Walker, a wicked world, and we ought all of us to have religion. Religion is a good thing to live by, and we all want it when we die. Yes, sir, when the great trumpet blows, we ought to be ready. And a man in your business of buying and selling slaves needs religion more than anybody else, for it makes you treat your people as you should. Now, there is Mr. Haskins,—he is a slave-trader, like yourself. Well, I converted him. Before he got religion, he was one of the worst men to his niggers I ever saw; his heart was as hard as stone. But religion has made his heart as soft as a piece of cotton. Before I converted him he would sell husbands from their wives, and seem to take delight in it; but now he won't sell a man from his wife, if he can get any one to buy both of them together. I tell you, sir, religion has done a wonderful work for him.''

Walk. "I know, Mr. Pinchen, that I ought to have religion, and I feel that I am a great sinner; and whenever I get with good pious people like you and the Doctor, it always makes me feel that I am a desperate sinner. I feel it the more, because I've got a religious turn of mind. I know that I would be happier with religion, and the first spare time I get, I am going to try to get it. I'll go to a protracted meeting, and I won't stop till I get religion.''

The departure of the trader with his property left a sadness even amongst the white members of the family, and special sympathy was felt for Hannah for the loss of her husband by the sale. However, Mrs. Gaines took it coolly, for as Sam was a field hand, she had often said she wanted her to have one of the house servants, and as Cato was without a wife, this seemed to favor her plans. Therefore, a week later, as Hannah entered the sitting-room one evening, she said to her:—"You need not tell me, Hannah, that you don't want another husband, I know better. Your master has sold Sam, and he's gone down the river, and you'll never see him again. So go and put on your calico dress, and meet me in the kitchen. I intend for you to *jump the broomstick* with Cato. You need not tell me you don't want another man. I know there's no woman living that can be happy and satisfied without a husband.''

Hannah said: "Oh, missis, I don't want to jump de broomstick wid Cato. I don't love Cato; I can't love him.''

Mrs. G. "Shut up, this moment! What do you know about love? I didn't love your master when I married him, and people don't marry for love now. So go and put on your calico dress, and meet me in the kitchen.''

As the servant left for the kitchen, the mistress remarked: "I am glad that the Doctor has sold Sam, for now I'll have her marry Cato, and I'll have them both in the house under my eyes.''

As Hannah entered the kitchen, she said: "Oh, Cato, do go and tell missis dat you don't want to jump de broomstick wid me,—dat's a good man. Do, Cato; kase I nebber can love you. It was only las week dat massa sold my Sammy, and I don't want any udder man. Do go tell missis dat you don't want me.'' To which Cato replied: "No, Hannah, I ain't a-gwine to tell missis no such thing, kase I does want you, and I ain't a-gwine to tell a lie for you ner nobody else. Dar, now you's got it! I don't see why you need to make so much fuss. I is better lookin' den Sam; an' I is a house servant, an' Sam was only a fiel hand; so you ought to feel proud of a change. So go and do as missis tells you.''

As the woman retired, the man continued: ''Hannah needn't try to get me to tell a lie; I ain't a-gwine to do it, kase I dose want her, an' I is bin wantin' her dis long time, an' soon as massa sold Sam, I knowed I would get her. By golly, I is gwine to be a married man. Won't I be happy? Now, ef I could only jess run away from ole massa, an' get to Canada wid Hannah, den I'd show 'em who I was. Ah! dat reminds me of my song 'bout ole massa and Canada, an' I'll sing it. Dis is my moriginal hyme. It comed into my head one night when I was fass asleep under an apple tree, looking up at de moon.''

While Hannah was getting ready for the nuptials, Cato amused himself by singing—

De happiest day I ever did see,
   I'm bound fer my heavenly home,
When missis give Hannah to me,
   Through heaven dis chile will roam.

Chorus.—Go away, Sam, you can't come a-nigh me,
      Gwine to meet my friens in hebben,
      Hannah is gwine along;
      Missis ses Hannah is mine,
      So Hannah is gwine along.

Chorus, *repeated.*

Father Gabriel, blow your horn,
   I'll take wings and fly away,
Take Hannah up in the early morn,
   An' I'll be in hebben by de break of day.

Chorus.—Go away, Sam, you can't come a-nigh me,
      Gwine to meet my friens in hebben,
      Hannah is gwine along;
      Missis ses Hannah is mine,
      So Hannah is gwine along.

Mrs. Gaines, as she approached the kitchen, heard the servant's musical voice and knew that he was in high glee; entering, she said, ''Ah! Cato, you're ready, are you? Where is Hannah?''

Cato. "Yes, missis; I is bin waitin' dis long time. Hannah has bin here tryin' to swade me to tell you dat I don't want her; but I telled her dat you sed I must jump de broomstick wid her, an' I is gwine to mind you."

Mrs. G. "That's right, Cato; servants should always mind their masters and mistresses, without asking a question."

Cato. "Yes, missis, I allers dose what you and massa tells me, an' axes nobody."

While the mistress went in search of Hannah, Dolly came in saying, "Oh, Cato, do go an' tell missis dat you don't want Hannah. Don't yer hear how she's whippin' her in de cellar? Do go an' tell missis dat you don't want Hannah, and den she'll stop whippin' her."

Cato. "No, Dolly, I ain't a gwine to do no such a thing, kase ef I tell missis dat I don't want Hannah, den missis will whip me; an' I ain't a-gwine to be whipped fer you, ner Hannah, ner nobody else. No, I'll jump the broomstick wid every woman on de place, ef missis wants me to, before I'll be whipped."

Dolly. "Cato, ef I was in Hannah's place, I'd see you in de bottomless pit before I'd live wid you, you great, big, wall-eyed, empty-headed, knock-kneed fool. You're as mean as your devilish old missis."

Cato. "Ef you don't quit dat busin' me, Dolly, I'll tell missis as soon as she comes in, an' she'll whip you, you know she will."

As Mrs. Gaines entered she said, "You ought to be ashamed of yourself, Hannah, to make me fatigue myself in this way, to make you do your duty. It's very naughty in you, Hannah. Now, Dolly, you and Susan get the broom, and get out in the middle of the room. There, hold it a little lower—a little higher; there, that'll do. Now, remember that this is a solemn occasion; you are going to jump into matrimony. Now, Cato, take hold of Hannah's hand. There, now, why couldn't you let Cato take hold of your hand before? Now, get ready, and when I count three, do you jump. Eyes on the *broomstick!* All ready. One, two, three, and over you go. There, now you're husband and wife, and if you don't live happily together, it's your own fault; for I am sure there's nothing to hinder it. Now, Hannah, come up to the house, and I'll give you some whiskey, and you can make some apple-toddy, and you and Cato can have a fine time. Now, I'll go back to the parlor.''

Dolly. "I tell you what, Susan, when I get married, I is gwine to have a preacher to marry me. I ain't a-gwine to jump de broomstick. Dat will do for fiel' hands, but house servants ought to be 'bove dat.''

Susan. "Well, chile, you can't spect any ting else from ole missis. She come from down in Carlina, from 'mong de poor white trash. She don't know any better. You can't speck nothin' more dan a jump from a frog. Missis says she is one ob de akastocacy; but she ain't no more of an akastocacy dan I is. Missis says she was born wid a silver spoon in her mouf; ef she was, I wish it had a-choked her, dat' what I wish.''

The mode of jumping the broomstick was the general custom in the rural districts of the South, forty years ago; and, as there was no law whatever in regard to the marriage of slaves, this custom had as binding force with the negroes, as if they had been joined by a clergyman; the difference being the one was not so high-toned as the other. Yet, it must be admitted that the blacks always preferred being married by a clergyman.

CHAPTER V.

Dr. Gaines and wife having spent the heated season at the North, travelling for pleasure and seeking information upon the mode of agriculture practised in the free States, returned home filled with new ideas which they were anxious to put into immediate execution, and, therefore, a radical change was at once commenced.

Two of the most interesting changes proposed were the introduction of a plow, which was to take the place of the heavy, unwieldy one then in use, and a washing-machine, instead of the hard hand-rubbing then practised. The first called forth much criticism amongst the men in the field, where it was christened the "Yankee Dodger," and during the first half a day of its use it was followed by a large number of the negroes, men and women wondering at its superiority over the old plow, and wanting to know where it was from.

But the excitement in the kitchen, amongst the women, over the washing-machine, threw the novelty of the plow entirely in the shade.

"An' so dat tub wid its wheels an' fixin' is to do de washin', while we's to set down an' look at it," said Dolly, as ten or a dozen servants stood around the new comer, laughing and making fun at its ungainly appearance.

"I don't see why massa didn't buy a woman, out dar whar de ting was made, an' fotch 'em along, so she could learn us how to wash wid it," remarked Hannah, as her mistress came into the kitchen to give orders about the mode of using the "washer."

"Now, Dolly," said the mistress, "we are to have new rules, hereafter, about the work. While at the North, I found that the women got up at four o'clock, on Monday mornings, and commenced the washing, which was all finished, and out on the lines, by nine o'clock. Now, remember that, hereafter, there is to be no more washing on Fridays, and ironing on Saturdays, as you used to do. And instead of six of you great, big women to do the washing, two of you with the 'washer,' can do the work.'' And out she went, leaving the negroes to the contemplation of the future.

"I wish missis had stayed at home, 'stead of goin' round de world, bringin' home new rules. Who she tinks gwine to get out of bed at four o'clock in de mornin', kase she fotch home dis wash-box,'' said Dolly, as she gave a knowing look at the other servants.

"De Lord knows dat dis chile ain't a-gwine to git out of her sweet bed at four o'clock in de mornin', for no body; you hears dat, don't you?'' remarked Winnie, as she gave a loud laugh, and danced out of the room.

Before the end of the week, Peter had run the new plow against a stump, and had broken it beyond the possibility of repair.

When the lady arose on Monday morning, at half-past nine, her usual time, instead of finding the washing out on the lines, she saw, to her great disappointment, the inside works of the ''washer'' taken out, and Dolly, the chief laundress, washing away with all her power, in the old way, rubbing with her hands, the perspiration pouring down her black face.

"What have you been doing, Dolly, with the 'washer?' '' exclaimed the mistress, as she threw up her hands in astonishment.

"Well, you see, missis,'' said the servant, ''dat merchine won't work no way. I tried it one way, den I tried it an udder way, an' still it would not work. So, you see, I got de screw-driver an' I took it to pieces. Dat's de reason I ain't got along faster wid de work.''

Mrs. Gaines returned to the parlor, sat down, and had a good cry, declaring her belief that ''negroes could not be made white folks, no matter what you should do with them.''

Although the ''patent plow'' and the ''washer'' had failed, Dr. and Mrs. Gaines had the satisfaction of knowing that one of their new ideas was to be put into successful execution in a few days.

While at the North, they had eaten at a farm-house,

some new cheese, just from the press, and on speaking of it, she was told by old Aunt Nancy, the black *mamma* of the place, that she understood all about making cheese. This piece of information gave general satisfaction, and a cheese-press was at once ordered from St. Louis.

The arrival of the cheese-press, the following week, was the signal for the new sensation. Nancy was at once summoned to the great house for the purpose of superintending the making of the cheese. A prouder person than the old negress could scarcely have been found. Her early days had been spent on the eastern shores of Maryland, where the blacks have an idea that they are, by nature, superior to their race in any other part of the habitable globe. Nancy had always spoken of the Kentucky and Missouri negroes as "low brack trash," and now, that all were to be passed over, and the only Marylander on the place called in upon this "great occasion," her cup of happiness was filled to the brim.

"What do you need, besides the cheese-press, to make the cheese with, Nancy?" inquired Mrs. Gaines, as the old servant stood before her, with her hands resting upon her hips, and looking at the half-dozen slaves who loitered around, listening to what was being said.

"Well, missis," replied Nancy, "I mus' have a runnet."

"What's a runnet?" inquired Mrs. Gaines.

"Why, you see, missis, you's got to have a sheep killed, and get out of it de maw, an' dat's what's called de runnet. An' I puts dat in de milk, an' it curdles the milk so it makes cheese."

"Then I'll have a sheep killed at once," said the mistress, and orders were given to Jim to kill the sheep. Soon after the sheep's carcass was distributed amongst the negroes, and "de runnet," in the hands of old Nancy.

That night there was fun and plenty of cheap talk in the negro quarters and in the kitchen, for it had been discovered amongst them that a calf's runnet, and not a sheep's, was the article used to curdle the milk for making cheese.

The laugh was then turned upon Nancy, who, after listening to all sorts of remarks in regard to her knowledge of cheese-making, said, in a triumphant tone, suiting the action to the words,—

"You niggers tink you knows a heap, but you don't know as much as you tink. When de sheep is killed, I knows dat you niggers would git de meat to eat. I knows dat."

With this remark Nancy silenced the entire group. Then putting her hand a-kimbo, the old woman sarcastically exclaimed: "To-morrow you'll all have calf's meat for dinner, den what will you have to say 'bout old Nancy?" Hearing no reply, she said: "Whar is you smart niggers now? Whar is you, I ax you?"

"Well, den, ef Ant Nancy ain't some punkins, dis chile knows nuffin," remarked Ike, as he stood up at full length, viewing the situation, as if he had caught a new idea. "I allers told yer dat Ant Nancy had moo in her head dan what yer catch out wid a fine-toof comb," exclaimed Peter.

"But how is you going to tell missis 'bout killin' de sheep?" asked Jim.

Nancy turned to the head man and replied: "De same mudder wit dat tole me to get some sheep fer you niggers will tell me what to do. De Lord always guides me through my troubles an' trials. Befoe I open my mouf, He always fills it."

The following day Nancy presented herself at the great house door, and sent in for her mistress. On the lady's appearing, the servant, putting on a knowing look, said: "Missis, when de moon is cold an' de water runs high in it, den I have to put calf's runnet in de milk, instead of sheep's. So, lass night, I see dat de moon is cold an' de water is runnin' high."

"Well, Nancy," said the mistress, "I'll have a calf killed at once, for I can't wait for a warm moon. Go and tell Jim to kill a calf immediately, for I must not be kept out of cheese much longer." On Nancy's return to the quarters, old Ned, who was past work, and who never did anything but eat, sleep and talk, heard the woman's explanation, and clapping his wrinkled hands exclaimed: "Well den, Nancy, you is wof moo den all de niggers on dis place, fer you gives us fresh meat ebbry day."

After getting the right runnet, and two weeks' work on the new cheese, a little, soft, sour, hard-looking thing, appearing like anything but a cheese, was exhibited at "Poplar Farm," to the great amusement of the blacks, and the disappointment of the whites, and especially Mrs. Gaines, who had frequently remarked that her "mouth was watering for the new cheese."

No attempt was ever made afterwards to renew the cheese-making, and the press was laid under the shed, by the side of the washing machine and the patent plow. While we had three or four trustworthy and faithful servants, it must be admitted that most of the negroes on "Poplar Farm" were always glad to shirk labor, and thought that to deceive the whites was a religious duty.

Wit and religion has ever been the negro's forte while in slavery. Wit with which to please his master, or to soften his anger when displeased, and religion to enable him to endure punishment when inflicted.

Both Dr. and Mrs. Gaines were easily deceived by their servants. Indeed, I often thought that Mrs. Gaines took peculiar pleasure in being misled by them; and even the Doctor, with his long experience and shrewdness, would allow himself to be carried off upon almost any pretext. For instance, when he retired at night, Ike, his body servant, would take his master's clothes out of the room, brush them off and return them in time for the Doctor to dress for breakfast. There was nothing in this out of the way; but the master would often remark that he thought Ike brushed his clothes too much, for they appeared to wear out a great deal faster than they had formerly. Ike, however, attributed the wear to the fact that the goods were wanting in soundness. Thus the master, at the advice of his servant, changed his tailor.

About the same time the Doctor's watch stopped at night, and when taken to be repaired, the watch-maker found it badly damaged, which he pronounced had been done by a fall. As the Doctor was always very careful with his time-piece, he could in no way account for the stoppage. Ike was questioned as to his handling of it, but he could throw no light upon the subject. At last, one night about twelve o'clock, a message came for the Doctor to visit a patient who had a sudden attack of cholera morbus. The faithful Ike was nowhere to be found, nor could any traces of the Doctor's clothes be discovered. Not even the watch, which was always laid upon the mantle-shelf, could be seen anywhere.

It seemed clear that Ike had run away with his master's

daily wearing apparel, watch and all. Yes, and further search showed that the boots, with one heel four inches higher than the other, had also disappeared. But go, the Doctor must; and Mrs. Gaines and all of us went to work to get the Doctor ready.

While Cato was hunting up the old boots, and Hannah was in the attic getting the old hat, Jim returned from the barn and informed his master that the sorrel horse, which he had ordered to be saddled, was nowhere to be found; and that he had got out the bay mare, and as there was no saddle on the place, Ike having taken the only one, he, Jim, had put the buffalo robe on the mare.

It was a bright moonlight night, and to see the Doctor on horseback without a saddle, dressed in his castaway suit, was, indeed, ridiculous in the extreme. However, he made the visit, saved the patient's life, came home and went snugly to bed. The following morning, to the Doctor's great surprise, in walked Ike, at his usual time, with the clothes in one hand and the boots nicely blacked in the other. The faithful slave had not seen any of the other servants, and consequently did not know of the master's discomfiture on the previous night.

"Were any of the servants off the place last night?" inquired the Doctor, as Ike laid the clothes carefully on a chair, and was setting down the boots.

"No, I speck not," answered Ike.

"Were you off anywhere last night?" asked the master.

"No, sir," replied the servant.

"What! not off the place at all?" inquired the Doctor sharply. Ike looked confused and evidently began to "smell a mice."

"Well, massa, I was not away only to step over to de prayer-meetin' at de Corners, a little while, dat's all," said Ike.

"Where's my watch?" asked the Doctor.

"I speck it's on de mantleshelf dar, whar I put it lass night, sir," replied Ike, and at the same time reached to the time-piece, where he had laid it a moment before, and holding it up triumphantly, "Here it is, sir, right where I left it lass night."

Ike was told to go, which he was glad to do. "What

shall I do with that fellow?'' said the Doctor to his wife, as the servant quitted the room.

Ike had scarcely reached the back yard when he met Cato, who told him of his absence on the previous night being known to his master. When Ike had heard all, he exclaimed, ''Well, den ef de ole boss knows it, dis nigger is kotched sure as you is born.''

''I would not be in your shoes, Ike, fer a heap, dis mornin','' said Cato.

''Well,'' replied Ike, ''I thank de Lord dat I is got religion to stand it.''

Dr. Gaines, as he dressed himself, found nothing out of the way until he came to look at the boots. The Doctor was lame from birth. Here he saw unmistakable evidence that the high heel had been taken off, and had been replaced by a screw put through the inside, and the seam waxed over. Dr. Gaines had often thought, when putting his boots on in the morning, that they appeared a little loose, and on speaking of it to his servant, the negro would attribute it to the blacking, which he said ''made de lether stretch.''

That morning when breakfast was over, and the negroes called in for family prayers, all eyes were upon Ike.

It has always appeared strange that the negroes should seemingly take such delight in seeing their fellow-servants in a ''bad fix.'' But it is nevertheless true, and Ike's ''bad luck'' appeared to furnish sport for old and young of his own race. At the conclusion of prayers, the Doctor said, ''Now, Ike, I want you to tell me the truth, and nothing but the truth, of your whereabouts last night, and why you wore away my clothes?''

''Well, massa,'' said Ike, ''I'm gwine to tell you God's truth.''

''That's what I want, Ike,'' remarked the master.

''Now,'' continued the negro, ''I ware de clothes to de dance, kase you see, massa, I knowed dat you didn't want your body servant to go to de ball looking poorer dressed den udder gentmen's boys. So you see I had no clothes myself, so I takes yours. I had to knock the heel off de lame leg boot, so dat I could ware it. An' den I took 'ole Sorrel,' kase he paces so fass an' so easy. No udder hoss could get me to de city in time fer de ball, ceptin' 'ole Sorrel.' You see, massa, ten miles is a good ways to go after you is gone to bed. Now, massa, I hope you'll forgive me dis time, an' I'll never do so any moo.''

During Ike's telling his story, his master kept his eyes rivetted upon him, and at its conclusion said: ''You first told me that you were at the prayer-meeting at the Corners; what did you do that for?''

''Well, massa,'' replied Ike, ''I knowed dat I ought to had gone to de prar-meetin', an' dat's de reason I said I was dar.''

''And you're a pretty Christian, going to a dance, instead of your prayer-meeting. This is the fifth time you've fallen from grace,'' said the master.

''Oh, no,'' quickly responded Ike; ''dis is only de fourf time dat I is back slid.''

''But this is not the first time that you have taken my clothes and worn them. And there's my watch, you could not tell the time, what did you want with that?'' said the Doctor.

''Yes, massa,'' replied Ike, ''I'll tell de truth; I wore de clothes afore dis time, an' I take de watch too, an' I let it fall, an' dat's de reason it stop dat time. An' I know I could not tell de time by de watch, but I guessed at it, an' dat made de niggers star at me, to see me have a watch.''

The announcement that Col. Lemmy was at the door cut short the further investigation of Ike's case. The Colonel was the very opposite to Dr. Gaines, believing that there was no good in the negro, except to toil, and feeling that all religious efforts to better the condition of the race was time thrown away.

The Colonel laughed heartily as the Doctor told how Ike had worn his clothes. He quickly inquired if the servant had been punished, and when informed that he had not, he said: ''The lash is worth more than all the religion in the world. Your boy, Ike, with the rest of the niggers around here, will go to a prayer meetin' and will tell how good they feel or how bad they feel, just as it may suit the case. They'll cry, groan, clap their hands, pat their feet, worry themselves into a lather of sweat, sing,

I'm a-gwine to keep a-climbin' high,
　　See de hebbenly land;

Till I meet dem er angels in a de sky
  See de hebbenly lan'.
Dem pooty angels I shall see,
  See de hebbenly lan';
Why don't de debbil let a-me be,
  See de hebbenly lan'.

"Yes, Doctor; these niggers will pray till twelve o'clock at night; break up their meeting and go home shouting and singing, 'Glory hallelujah!' and every darned one of them will steal a chicken, turkey, or pig, and cry out 'Come down, sweet chariot, an' carry me home to hebben!' yes, and still continue to sing till they go to sleep. You may give your slaves religion, and I'll give mine the whip, an' I'll bet that I'll get the most tobacco and hemp out of the same number of hands."

"I hardly think," said the Doctor after listening attentively to his neighbor, "that I can let Ike pass without some punishment. Yet I differ with you in regard to the good effects of religion upon all classes, more especially our negroes, for the African is preeminently a religious being; with them, I admit, there is considerable superstition. They have a permanent belief in good and bad luck, ghosts, fortune-telling, and the like; but we whites are not entirely free from such notions."

At the last sentence or two, the Colonel's eyes sparkled, and he began to turn pale, for it was well known that he was a firm believer in ghosts and fortune-telling.

"Now, Doctor," said Col. Lemmy, "every sensible man must admit the fact that ghosts exist, and that there is nothing in the world truer than that the future can be told. Look at Mrs. McWilliams' law-suit with Major Todd. She went to old Frank, the nigger fortune-teller, and asked him which lawyer she should employ. The old man gazed at her for a moment or two, and said, 'missis, you's got your mind on two lawyers,—a big man and a little man. Ef you takes de big man, you loses de case; ef you takes de little man, you wins de case.' Sure enough, she had in contemplation the employment of either McGuyer or Darby. The first is a large man; the latter was, as you know, a small man. So, taking the old negro's advice, she obtained the services of John F. Darby, and gained the suit."

"Yes," responded the Doctor, "I have always heard that the Widow McWilliams gained her case by consulting old Frank."

"Why, Doctor," continued the Colonel, in an animated manner, "When the races were at St. Louis, three years ago, I went to old Betty, the blind fortune-teller, to see which horse was going to win; and she said, 'Massa, bet your money on de gray mare.' Well, you see, everybody thought that Johnson's black horse would win, and piles of money was bet on him. However, I bet one hundred dollars on the gray mare, and, to the utter surprise of all, she won. When the race was over, I was asked how I come to bet on the mare, when everybody was putting their funds on the horse. I then told them that I never risked my money on any horse, till I found out which was going to win.

"Now, with regard to ghosts, just let me say to you, Doctor, that I saw the ghost of the peddler that was murdered over on the old road, just as sure as you are born."

"Do you think so?" asked the Doctor.

"Think so! Why, I know it, just as well as I know that I see you now. He had his pack on his back; and it was in the daytime, no night-work about it. He looked at me, and I watched him till he got out of sight. But wasn't I frightened; it made the hair stand up on my head, I tell you."

"Did he speak to you?" asked the Doctor.

"Oh, no! he didn't speak, but he had a sorrowful look, and, as he was getting out of sight, he turned and looked over his shoulder at me."

Most of the superstition amongst the whites, in our section, was the result of their close connection with the blacks; for the servants told the most foolish stories to the children in the nurseries, and they learned more, as they grew older, from the slaves in the quarters, or out on the premises.

CHAPTER VI.

Profitable and interesting amusements were always needed at the Corners, the nearest place to the "Poplar Farm." At the tavern, post-office, and the store, all the neighborhood assembled to read the news, compare notes, and to talk politics.

Shows seldom ventured to stop there, for want of sufficient patronage. Once in three months, however, they had a "Gander Snatching," which never failed to draw together large numbers of ladies as well as gentlemen, the *elite*, as well as the common. The getter-up of this entertainment would procure a gander of the wild goose species. This bird had a long neck, which was large as it rose above the breast, but tapered gradually, for more than half the length, until it became small and serpent-like in form, terminating in a long, slim head, and peaked bill. The head and neck of the gander was well-greased; the legs were tied together with a strong cord, and the bird was then fastened by its legs, to a swinging limb of a tree. The *Snatchers* were to be on horse-back, and were to start fifteen or twenty rods from the gander, riding at full speed, and, as they passed along under the bird, they had the right to pull his head off if they could. To accelerate the speed of the horses, a man was stationed a few feet from the gander, with orders to give every horse a cut with his whip, as he went by.

Sometimes the bird's head would be caught by ten or a dozen before they would succeed in pulling it off, which was necessary; often by the sudden jump of the animal, or the rider having taken a little too much wine, he would fall from his horse, which event would give additional interest to the "Snatching."

The poor gander would frequently show far more sagacity than its torturers. After having its head caught once or twice, the gander would draw up its head, or dodge out of the way. Sometimes the snatcher would have in his hand a bit of sand-paper, which would enable him to make a tighter grasp. But this mode was generally considered unfair, and, on one occasion, caused a duel in which both parties were severely wounded.

But the most costly and injurious amusement that the people in our section entered into was that of card-playing, a species of gambling too much indulged in throughout the entire South. This amusement causes much sadness, for it often occurs that gentlemen lose large sums at the gambling-table, frequently seriously embarrassing themselves, sometimes bringing ruin upon whole families.

Mr. Oscar Smith, residing near "Poplar Farm," took a trip to St. Louis, thence to New Orleans and back. On the steamer he was beguiled into gaming.

"Go call my boy, steward," said Mr. Smith, as he took his cards one by one from the table.

In a few moments a fine-looking, bright-eyed mulatto boy, apparently about fifteen years of age, was standing by his master's side at the table.

"I will see you and five hundred dollars better," said Smith, as his servant Jerry approached the table.

"What price do you set on that boy?" asked Johnson, as he took a roll of bills from his pocket.

"He will bring a thousand dollars, any day, in the New Orleans market," replied Smith.

"Then you bet the whole of the boy, do you?"

"Yes."

"I call you, then," said Johnson, at the same time spreading his cards out upon the table.

"You have beat me," said Smith, as soon as he saw the cards.

Jerry, who was standing on top of the table, with the bank-notes and silver dollars round his feet, was now ordered to descend from the table.

"You will not forget that you belong to me," said Johnson; as the young slave was stepping from the table to a chair.

"No, sir," replied the chattel.

"Now go back to your bed, and be up in time to-morrow morning to brush my clothes and clean my boots, do you hear?''

"Yes, sir,'' responded Jerry, as he wiped the tears from his eyes.

As Mr. Smith left the gaming-table, he said: "I claim the right of redeeming that boy, Mr. Johnson. My father gave him to me when I came of age, and I promised not to part with him.''

"Most certainly, sir, the boy shall be yours whenever you hand me over a cool thousand,'' replied Johnson.

The next morning, as the passengers were assembling in the breakfast saloons, and upon the guards of the vessel, and the servants were seen running about waiting upon or looking for their masters, poor Jerry was entering his new master's state-room with his boots.

The genuine wit of the negro is often a marvel to the whites, and this wit or humor, as it may be called, is brought out in various ways. Not unfrequently is it exhibited by the black, when he really means to be very solemn.

Thus our Sampey met Davidson's Joe, on the road to the Corners, and called out to him several times without getting an answer. At last, Joe, appearing much annoyed, stopped, looked at Sampey in an attitude of surprise, and exclaimed: "Ain't you got no manners? Whare's your eyes? Don't you see I is a funeral?''

It was not till then that Sampey saw that Joe had a box in his arms, resembling a coffin, in which was a deceased negro child. The negro would often show his wit to the disadvantage of his master or mistress.

When visitors were at "Poplar Farm,'' Dr. Gaines would frequently call in Cato to sing a song or crack a joke, for the amusement of the company. On one occasion, requesting the servant to give a toast, at the same time handing the negro a glass of wine, the latter took the glass, held it up, looked at it, began to show his ivory, and said:

"De big bee flies high,
    De little bee makes de honey,
  De black man raise de cotton,
      An' de white man gets de money.''

The same servant going to meeting one Sabbath, was met on the road by Major Ben. O'Fallon, who was riding on horseback, with a hoisted umbrella to keep the rain off. The Major, seeing the negro trudging along bare-headed and with something under his coat, supposing he had stolen some article which he was attempting to hide, said, "What's that you've got under your coat, boy?"

"Nothin', sir, but my hat," replied the slave, and at the same time drawing forth a second-hand beaver.

"Is it yours?" inquired the Major.

"Yes, sir," was the quick response of the negro.

"Well," continued the Major, "if it is yours, why don't you wear it and save your head from the rain?"

"Oh!" replied the servant, with a smile of seeming satisfaction, "de head belongs to massa an' de hat belongs to me. Let massa take care of his property, an' I'll take care of mine."

Dr. Gaines, while taking a neighbor out to the pig sty, to show him some choice hogs that he intended for the next winter's bacon, said to Dolly who was feeding the pigs: "How much lard do you think you can get out of that big hog, Dolly?"

The old negress scratched her wooly head, put on a thoughtful look, and replied, "I specks I can get a pail full, ef de pail aint too big."

"I reckon you can," responded the master.

The ladies are not without their recreation, the most common of which is snuff-dipping. A snuff-box or bottle is carried, and with it a very small stick or cane, which has been chewed at the end until it forms a small mop. The little dippers or sticks are sold in bundles for the use of the ladies, and can be bought simply cut in the requisite lengths or chewed ready for use. This the dipper moistens with saliva, and dips into the snuff-box, and then lifts the mop thus loaded inside the lips. In some parts they courteously hand round the snuff and dipper, or place a plentiful supply of snuff on the table, into which all the company may dip.

Amongst even the better classes of whites, the ladies would often assemble in considerable numbers, especially during revival meeting times, place a wash-dish in the middle of the room, all gather around it, commence snuff-dipping, and all using the wash-dish as a common spittoon.

Every well bred lady carries her own snuff-box and dipper. Generally during church service, where the clergyman is a little prosy, snuff-dipping is indispensible.

CHAPTER VII.

Forty years ago, in the Southern States, superstition held an exalted place with all classes, but more especially with the blacks and uneducated, or poor, whites. This was shown more clearly in their belief in witchcraft in general, and the devil in particular. To both of these classes, the devil was a real being, sporting a club-foot, horns, tail, and a hump on his back.

The influence of the devil was far greater than that of the Lord. If one of these votaries had stolen a pig, and the fear of the Lord came over him, he would most likely ask the Lord to forgive him, but still cling to the pig. But if the fear of the devil came upon him, in all probability he would drop the pig and take to his heels.

In those days the city of St. Louis had a large number who had implicit faith in Voudooism. I once attended one of their midnight meetings. In the pale rays of the moon the dark outlines of a large assemblage was visible, gathered about a small fire, conversing in different tongues. They were negroes of all ages,—women, children, and men. Finally, the noise was hushed, and the assembled group assumed an attitude of respect. They made way for their queen, and a short, black, old negress came upon the scene, followed by two assistants, one of whom bore a cauldron, and the other, a box.

The cauldron was placed over the dying embers, the queen drew forth, from the folds of her gown, a magic wand, and the crowd formed a ring around her. Her first act was to throw some substance on the fire, the flames shot up with a lurid glare—now it writhed in serpent coils, now it darted upward in forked tongues, and then it gradually transformed itself into a veil of dusky vapors. At this stage, after a certain amount of gibberish and wild gesticulation from the queen, the box was opened, and frogs, lizards, snakes, dog liver, and beef hearts drawn forth and thrown into the cauldron. Then followed more gibberish and gesticulation, when the congregation joined hands, and began the wildest dance imaginable, keeping it up until the men and women sank to the ground from mere exhaustion.

In the ignorant days of slavery, there was a general belief that a horse-shoe hung over the door would insure good luck. I have seen negroes, otherwise comparatively intelligent, refuse to pick up a pin, needle, or other such object, dropped by a negro, because, as they alleged, if the person who dropped the articles had a spite against them, to touch anything they dropped would voudou them, and make them seriously ill.

Nearly every large plantation, with any considerable number of negroes, had at least one, who laid claim to be a fortune-teller, and who was regarded with more than common respect by his fellow-slaves. Dinkie, a full-blooded African, large in frame, coarse featured, and claiming to be a descendant of a king in his native land, was the oracle on the "Poplar Farm." At the time of which I write, Dinkie was about fifty years of age, and had lost an eye, and was, to say the least, a very ugly-looking man.

No one in that section was considered so deeply immersed in voudooism, gooperism, and fortune-telling, as he. Although he had been many years in the Gaines family, no one could remember the time when Dinkie was called upon to perform manual labor. He was not sick, yet he never worked. No one interfered with him. If he felt like feeding the chickens, pigs, or cattle, he did so. Dinkie hunted, slept, was at the table at meal time, roamed through the woods, went to the city, and returned when he pleased, with no one to object, or to ask a question. Everybody treated him with respect. The whites, throughout the neighborhood, tipped their hats to the old one-eyed negro, while the policemen, or patrollers, permitted him to pass without a challenge. The negroes, everywhere, stood in mortal fear of "Uncle Dinkie." The blacks who saw him every day, were always thrown upon their good behavior, when in his presence. I once asked a negro why they appeared to be afraid of Dinkie.

He looked at me, shrugged his shoulders, smiled, shook his head and said,—

"I ain't afraid of de debble, but I ain't ready to go to him jess yet." He then took a look around and behind, as if he feared some one would hear what he was saying, and then continued: "Dinkie's got de power, ser; he knows things seen and unseen, an' dat's what makes him his own massa."

It was literally true, this man was his own master. He wore a snake's skin around his neck, carried a petrified frog in one pocket, and a dried lizard in the other.

A slave speculator once came along and offered to purchase Dinkie. Dr. Gaines, no doubt, thought it a good opportunity to get the elephant off his hands, and accepted the money. A day later, the trader returned the old negro, with a threat of a suit at law for damages.

A new overseer was employed, by Dr. Gaines, to take charge of "Poplar Farm." His name was Grove Cook, and he was widely known as a man of ability in managing plantations, and in raising a large quantity of produce from a given number of hands. Cook was called a "hard overseer." The negroes dreaded his coming, and, for weeks before his arrival, the overseer's name was on every slave's tongue.

Cook came, he called the negroes up, men and women; counted them, looked them over as a purchaser would a drove of cattle that he intended to buy. As he was about to dismiss them he saw Dinkie come out of his cabin. The sharp eye of the overseer was at once on him.

"Who is that nigger?" inquired Cook.

"That is Dinkie," replied Dr. Gaines.

"What is his place?" continued the overseer.

"Oh, Dinkie is a gentleman at large!" was the response.

"Have you any objection to his working?"

"None, whatever."

'Well, sir," said Cook, "I'll put him to work tomorrow morning."

Dinkie was called up and counted in.

At the roll call, the following morning, all answered except the conjurer; he was not there.

The overseer inquired for Dinkie, and was informed that he was still asleep.

"I will bring him out of his bed in a hurry," said Cook, as he started towards the negro's cabin. Dinkie appeared at his door, just as the overseer was approaching.

"Follow me to the barn," said the impatient driver to the negro. "I make it a point always to whip a nigger, the first day that I take charge of a farm, so as to let the hands know who I am. And, now, Mr. Dinkie, they tell me that you have not had your back tanned for many years; and, that being the case, I shall give you a flogging that you will never forget. Follow me to the barn." Cook started for the barn, but turned and went into his house to get his whip.

At this juncture, Dinkie gave a knowing look to the other slaves, who were standing by, and said, "Ef he lays the weight ob his finger on me, you'll see de top of dat barn come off."

The reappearance of the overseer, with the large negro whip in one hand, and a club in the other, with the significant demand of "follow me," caused a deep feeling in the breast of every negro present.

Dr. Gaines, expecting a difficulty between his new driver and the conjurer, had arisen early, and was standing at his bedroom window looking on.

The news that Dinkie was to be whipped, spread far and near over the place, and had called forth men, women, and children. Even Uncle Ned, the old negro of ninety years, had crawled out of his straw, and was at his cabin door. As the barn doors closed behind the overseer and Dinkie, a death-like silence pervaded the entire group, who, instead of going to their labor, as ordered by the driver, were standing as if paralyzed, gazing intently at the barn, expecting every moment to see the roof lifted.

Not a word was spoken by anyone, except Uncle Ned, who smiled, shook his head, put on a knowing countenance, and said, "My word fer it, de oberseer ain't agwine to whip Dinkie."

Five minutes, ten minutes, fifteen minutes passed, and the usual sound of "Oh, pray, massa! Oh, pray, massa!" heard on the occasion of a slave being punished, had not yet proceeded from the barn.

Many of the older negroes gathered around Uncle Ned,

for he and Dinkie occupied the same cabin, and the old, superannuated slave knew more about the affairs of the conjurer, than anyone else. Ned told of how, on the previous night, Dinkie had slept but little, had closely inspected the snake's skin around his neck, the petrified frog and dried lizard, in his pockets, and had rubbed himself all over with goopher; and when he had finished, he knelt, and exclaimed,—

"Now, good and lovely devil, for more than twenty years, I have served you faithfully. Before I got into your service, de white folks bought an' sold me an' my old wife an' chillen, an' whip me, and half starve me. Dey did treat me mighty bad, dat you knows. Den I used to pray to de Lord, but dat did no good, kase de white folks don't fear de Lord. But dey fears you, an' ever since I got into your service, I is able to do as I please. No white dares to lay his hand on me; and dis is all owing to de power dat you give me. Oh, good and lovely devil! please to continer dat power. A new oberseer is to come here to-morrow, an' he wants to get me in his hands. But, dear devil, I axe you to stand by me in dis my trial hour, an' I will neber desert you as long as I live. Continer dis power; make me strong in your cause; make me to be more faithful to you, an' let me still be able to conquer my enemies, an' I will give you all de glory, and will try to deserve a seat at your right hand."

With bated breath, everyone listened to Uncle Ned. All had the utmost confidence in Dinkie's "power." None believed that he would be punished, while a large number expected to see the roof of the barn burst off at any moment. At last the suspense was broken. The barn door flew open; the overseer and the conjurer came out together, walking side by side, and separated when half-way up the walk. As they parted, Cook went to the field, and Dinkie to his cabin.

The slaves all shook their heads significantly. The fact that the old negro had received no punishment was evidence of his victory over the slave driver. But how the feat had been accomplished, was a mystery. No one dared to ask Dinkie, for he was always silent, except when he had something to communicate. Everyone was afraid to inquire of the overseer.

There was, however, one faint chance of getting an

inkling of what had occurred in the barn, and that was through Uncle Ned. This fact made the old, superannuated slave the hero and centre of attraction, for several days. Many were the applications made to Ned for information, but the old man did not know, or wished to exaggerate the importance of what he had learned.

"I tell you," said Dolly, "Dinkie is a power."

"He's nobody's fool," responded Hannah.

"I would not make him mad wid me, fer dis whole world," ejaculated Jim.

Just then, Nancy, the cook, came in brim full of news. She had given Uncle Ned some "cracklin bread," which had pleased the old man so much that he had opened his bosom, and told her all that he got from Dinkie. This piece of information flew quickly from cabin to cabin, and brought the slaves hastily into the kitchen.

It was night. Nancy sat down, looked around, and told Billy to shut the door. This heightened the interest, so that the fall of a pin could have been heard. All eyes were upon Nancy, and she felt keenly the importance of her position. Her voice was generally loud, with a sharp ring, which could be heard for a long distance, especially in the stillness of the night. But now, Nancy spoke in a whisper, occasionally putting her finger to her mouth, indicating a desire for silence, even when the breathing of those present could be distinctly heard.

"When dey got in de barn, de oberseer said to Dinkie, 'Strip yourself; I don't want to tear your clothes with my whip. I'm going to tear your black skin.'

"Den, you see, Dinkie told de oberseer to look in de east corner ob de barn. He looked, an' he saw hell, wid all de torments, an' de debble, wid his cloven foot, a-struttin' about dar, jes as ef he was cock ob de walk. An' Dinkie tole Cook, dat ef he lay his finger on him, he'd call de debble up to take him away."

"An' what did Cook say to dat?" asked Jim.

"Let me 'lone; I didn't tell you all," said Nancy. "Den you see de oberseer turn pale in de face, an' he say to Dinkie, 'Let me go dis time, an' I'll nebber trouble you any more.'"

This concluded Nancy's story, as related to her by old Ned, and religiously believed by all present. Whatever caused the overseer to change his mind in regard to the flogging of Dinkie, it was certain that he was most thoroughly satisfied to let the old negro off without the threatened punishment; and, although he remained at "Poplar Farm," as overseer, for five years, he never interfered with the conjurer again.

It is not strange that ignorant people should believe in characters of Dinkie's stamp; but it is really marvellous that well-educated men and women should give any countenance whatever, to such delusions as were practised by the oracle of "Poplar Farm."

The following illustration may be taken as a fair sample of the easy manner in which Dinkie carried on his trade.

Miss Martha Lemmy, being on a visit to Mrs. Gaines, took occasion during the day to call upon Dinkie. The conjurer knew the antecedents of his visitor, and was ready to give complete satisfaction in his particular line. When the young lady entered the old man's cabin, he met her, bade her be welcome, and tell what she had come for. She took a seat on one stool, and he on another. Taking the lady's right hand in his, Dinkie spit into its palm, rubbed it, looked at it, shut his one eye, opened it, and said: "I sees a young gentman, an' he's rich, an' owns plenty of land an' a heap o' niggers; an', lo! Miss Marfa, he loves you."

The lady drew a long breath of seeming satisfaction, and asked, "Are you sure that he loves me, Uncle Dinkie?"

"Oh! Miss Marfa, I knows it like a book."

"Have you ever seen the gentleman?" the lady inquired.

The conjurer began rubbing the palm of the snow-white hand, talked to himself in an undertone, smiled, then laughed out, and saying: "Why, Miss Marfa, as I lives it's Mr. Scott, an' he's thinkin' 'bout you now; yes, he's got his mind on you dis bressed minute. But how he's changed sense I seed him de lass time. Now he's got side whiskers an' a mustacher on his chin. But, let me see. Here is somethin' strange. De web looks a little smoky, an' when I gets to dat spot, I can't get along till a little silver is given to me."

Here the lady drew forth her purse and gave the old

man a half dollar piece that made his one eye fairly twinkle.

He resumed: "Ah! now de fog is cleared away, an' I see dat Mr. Scott is settin in a rockin-cheer, wid boff feet on de table, an' smokin' a segar."

"Do you think Mr. Scott loves me?" inquired the lady.

"O! yes," responded Dinkie; "he jess sets his whole heart on you. Indeed, Miss Marfa, he's almos' dyin' 'bout you."

"He never told me that he loved me," remarked the lady.

"But den, you see, he's backward, he ain't got his eye-teef cut yet in love matters. But he'll git a little bolder ebbry time he sees you," replied the negro.

"Do you think he'll ever ask me to marry him?"

"O! yes, Miss Marfa, he's sure to do dat. As he sets dar in his rockin-cheer, he looks mighty solem-colly—looks like he wanted to ax you to haf him now."

"Do you think that Mr. Scott likes any other lady, Uncle Dinkie?" asked Miss Lemmy.

"Well, Miss Marfa, I'll jess consult de web an' see." And here the conjurer shut his one eye, opened it, shut it again, talked to himself in an undertone, opened his eye, looked into the lady's hand, and exclaimed: "Ah! Miss Marfa, I see a lady in de way, an' she's got riches; but de web is smoky, an' it needs a little silver to clear it up."

With tears in her eyes, and almost breathless, Miss Lemmy hastily took from her pocket her purse, and handed the old man another piece of money, saying: "Please go on."

Dinkie smiled, shook his head, got up and shut his cabin door, sat down, and again took the lady's hand in his.

"Yes, I see," said he, "I see it's a lady; but bless you soul, Miss Marfa, it's a likeness of you dat Mr. Scott is lookin' at; dat's all."

This morsel of news gave great relief, and Miss Lemmy dried her eyes with joy.

Dinkie then took down the old rusty horseshoe from over his cabin door, held it up, and said: "Dis horseshoe neffer lies." Here he took out of his pocket a bag made of the skin of the rattlesnake, and took from it some goopher, sprinkled it over the horseshoe, saying: "Dis is de stuff, Miss Marfa, dat's gwine to make you Mr. Scott's conqueror. Long as you keeps dis goopher 'bout you he can't get away from you; he'll ax you fer a kiss, de berry next time he meets you, an' he can't help hisself fum doin' it. No woman can get him fum you so long as you keep dis goopher 'bout you."

Here Dinkie lighted a tallow candle, looked at it, smiled, shook his head,—"You's gwine to marry Mr. Scott in 'bout one year, an' you's gwine to haf thirteen children—sebben boys an' six gals, an' you's gwine to haf a heap of riches."

Just then, Dinkie's interesting revelations were cut short by Ike and Cato bringing along Peter, who, it was said, had been killed by the old bell sheep.

It appears that Peter had a way of playing with the old ram, who was always ready to butt at any one who got in his way. When seeing the ram coming, Peter would get down on his hands and knees and pretend that he was going to have a butting match with the sheep. And when the latter would come full-tilt at him, Peter would dodge his head so as to miss the ram, and the latter would jump over the boy, turn around angrily, shake his head and start for another butt at Peter.

This kind of play was repeated sometimes for an hour or more, to the great amusement of both whites and blacks. But, on this occasion, Peter was completely caught. As he was on his hands and knees, the ram started on his usual run for the boy; the latter, in dodging his head, run his face against a stout stub of dry rye stalk, which caused him to quickly jerk up his head, just in time for the sheep to give him a fair butt squarely in the forehead, which knocked Peter senseless. The ram, elated with his victory, began to back himself for another lick at Peter, when the men, seeing what had happened to the poor boy, took him up and brought him to Dinkie's cabin to be resuscitated, or "brought to," as they termed it.

Nearly an hour passed in rubbing the boy, before he began to show signs of consciousness. He "come to," but he never again accepted a butting match with the ram.

CHAPTER VIII.

Cruelty to negroes was not practised in our section. It is true there were some exceptional cases, and some individuals did not take the care of their servants at all times, that economy seemed to demand. Yet a certain degree of punishment was actually needed to insure respect to the master, and good government to the slave population. If a servant disobeyed orders, it was necessary that he should be flogged, to deter others from following the bad example. If a servant ran away, he must be caught and brought back, to let the others see that the same fate awaited them if they made similar attempts.

While the keeping of bloodhounds, for running down and catching negroes, was not common, yet a few were kept by Mr. Tabor, an inferior white man, near the Corners, who hired them out, or hunted the runaway, charging so much per day, or a round sum for the *catch*.

Jerome, a slave owned by the Rev. Mr. Wilson, when about to be punished by his master, ran away. Tabor and his dogs were sent for. The slave-catcher came, and at once set his dogs upon the trail. The parson and some of the neighbors went along for the fun that was in store.

These dogs will attack a negro, at their master's bidding, and cling to him as a bull-dog will cling to a beast. Many are the speculations as to whether the negro will be secured alive or dead, when these dogs get on his track. However, on this occasion, there was not much danger of ill-treatment, for Mr. Wilson was a clergyman, and was of a humane turn, and bargained with Tabor not to injure the slave if he could help it.

The hunters had been in the wood a short time, ere they got on the track of two slaves, one of whom was Jerome. The negroes immediately bent their steps toward the swamp, with the hope that the dogs would, when put upon the scent, be unable to follow them through the water. Nearer and nearer the whimpering pack pressed on; their delusion began to dispel.

All at once the truth flashed upon the minds of the fugitives like a glare of light,—that it was Tabor with his dogs! They at last reached the river, and in the negroes plunged, followed by the catch-dog. Jerome was finally caught, and once more in the hands of his master; while the other man found a watery grave. They returned, and the preacher sent his slave to the city jail for safe-keeping.

While the planters would employ Tabor, without hesitation, to hunt down their negroes, they would not receive him into their houses as a visitor any sooner than they would one of their own slaves. Tabor was, however, considered one of the better class of poor whites, a number of whom had a religious society in that neighborhood. The pastor of the poor whites was the Rev. Martin Louder, somewhat of a genius in his own way. The following sermon, preached by him, about the time of which I write, will well illustrate the character of the people for whom he labored.

More than two long, weary hours had now elapsed since the audience had been convened, and the people began to exhibit slight signs of fatigue. Some few scrapings and rasping of cowhide boots on the floor, an audible yawn or two, a little twisting and turning on the narrow, uncomfortable seats, while, in one or two instances, a somnolent soul or two snored outright. These palpable signs were not lost upon our old friend Louder. He cast an eye (emphatically, an eye) over the assemblage, and then—he spoke:—

"My dear breethering, and beloved sistering! You've ben a long time a settin' on your seats. You're tired, I know, an' I don't expect you want to hear the ole daddy preach. Ef you don't want to hear the ole man, jist give him the least bit of a sign. Cough. Hold up your hand. Ennything, an' Louder'll sit rite down. He'll dry up in a minit."

At this juncture of affairs, Louder paused for a reply. He glanced furtively over the audience, in search of the individual who might be "tired of settin' on his seat," but no sign was made: no such malcontent came within the visual range.

"Go on, Brother Louder!" said a sonorous voice in the "amen corner" of the house. Thus encouraged, the speaker proceeded in his remarks:—

"Well, then, breethering, sense you say so, Louder'll perceed; but he don't intend to preach a reg'lar sermon, for it's a gittin' late, and our sect which hit don't believe in eatin' cold vittles on the Lord's day. My breethering, ef the ole Louder gits outen the rite track, I want you to call him back. He don't want to teach you any error. He don't want' to preach nuthin' but what's found between the leds of this blessed Book."

"My dear breethering, the Lord raised up his servant, Moses, that he should fetch his people Isrel up outen that wicked land—ah. Then Moses, he went out from the face of the Lord, and departed hence unto the courts of the old tyranickle king—ah. An' what sez you, Moses? Ah, sez he, Moses sez, sez he to that wicked old Faro: Thus sez the Lord God of hosts, sez he: Let my Isrel go—ah. An' what sez the ole, hard-hearted king—ah? Ah! sez Faro, sez he, who is the Lord God of hosts, sez he, that I should obey his voice—ah? An' now what sez you, Moses—ah. Ah, Moses sez, sez he: Thus saith the Lord God of Isrel, let my people go, that they mought worship me, sez the Lord, in the wilderness—ah. But—ah! my beloved breethering an' my harden', impenitent frien's—ah, did the ole, hard-hearted king harken to the words of Moses, and let my people go—ah? Nary time."

This last remark, made in an ordinary, conversational tone of voice, was so sudden and unexpected that the change, the transition from the singing state was electrical.

"An' then, my beloved breethering an' sistering, what next—ah? What sez you, Moses, to Faro—that contrary ole king—ah? ah, Moses sez to Faro, sez he, Moses sez, sez he: Thus seth the Lord God of Isrel: Let my people go, sez the Lord, leest I come, sez he, an' smite you with a cuss—ah! An' what sez Faro, the ole tyranickle king—ah? Ah, sez he, sez ole Faro, Let their tasks be doubled, and leest they mought grumble, sez he, those bricks shall be made without straw—ah! [Vox naturale.] Made 'em pluck up grass an' stubble outen the fields, breethering, to mix with their mud. Mity hard on the pore critters; warn't it, Brother Flood Gate?" [The individual thus interrogated replied, "Jess so;" and "ole Louder" moved along.]

An' what next—ah? Did the ole king let my people Isrel go—ah? No, my dear breethering, he retched out his pizen hand, and he hilt 'em fash—ah. Then the Lord was wroth with that wicked ole king—ah. An' the Lord, he sed to Moses, sez he: Moses, stretch forth now thy rod over the rivers an' the ponds of this wicked land—ah; an' behold, sez he, when thou stretch out thy rod, sez the Lord, all the waters shall be turned into blood—ah! Then Moses, he tuck his rod, an' he done as the Lord God of Isrel had commanded his servant Moses to do—ah. An' what then, say you, my breethering—ah? Why, lo an' behold! the rivers of that wicked land was all turned into blood—ah; an' all the fish an' all the frogs in them streams an' waters died—ah!"

"Yes!" said the speaker, lowering his voice to a natural tone, and glancing out of the open window at the dry and dusty road, for we were at the time suffering from a protracted drouth: "An' I believe the frogs will all die now, unless we get some rain purty soon. What do you think about it, Brother Waters?" [This interrogatory was addressed to a fine, portly-looking old man in the congregation. Brother W. nodded assent, and old Louder resumed the thread of his discourse.] "Ah, my beloved breethering, that was a hard time on old Faro an' his wicked crowd—ah. For the waters was loathking obey the voice of the Lord, and let my people Isrel go—ah? Ah, no, my breethering, not by a long sight—ah. For he hilt out agin the Lord, and obeyed not his voice—ah. Then the Lord sent a gang of bull-frogs into that wicked land—ah. An' they went hoppin' an' lopin' about all over the country, into the vittles, an' everywhere else—ah. My breethering, the old Louder thinks that was a des'-prit time—ah. But all woodent do—ah. Ole Faro was as stubborn as one of Louder's mules—ah, an' he wooden let the chosen seed go up outen the land of bondage—ah. Then the Lord sent a mighty hail, an', arter that, his devourin' locuses—ah! An' they et up blamed nigh everything on the face of the eth—ah."

"Let not yore harts be trubbled, for the truth is mitay and must prevale—ah. Brother Creek, you don't seem to be doin' much of ennything, suppose you raise a tune!"

This remark was addressed to a tall, lank, hollow-jawed old man, in the congregation, with a great shock of "grizzled gray" hair.

"Wait a minit, Brother Louder, till I git on my glasses!" was the reply of Brother Creek, who proceeded to draw from his pocket an oblong tin case, which opened and shut with a tremendous snap, from which he drew a pair of iron-rimmed spectacles. These he carefully "dusted" with his handkerchief, and then turned to the hymn which the preacher had selected and read out to the congregation. After considerable deliberation, and some clearing of the throat, hawking, spitting, etc., and other preliminaries, Brother Creek, in a quavering, split sort of voice, opened out on the tune.

Louder seemed uneasy. It was evident that he feared a failure on the part of the worthy brother. At the end of the first line, he exclaimed:—

" 'Pears to me, Brother Creek, you hain't got the right miter."

Brother Creek suspended operations a moment, and replied, "I am purty kerrect, ginerally, Brother Louder, an' I'm confident she'll come out all right!"

"Well," said Louder, "we'll try her agin," and the choral strain, under the supervision of Brother Creek, was resumed in the following words:—

> "When I was a mourner just like you,
>   Washed in the blood of the Lamb,
> I fasted and prayed till I got through,
>   Washed in the blood of the Lamb.
>
> CHORUS. "Come along, sinner, and go with us;
>   If you don't you will be cussed.
>
> "Religion's like a blooming rose,
>   Washed in the blood of the Lamb,
> As none but those that feel it knows,
>   Washed in the blood of the Lamb."—*Cho.*

The singing, joined in by all present, brought the enthusiasm of the assembly up to white heat, and the shouting, with the loud "Amen," "God save the sinner," "Sing it, brother, sing it," made the welkin ring.

CHAPTER IX.

While the "peculiar institution" was a great injury to both master and slaves, yet there was considerable truth in the oft-repeated saying that the slave "was happy." It was indeed, a low kind of happiness, existing only where masters were disposed to treat their servants kindly, and where the proverbial light-heartedness of the latter prevailed. History shows that of all races, the African was best adapted to be the "hewers of wood, and drawers of water."

Sympathetic in his nature, thoughtless in his feelings, both alimentativeness and amativeness large, the negro is better adapted to follow than to lead. His wants easily supplied, generous to a fault, large fund of humor, brimful of music, he has ever been found the best and most accommodating of servants. The slave would often get rid of punishment by his wit; and even when being flogged, the master's heart has been moved to pity, by the humorous appeals of his victim. House servants in the cities and villages, and even on plantations, were considered privileged classes. Nevertheless, the field hands were not without their happy hours.

An old-fashioned corn-shucking took place once a year, on "Poplar Farm," which afforded pleasant amusement for the out-door negroes for miles around. On these occasions, the servants, on all plantations, were allowed to attend by mere invitation of the blacks where the corn was to be shucked.

As the grain was brought in from the field, it was left in a pile near the corn-cribs. The night appointed, and invitations sent out, slaves from plantations five or six miles away, would assemble and join on the road, and in large bodies march along, singing their melodious plantation songs.

To hear three or four of these gangs coming from different directions, their leaders giving out the words, and the whole company joining in the chorus, would indeed surpass anything ever produced by "Haverly's Minstrels," and many of their jokes and witticisms were never equalled by Sam Lucas or Billy Kersands.

A supper was always supplied by the planter on whose farm the shucking was to take place. Often when approaching the place, the singers would speculate on what they were going to have for supper. The following song was frequently sung:—

"All dem puty gals will be dar,
    Shuck dat corn before you eat.
Dey will fix it fer us rare,
    Shuck dat corn before you eat.
I know dat supper will be big,
      Shuck dat corn before you eat.
I think I smell a fine roast pig,
    Shuck dat corn before you eat.
A supper is provided, so dey said,
    Shuck dat corn before you eat.
I hope dey'll have some nice wheat bread,
    Shuck dat corn before you eat.
I hope dey'll have some coffee dar,
    Shuck dat corn before you eat.
I hope dey'll have some whisky dar,
    Shuck dat corn before you eat.
I think I'll fill my pockets full,
    Shuck dat corn before you eat.
Stuff dat coon an' bake him down,
    Shuck dat corn before you eat.
I speck some niggers dar from town,
    Shuck dat corn before you eat.
Please cook dat turkey nice an' brown.
    Shuck dat corn before you eat.
By de side of dat turkey I'll be foun',
    Shuck dat corn before you eat.
I smell de supper, dat I do,
    Shuck dat corn before you eat.
On de table will be a stew,
    Shuck dat corn, etc."

Burning pine knots, held by some of the boys, usually furnished light for the occasion. Two hours is generally sufficient time to finish up a large shucking; where five hundred bushels of corn is thrown into the cribs as the shuck is taken off. The work is made comparatively light by the singing, which never ceases till they go to the supper table. Something like the following is sung during the evening:

"De possum meat am good to eat,
     Carve him to de heart;
 You'll always find him good and sweet,
     Carve him to de heart;
 My dog did bark, and I went to see,
     Carve him to de heart;
 And dar was a possum up dat tree,
     Carve him to de heart.

Chorus: "Carve dat possum, carve dat possum chil-
          dren,
     Carve dat possum, carve him to de heart;
 Oh, carve dat possum, carve dat possum children,
     Carve dat possum, carve him to de heart.

"I reached up for to pull him in,
     Carve him to de heart;
 De possum he began to grin,
     Carve him to de heart;
 I carried him home and dressed him off,
     Carve him to de heart;
 I hung him dat night in de frost,
     Carve him to de heart.

Chorus: "Carve dat possum, etc.

"De way to cook de possum sound,
     Carve him to de heart;
 Fust par-bile him, den bake him brown,
     Carve him to de heart;
 Lay sweet potatoes in de pan,
     Carve him to de heart;
 De sweetest eatin' in de lan,'
     Carve him to de heart.

Chorus: "Carve dat possum, etc."

Should a poor supper be furnished, on such an occasion, you would hear remarks from all parts of the table,—

"Take dat rose pig 'way from dis table."

"What rose pig? you see any rose pig here?"

"Ha, ha, ha! Dis ain't de place to see rose pig."

"Pass up some dat turkey wid clam sauce."

"Don't talk about dat turkey; he was gone afore we come."

"Dis is de las' time I shucks corn at dis farm."

"Dis is a cheap farm, cheap owner, an' a cheap supper."

"He's talkin' it, ain't he?"

"Dis is de tuffest meat dat I is been called upon to eat fer many a day; you's got to have teeth sharp as a saw to eat dis meat."

"Spose you ain't got no teef, den what you gwine to do?"

"Why, ef you ain't got no teef you muss *gum it!*"

"Ha, ha, ha!" from the whole company, was heard.

On leaving the corn-shucking farm, each gang of men, headed by their leader, would sing during the entire journey home. Some few, however, having their dogs with them, would start on the trail of a coon, possum, or some other game, which might keep them out till nearly morning.

To the Christmas holidays, the slaves were greatly indebted for winter recreation; for long custom had given to them the whole week from Christmas day to the coming in of the New Year.

On "Poplar Farm," the hands drew their share of clothing on Christmas day for the year. The clothing for both men and women was made up by women kept for general sewing and housework. One pair of pants, and two shirts, made the entire stock for a male field hand.

The women's garments were manufactured from the same goods that the men received. Many of the men worked at night for themselves, making splint and corn brooms, baskets, shuck mats, and axe-handles, which they would sell in the city during Christmas week. Each slave was furnished with a pass, something like the following:—

"Please let my boy, Jim, pass anywhere in this county, until Jan. 1, 1834, and oblige.

"Respectfully,
JOHN GAINES, M.D.
" 'Poplar Farm,' St. Louis County, Mo."

With the above precious document in his pocket, a load of baskets, brooms, mats, and axe-handles on his back, a bag hanging across his shoulders, with a jug in each end—one for the whiskey, and the other for the molasses,—the slaves trudged off to town at night, singing,

"Hurra, for good ole massa,
    He give me de pass to go to de city.
  Hurra, for good ole missis,
      She bile de pot, and giv me de licker.
        Hurra, I'm goin to de city."

"When de sun rise in de mornin',
    Jes' above de yaller corn,
  You'll fin' dis nigger has take warnin',
    An's gone when de driver blows his horn.

"Hurra, for good ole massa,
    He giv me de pass to go to de city.
  Hurra for good ole missis,
      She bile de pot, and give me de licker.
        Hurra, I'm goin to de city."

Both the Methodists and Baptists,—the religious denominations to which the blacks generally belong,—never fail to be in the midst of a revival meeting during the holidays, and most of the slaves from the country hasten to these gatherings. Some, however, spend their time at the dances, raffles, cock-fights, foot-races, and other amusements that present themselves.

CHAPTER X.

A young and beautiful lady, closely veiled and attired in black, arrived one morning at "Poplar Farm," and was shown immediately into a room in the eastern wing, where she remained, attended only by old Nancy. That the lady belonged to the better class was evident from her dress, refined manners, and the inviolable secrecy of her stay at the residence of Dr. Gaines. At last the lady gave birth to a child, which was placed under the care of Isabella, a quadroon servant, who had recently lost a baby of her own.

The lady left the premises as mysteriously as she had come, and nothing more was ever seen or heard of her, certainly not by the negroes. The child, which was evidently of pure Anglo-Saxon blood, was called Lola, and grew up amongst the negro children of the place, to be a bright, pretty girl, to whom her adopted mother seemed very much attached. At the time of which I write, Lola was eight years old, and her presence on the plantation began to annoy the white members of Dr. Gaines' family, especially when strangers visited the place.

The appearance of Mr. Walker, the noted slave speculator, on the plantation, and whom it was said, had been sent for, created no little excitement amongst the slaves; and great was the surprise to the blacks, when they saw the trader taking Isabella and Lola with him at his departure. Unable to sell the little white girl at any price, Mr. Walker gave her to Mr. George Savage, who having no children of his own adopted the child.

Isabella was sold to a gentleman, who took her to Washington. The grief of the quadroon at being separated from her adopted child was intense, and greatly annoyed her new master, who determined to sell her on his arrival home. Isabella was sold to the slave-trader, Jennings, who placed the woman in one of the private slave-pens, or prisons, a number of which then disgraced the national capital.

Jennings intended to send Isabella to the New Orleans market, as soon as he purchased a sufficient number. At the dusk of the evening, previous to the day she was to be sent off, as the old prison was being closed for the night, Isabella suddenly darted past the keeper, and ran for her life. It was not a great distance from the prison to the long bridge which passes from the lower part of the city, across the Potomac to the extensive forests and woodlands of the celebrated Arlington Heights, then occupied by that distinguished relative and descendant of the immortal Washington, Mr. Geo. W. Custis. Thither the poor fugitive directed her flight. So unexpected was her escape, that she had gained several rods [at] the start before the keeper had secured the other prisoners, and rallied his assistants to aid in the pursuit. It was at an hour, and in a part of the city where horses could not easily be obtained for the chase; no bloodhounds were at hand to run down the flying woman, and for once it seemed as if there was to be a fair trial of speed and endurance between the slave and the slave-catchers.

The keeper and his force raised the hue-and-cry on her path as they followed close behind; but so rapid was the flight along the wide avenue, that the astonished citizens, as they poured forth from their dwellings to learn the cause of alarm, were only able to comprehend the nature of the case in time to fall in with the motley throng in pursuit, or raise an anxious prayer to heaven, as they refused to join in the chase (as many a one did that night), that the panting fugitive might escape, and the merciless soul-dealer for once be disappointed of his prey. And now, with the speed of an arrow, having passed the avenue, with the distance between her and her pursuers constantly increasing, this poor, hunted female gained the "Long Bridge," as it is called, where interruption seemed improbable. Already her heart began to beat high with the hope of success. She had only to pass three-quarters of a mile across the bridge, when she could bury herself in a vast forest, just at the time when the curtain of night would close around her, and protect her from the pursuit of her enemies.

But God, by His providence, had otherwise determined. He had ordained that an appalling tragedy should be enacted that night within plain sight of the President's house, and the Capitol of the Union, which would be an evidence, wherever it should be known, of the unconquerable love of liberty which the human heart may inherit, as well as a fresh admonition to the slave-dealer of the cruelty and enormity of his crimes.

Just as the pursuers passed the high draw, soon after entering upon the bridge, they beheld three men slowly approaching from the Virginia side. They immediately called to them to arrest the fugitive, proclaiming her a runaway slave. True to their Virginia instincts, as she came near, they formed a line across the narrow bridge to intercept her. Seeing that escape was impossible in that quarter, she stopped suddenly, and turned upon her pursuers.

On came the profane and ribald gang, faster than ever, already exulting in her capture, and threatening punishment for her flight. For a moment, she looked wildly and anxiously around to see if there was no hope of escape, on either hand; far down below, rolled the deep, foaming waters of the Potomac, and before and behind were the rapidly approaching steps and noisy voices of her pursuers.

Seeing how vain would be any further effort to escape, her resolution was instantly taken. She clasped her hands convulsively together, raised her tearful and imploring eyes towards heaven, and begged for the mercy and compassion there, which was unjustly denied her on earth; then, with a single bound, vaulted over the railing of the bridge, and sank forever beneath the angry and foaming waters of the river.

In the meantime Mr. and Mrs. Savage were becoming more and more interested in the child, Lola, whom they had adopted, and who was fast developing into an intellectual and beautiful girl, whose bright, sparkling hazel eyes, snow-white teeth and alabaster complexion caused her to be admired by all. In time, Lola became highly educated, and was duly introduced into the best society.

The cholera of 1832, in its ravages, swept off many of St. Louis' most valued citizens, and among them, Mr. George Savage. Mrs. Savage, who was then in ill-

health, regarded Lola with even greater solicitude, than
during the lifetime of her late husband. Lola had been
amply provided for by Mr. Savage, in his will. She was
being courted by Mr. Martin Phelps, previous to the
death of her adopted father, and the failing health of Mrs.
Savage hastened the nuptials.

The marriage of Mr. Phelps and Miss Savage partook
more of a private than of a public affair, owing to the
recent death of Mr. Savage. Mr. Phelps' residence was
at the outskirts of the city, in the vicinity of what was
known as the "Mound," and was a lovely spot. The lady
had brought considerable property to her husband.

One morning in the month of December, and only about
three months after the marriage of the Phelps's, two men
alighted from a carriage, at Mr. Phelps' door, rang the
bell, and were admitted by the servant. Mr. Phelps hastened from the breakfast-table, as the servant informed
him of the presence of the strangers.

On entering the sitting-room, the host recognized one
of the men as Officer Mull, while the other announced
himself as James Walker, and said,—

"I have come, Mr. Phelps, on rather an unpleasant
errand. You've got a slave in your house that belongs to
me."

"I think you are mistaken, sir," replied Mr. Phelps;
"my servants are all hired from Major Ben. O'Fallon."

Walker put on a sinister smile, and blandly continued,
"I see, sir, that you don't understand me. Ten years ago
I bought a slave child from Dr. Gaines, and lent her to
Mr. George Savage, and I understand she's in your employ, and I've come to get her," and here the slave speculator took from his side pocket a large sheepskin pocket
book, and drew forth the identical bill of sale of Lola,
given to him by Dr. Gaines at the time of the selling of
Isabella and the child.

"Good heavens!" exclaimed Mr. Phelps, "that paper,
if it means anything, it means my wife."

"I can't help what it means," remarked Walker:
"here's the bill of sale, and here's the officer to get me
my nigger."

"There must be a mistake here. It is true that my wife
was the adopted daughter of the late Mr. George Savage,

but there is not a drop of negro blood in her veins; and I doubt, sir, if you have ever seen her.''

"Well, sir," said Walker, "jest bring her in the room, and I guess she'll know me."

Feeling confident that the bill of sale had no reference to his wife, Mr. Phelps rang the bell, and told the boy that answered it to ask his mistress to come in. A moment or two later, and the lady entered the room.

"My dear," said Mr. Phelps, "are you acquainted with either of these gentlemen?"

The lady looked, hesitated, and replied, "I think not."

Then Walker arose, stepped towards the window, where he could be seen to better advantage, and said, "Why, Lola, have you forgotten me, it's only about ten years since I brought you from 'Poplar Farm,' and lent you to Mr. Savage. Ha, ha, ha!"

This coarse laugh of the rough, uneducated negro-trader had not ceased, when Lola gave a heart-rending shriek, and fell fainting upon the floor.

"I thought she'd know me when I jogged her memory," said Walker, as he re-seated himself.

Mr. Phelps sprang to his wife, and lifted her from the floor, and placed her upon the sofa.

"Throw a little of Adam's ale in her face, and that'll bring her to. I've seen 'em faint afore; but they allers come to," said the trader.

"I thank you, sir, but I will attend to my own affairs," said Mr. Phelps, in a rather petulant tone.

"Yes," replied Walker; "but she's mine, and I want to see that she comes to."

As soon as she revived, Mr. Phelps led his wife from the room. A conference of an hour took place on the return of Mr. Phelps to the parlor, which closed with the understanding that a legal examination of the papers should settle the whole question the next day.

At the appointed time, on the following morning, one of the ablest lawyers in the city, Col. Strawther, pronounced the bill of sale genuine, for it had been drawn up by Justice McGuyer, and witnessed by George Kennelly and Wilson P. Hunt.

For this claim, Walker expressed a willingness to sell the woman for two thousand dollars. The payment of the money would have been a small matter, if it had not carried with it the proof that Lola was a slave, which was undeniable evidence that she had negro blood in her veins.

Yet such was the result, for Dr. Gaines had been dead these three years, and whoever Lola's mother was, even if living, she would not come forth to vindicate the free birth of her child.

Mr. Phelps was a man of fine sensibility and was affectionately attached to his wife. However, it was a grave question to be settled in his mind, whether his honor as a Southern gentleman, and his standing in society would allow him to acknowledge a woman as his wife, in whose veins coursed the accursed blood of the negro slave.

Long was the struggle between love and duty, but the shame of public gaze and the ostracism of society decided the matter in favor of duty, and the young and lovely wife was informed by the husband that they must separate, never to meet again. Indescribable were the feelings of Lola, as she begged him, upon her knees, not to leave her. The room was horrible in its darkness,—her mind lost its reasoning powers for a time. At last consciousness returned, but only to awaken in her the loneliness of her condition, and the unfriendliness of that law and society that dooms one to everlasting disgrace for a blood taint, which the victim did not have.

Ten days after the proving of the bill of sale, the innocent Lola died of a broken heart, and was interred in the negro burial ground, with not a white face to follow the corpse to its last resting-place. Such is American race prejudice.

CHAPTER XI.

The invention of the Whitney cotton gin, nearly fifty years ago, created a wonderful rise in the price of slaves in the cotton States. The value of able-bodied men, fit for field-hands, advanced from five hundred to twelve hundred dollars, in the short space of five years. In 1850, a prime field-hand was worth two thousand dollars. The price of women rose in proportion; they being valued at about three hundred dollars less each than the men. This change in the price of slaves caused a lucrative business to spring up, both in the breeding of slaves and the sending of them to the States needing their services. Virginia, Kentucky, Missouri, Tennessee, and North Carolina became the slave-raising sections; Virginia, however, was always considered the banner State. To the traffic in human beings, more than to any other of its evils, is the institution indebted for its overthrow.

From the picture on the heading of *The Liberator,* down to the smallest tract printed against slavery, the separation of families was the chief object of those exposing the great American sin. The tearing asunder of husbands and wives, of parents and children, and the gangs of men and women chained together, *en route* for the New Orleans' market, furnished newspaper correspondents with items that never wanted readers. These newspaper paragraphs were not unfrequently made stronger by the fact that many of the slaves were as white as those who offered them for sale, and the close resemblance of the victim to the trader, often reminded the purchaser that the same blood coursed through the veins of both.

The removal of Dr. Gaines from "Poplar Farm" to St. Louis, gave me an opportunity of seeing the worst features of the internal slave-trade. For many years Missouri

drove a brisk business in the selling of her sons and
daughters, the greater number of whom passed through
the city of St. Louis. For a long time, James Walker was
the principal speculator in this species of property. The
early life of this man had been spent as a drayman, first
working for others, then for himself, and eventually purchasing men who worked with him. At last, disposing of
his horses and drays, he took his faithful men to the Louisiana market and sold them. This was the commencement of a career of cruelty, that, in all probability, had
no equal in the annals of the American slave trade.

A more repulsive-looking person could scarcely be
found in any community of bad-looking men than Walker.
Tall, lean, and lank, with high cheek-bones, face much
pitted with the small-pox, gray eyes, with red eyebrows,
and sandy whiskers, he indeed stood alone without mate
or fellow in looks. He prided himself upon what he called
his goodness of heart, and was always speaking of his
humanity.

Walker often boasted that he never separated families
if he could "persuade the purchaser to take the whole
lot." He would always advertise in the New Orleans'
papers that he would be there with a prime lot of able-
bodied slaves, men and women, fit for field-service, with
a few extra ones calculated for house servants,—all between the ages of fifteen and twenty-five years; but like
most men who make a business of speculating in human
beings, he often bought many who were far advanced in
years, and would try to pass them off for five or six years
younger than they were. Few persons can arrive at anything approaching the real age of the negro, by mere
observation, unless they are well acquainted with the
race. Therefore, the slave-trader frequently carried out
the deception with perfect impunity.

As soon as the steamer would leave the wharf, and was
fairly on the bosom of the broad Mississippi, the speculator would call his servant Pompey to him, and instruct
him as to getting the slaves ready for the market. If any
of the blacks looked as if they were older than they were
advertised to be, it was Pompey's business to fit them for
the day of sale.

Pomp, as he was usually called by the trader, was of
real negro blood, and would often say, when alluding to

himself, "Dis nigger am no counterfeit, he is de ginuine artikle. Dis chile is none of your haf-and-haf, dere is no bogus about him."

Pompey was of low stature, round face, and, like most of his race, had a set of teeth, which, for whiteness and beauty, could not be surpassed; his eyes were large, lips thick, and hair short and woolly. Pomp had been with Walker so long, and seen so much of buying and selling of his fellow-creatures, that he appeared perfectly indifferent to the heart-rending scenes which daily occurred in his presence. Such is the force of habit:—

> "Vice is a monster of such frightful mien,
>   That to be hated, needs but to be seen;
>   But seen too oft, familiar with its face,
>   We first endure, then pity, then embrace."

Before reaching the place of destination, Pompey would pick out the older portion and say, "I is de chap dat is to get you ready for de Orleans market, so dat you will bring marser a good price. How old is you?" addressing himself to a man that showed some age.

"Ef I live to see next corn-plantin' time, I'll be forty."

"Dat may be," replied Pompey, "but now you is only thirty years old; dat's what marser says you is to be."

"I know I is mo' dan dat," responded the man.

"I can't help nuffin' 'bout dat," returned Pompey; "but when you get in de market, an' any one ax you how old you is, an' you tell um you is forty, massa will tie you up, an' when he is done whippin' you, you'll be glad to say you's only thirty."

"Well den, I reckon I is only thirty," said the slave.

"What is your name?" asked Pompey of another man in the group.

"Jeems," was the response.

"Oh! Uncle Jim, is it?"

"Yes."

"Den you muss' hab all dem gray whiskers shaved off, and dem gray hairs plucked out of your head. De fack is, you's got ole too quick." This was all said by Pompey in a manner which showed that he knew his business.

"How ole is you?" asked Pompey of a tall, strong-looking man.

"I am twenty-nine, nex' Christmas Eve," said the man.

"What's your name?"

"My name is Tobias," replied the slave.

"Tobias!" ejaculated Pompey, with a sneer, that told that he was ready to show his brief authority. "Now you's puttin' on airs. Your name is Toby, an' why can't you tell the truf? Remember, now, dat you is twenty-three years ole; an' afore you goes in de market your face muss' be greased; fer I see you's one of dem kind o' ashy niggers, an' a little grease will make your face look black an' slick, an' make you look younger."

Pompey reported to his master the condition of affairs, when the latter said, "Be sure that the niggers don't forget what you have taught them, for our luck depends a great deal upon the appearance of our stock."

With this lot of slaves was a beautiful quadroon, a girl of twenty years, fair as most white women, with hair a little wavy, large black eyes, and a countenance that betokened intelligence beyond the common house servant. Her name was Marion, and the jealousy of the mistress, so common in those days, was the cause of her being sold.

Not far from Canal Street, in the city of New Orleans, in the old days of slavery, stood a two-story, flat building, surrounded by a stone wall, some twelve feet high, the top of which was covered with bits of glass, and so constructed as to prevent even the possibility of any one's passing over it without sustaining great injury. Many of the rooms in this building resembled the cells of a prison, and in a small apartment, near the "office," were to be seen any number of iron collars, hobbles, hand-cuffs, thumb-screws, cowhides, chains, gags, and yokes.

A back-yard, enclosed by a high wall, looked like the play-ground attached to one of our large New England schools, in which were rows of benches and swings. Attached to the back premises was a good-sized kitchen, where, at the time of which we write, two old negresses were at work, stewing, boiling, and baking, and occasionally wiping the perspiration from their furrowed and swarthy brows.

The slave-trader, Walker, on his arrival at New Orleans, took up his quarters here, with his gang of human cattle, and the morning after, at ten o'clock, they were exhibited for sale. First of all, came the beautiful Marion, whose pale countenance and dejected look, told how many sad hours she had passed since parting with her mother. There, too, was a poor woman, who had been separated from her husband, and another woman, whose looks and manners were expressive of deep anguish, sat by her side. There was "Uncle Jeems," with his whiskers off, his face shaven clean, and the gray hairs plucked out, ready to be sold for ten years younger than he was. Toby was also there, with his face shaven and greased, ready for inspection.

The examination commenced, and was carried on in such a manner as to shock the feelings of any one not entirely devoid of the milk of human kindness.

"What are you wiping your eyes for?" inquired a fat, red-faced man, with a white hat set on one side of his head and a cigar in his mouth, of a woman who sat on one of the benches.

"Because I left my man behind."

"Oh, if I buy you, I will furnish you with a better man than you left. I've got lots of young bucks on my farm," responded the man.

"I don't want and never will have another man," replied the woman.

"What's your name?" asked a man, in a straw hat, of a tall negro, who stood with his arms folded across his breast, leaning against the wall.

"My name is Aaron, sar."

"How old are you?"

"Twenty-five."

"Where were you raised?"

"In ole Virginny, sar."

"How many men have owned you?"

"Four."

"Do you enjoy good health?"

"Yes, sar."

"How long did you live with your first owner?"

"Twenty years."

"Did you ever run away?"

"No, sar."

"Did you ever strike your master?"

"No sar."

"Were you ever whipped much?"

"No, sar; I spose I didn't desarve it, sar."

"How long did you live with your second master?"

"Ten years, sar."

"Have you a good appetite?"

"Yes, sar."

"Can you eat your allowance?"

"Yes, sar,—when I can get it."

"Where were you employed in Virginia?"

"I worked in de tobacker fiel'."

"In the tobacco field, eh?"

"Yes, sar."

"How old did you say you was?"

"Twenty-five, sar, nex' sweet-'tater-diggin' time."

"I am a cotton-planter, and if I buy you, you will have to work in the cotton field. My men pick one hundred and fifty pounds a day, and the women one hundred and forty pounds; and those who fail to perform their task receive five stripes for each pound that is wanting. Now do you think you could keep up with the rest of the hands?"

"I don't know, sar, but I reckon I'd have to."

"How long did you live with your third master?"

"Three years, sar," replied the slave.

"Why, that makes you thirty-three; I thought you told me you were only twenty-five."

Aaron now looked first at the planter, then at the trader, and seemed perfectly bewildered. He had forgotten the lesson given him by Pompey, relative to his age; and the planter's circuitous questions—doubtless to find out the slave's real age—had thrown the negro off his guard.

"I must see your back, so as to know how much you have been whipped, before I think of buying."

Pompey, who had been standing by during the examination, thought that his services were now required, and, stepping forth with a degree of officiousness, said to Aaron:—"Don't you hear de gemman tell you he wants to zamin you? Cum, unharness you-seff, ole boy, an' don't be standin' dar."

Aaron was examined, and pronounced "sound"; yet the conflicting statement about his age was not satisfactory.

On the following trip down the river, Walker halted at Vicksburg, with a "prime lot of slaves," and a circumstance occurred which shows what the slaves in those days would resort to, to save themselves from flogging, while, at the same time, it exhibits the quick wit of the race.

While entertaining some of his purchasers at the hotel, Walker ordered Pompey to hand the wine around to his guests. In doing this, the servant upset a glass of wine upon a gentleman's lap. For this mishap, the trader determined to have his servant punished. He, therefore, gave Pompey a sealed note, and ordered him to take it to the slave prison. The servant, suspecting that all was not right, hastened to open the note before the wafer had dried; and passing the steamboat landing, he got a sailor to read the note, which proved to be, as Pompey had suspected, an order to have him receive "thirty-nine stripes upon the bare back."

Walker had given the man a silver dollar, with orders to deliver it, with the note, to the jailor, for it was common in those days for persons who wanted their servants punished and did not wish to do it themselves, to send them to the "slave pen," and have it done; the price for which was one dollar. How to escape the flogging, and yet bring back to his master the evidence of having been punished, perplexed the fertile brain of Pompey. However, the servant was equal to the occasion. Standing in front of the "slave pen," the negro saw another well dressed colored man coming up the street, and he determined to inquire in regard to how they did the whipping there.

"How de do, sar," said Pompey, addressing the colored brother. "Do you live here?"

"Oh! no," replied the stranger, "I am a free man, and belong in Pittsburgh, Pa."

"Ah! ha, den you don't live here," said Pompey.

"No, I left my boat here last week, and I have been trying every day to get something to do. I'm pretty well out of money, and I'd do almost anything just now."

A thought flashed upon Pompey's mind—this was his occasion.

"Well," said the slave, "ef you want a job, whar you can make some money quick, I specks I can help you."

"If you will," replied the free man, you'll do me a great favor."

"Here, then," said Pompey, "take dis note, an' go in to dat prison, dar, an' dey will give you a trunk, bring it out, an' I'll tell you where to carry it to, an' here's a dollar; dat will pay you, won't it?"

"Yes," replied the man, with many thanks; and taking the note and the shining coin, with smiles, he went to the "Bell Gate," and gave the bell a loud ring. The gate flew open, and in he went.

The man had scarcely disappeared, ere Pompey had crossed the street, and was standing at the gate, listening to the conversation then going on between the jailor and the free colored man.

"Where is the dollar that you got with this note?" asked the "*whipper,*" as he finished reading the epistle.

"Here it is, sir; he gave it to me," said the man, with no little surprise.

"Hand it here," responded the jailor, in a rough voice. "There, now; take this nigger, Pete, and strap him down upon the stretcher, and get him ready for business."

"What are you going to do to me!" cried the horrified man, at the jailor's announcement.

"You'll know, damn quick!" was the response.

The resistance of the innocent man caused the "whipper" to call in three other sturdy blacks, and, in a few minutes, the victim was fastened upon the stretcher, face downwards, his clothing removed, and the strong-armed white negro-whipper standing over him with uplifted whip.

The cries and groans of the poor man, as the heavy instrument of torture fell upon his bare back, aroused Pompey, who retreated across the street, stood awaiting the result, and wondering if he could obtain, from the injured man, the receipt which the jailor always gives the slave to take back to his master as evidence of his having been punished.

As the gate opened, and the colored brother made his appearance, looking wildly about for Pompey, the latter called out, "Here I is, sar!"

Maddened by the pain from the excoriation of his bleeding back, in the surprise and astonishment at the quickness with which the whole thing had been accomplished, the man ran across the street, upbraiding in the most furious manner his deceiver, who also appeared amazed at the epithets bestowed upon him.

"What have I done to you?" asked Pompey, with a seriousness that was indeed amusing.

"What hain't you done!" said the man, the tears streaming down his face. "You've got my back cut all to pieces," continued the victim.

"What did you let 'em whip you for?" said Pompey, with a concealed smile.

"You knew that note was to get somebody whipped, and you put it on me. And here is a piece of paper that he gave me, and told me to give it to my master. Just as if I had a master."

"Well, responded Pompey, "I have a half a dollar, an' I'll give that to you, ef you'll give me the paper."

Seeing that he could make no better bargain, the man gave up the receipt, taking in exchange the silver coin.

"Now," said Pompey, "I'm mighty sorry for ye, an' ef ye'll go down to de house, I'll pray for ye. I'm powerful in prayer, dat I is." However the free man declined Pompey's offer.

"I reckon you'll behave yourself and not spill the wine over gentlemen again," said Walker, as Pompey handed him the note from the jailor. "The next time you commit such a blunder, you'll not get off so easy," continued the speculator.

Pompey often spoke of the appearance of "my fren'," as he called the colored brother, and would enjoy a hearty laugh, saying, "He was a free man, an' could afford to go to bed, an' lay dar till he got well."

Strangers to the institution of slavery, and its effects upon its victims, would frequently speak with astonishment of the pride that slaves would show in regard to their own value in the market. This was especially so, at auction sales where town or city servants were sold.

"What did your marser pay for you?" would often be asked by one slave of another.

"Eight hundred dollars."

"Eight hundred dollars! Ha, ha! Well, ef I didn't sell for mo' dan eight hundred dollars, I'd neber show my head agin 'mong 'spectable people."

"You got so much to say 'bout me sellin' cheap, now I want to know how much your boss paid fer you?"

"My boss paid fifteen hundred dollars cash, for me; an' it was a rainy day, an' not many out to de auction, or he'd had to pay a heap mo', let me tell you. I'm none of your cheap niggers, I ain't."

"Hy, uncle! Did dey sell you, 'isterday? I see you down dar to de market."

"Yes, dey sole me."

"How much did you fetch?"

"Eighteen hundred dollars."

"Dat was putty smart fer man like you, ain't it?"

"Well, I dunno; it's no mo' dan I is wuf; fer you muss' 'member, I was raised by de Christy's. I'm none of yer common niggers, sellin' fer a picayune. I tink my new boss got me mighty cheap."

"An' so you sole, las' Sataday, fer nine hundred dollars; so I herd."

"Well, what on it?"

"All I got to say is, ef I was sole, to-morrow, an' didn't bring more dan nine hundred dollars, I'd never look a decent man in de face agin."

These, and other sayings of the kind, were often heard in any company of colored men, in our Southern towns.

CHAPTER XII.

Throughout the Southern States, there are still to be found remnants of the old time Africans, who were stolen from their native land and sold in the Savannah, Mobile, and New Orleans markets, in defiance of all law. The last-named city, however, and its vicinity, had a larger portion of these people than any other section. New Orleans was their centre, and where their meetings were not uninteresting.

Congo Square takes its name, as is well known, from the Congo negroes who used to perform their dance on its sward every Sunday. They were a curious people, and brought over with them this remnant of their African jungles. In Louisiana there were six different tribes of negroes, named after the section of the country from which they came, and their representatives could be seen on the square, their teeth filed, and their cheeks still bearing tattoo marks. The majority of our city negroes came from the Kraels, a numerous tribe who dwell in stockades. We had here the Minahs, a proud, dignified, warlike race; the Congos, a treacherous, shrewd, relentless people; the Mandringas, a branch of the Congos; the Gangas, named after the river of that name, from which they had been taken; the Hiboas, called by the missionaries the "Owls," a sullen, intractable tribe, and the Foulas, the highest type of the African, with but few representatives here.

These were the people that one would meet on the square many years ago. It was a gala occasion, these Sundays in those years, and not less than two or three thousand people would congregate there to see the dusky dancers. A low fence enclosed the square, and on each street there was a little gate and turnstile. There were no trees then, and the ground was worn bare by the feet of the people. About three o'clock the negroes began to gather, each nation taking their places in different parts of the square. The Minahs would not dance near the Congos, nor the Mandringas near the Gangas. Presently the music would strike up, and the parties would prepare for the sport. Each set had its own orchestra. The instruments were a peculiar kind of banjo, made of a Louisiana gourd, several drums made of a gum stump dug out, with a sheepskin head, and beaten with the fingers, and two jaw-bones of a horse, which when shaken would rattle the loose teeth, keeping time with the drums. About eight negroes, four male and four female, would make a set, and generally they were but scantily clad.

It took some little time before the tapping of the drums would arouse the dull and sluggish dancers, but when the point of excitement came, nothing can faithfully portray the wild and frenzied motions they go through. Backward and forward, this way and that, now together and now apart, every motion intended to convey the most sensual ideas. As the dance progressed, the drums were thrummed faster, the contortions became more grotesque, until sometimes, in frenzy, the women and men would fall fainting to the ground. All this was going on with a dense crowd looking on, and with a hot sun pouring its torrid rays on the infatuated actors of this curious ballet. After one set had become fatigued, they would drop out to be replaced by others, and then stroll off to the groups of some other tribe in a different portion of the square. Then it was that trouble would commence, and a regular set-to with short sticks followed, between the men, and broken heads ended the day's entertainment.

On the sidewalks, around the square, the old negresses, with their spruce-beer and peanuts, cocoa-nuts and pop-corn, did a thriving trade, and a now and then, beneath petticoats, bottles of tafia, a kind of Louisiana rum, peeped out, of which the *gendarmes* were oblivious. When the sun went down, a stream of people poured out of the turn-stiles, and the *gendarmes*, walking through the square, would order the dispersion of the negroes, and by gun-fire, at nine o'clock, the place was well-nigh deserted. These dances were kept up until within the memory of men still living, and many who believe in them, and who would gladly revive them, may be found in every State in the Union.

The early traditions, brought down through the imported Africans, have done much to keep alive the belief that the devil is a personal being, with hoofs, horns, and having powers equal with God. These ideas give influence to the conjurer, goopher doctor, and fortune-teller.

While visiting one of the upper parishes, not long since, I was stopping with a gentleman who was accustomed to make weekly visits to a neighboring cemetery, sitting for hours amongst the graves, at which occurrence the wife felt very sad.

I inquired of her the object of her husband's strange freak.

"Oh!" said she, "he's influenced out there by angels."

"Has he gone to the cemetery now?" I asked.

"Yes," was the reply.

"I think I can cure him of it, if you will promise to keep the whole thing a secret."

"I will," was the reply.

"Let me have a sheet, and unloose your dog, and I will put the cure in motion," I said. Rolla, the big Newfoundland dog, was unfastened, the sheet was well fitted around his neck, tightly sewed, and the pet told to go hunt his master.

Taking the trail, the dog at once made for the cemetery. Screams of "Help, help! God save me!" coming from the direction of the tombs, aroused the neighborhood. The cries of the man frightened the dog, and he returned home in haste; the sheet, half torn, was removed, and Rolla again fastened in his house.

Very soon Mr. Martin was led in by two friends, who picked him up from the sidewalk, with his face considerably bruised. His story was, that "The devil had chased him out of the cemetery, tripped him up on the sidewalk, and hence the flow of blood from the wound on his face."

The above is a fair index to most of the ghost stories.

CHAPTER XIII.

Forty years ago, the escapes of slaves from the South, although numerous, were nevertheless difficult, owing to the large rewards offered for their apprehension, and the easy mode of extradition from the Northern States. Little or no difficulty was experienced in capturing and returning a slave from Ohio, Indiana, Illinois, or Pennsylvania, the four States through which the fugitives had to pass in their flight to Canada. The Quaker element in all of the above States showed itself in the furnishing of food to the flying bondman, concealing him for days, and even weeks, and at last conveying him to a place of safety, or carrying him to the Queen's dominions.

Instinct seemed to tell the negro that a drab coat and a broad-brimmed hat covered a benevolent heart, and we have no record of his ever having been deceived. It is possible that the few Friends scattered over the slave States, and the fact that they were never known to own a slave, gave the blacks a favorable impression of this sect, before the victim of oppression left his sunny birth-place.

A brave and manly slave resolved to escape from Natchez, Miss. This slave, whose name was Jerome, was of pure African origin, was perfectly black, very fine-looking, tall, slim, and erect as any one could possibly be. His features were not bad, lips thin, nose prominent, hands and feet small. His brilliant black eyes lighted up his whole countenance. His hair, which was nearly straight, hung in curls upon his lofty brow. George Combe or Fowler would have selected his head for a model. He was brave and daring, strong in person, fiery in spirit, yet kind and true in his affections, earnest in whatever he undertook.

To reach the free States or Canada, by travelling by night and lying by during the day, from a State so far

south as Mississippi, no one would think for a moment
of attempting to escape. To remain in the city would be
a suicidal step. The deep sound of the escape of steam
from a boat, which was at that moment ascending the
river, broke upon the ears of the slave. "If that boat is
going up the river," said he, "why not I conceal myself
on board, and try to escape?" He went at once to the
steamboat landing, where the boat was just coming in.
"Bound for Louisville,' said the captain, to one who was
making inquiries. As the passengers were rushing on
board, Jerome followed them, and proceeded to where
some of the hands were stowing away bales of goods, he
took hold and aided them.

"Jump down into the hold, there, and help the men,"
said the mate to the fugitive, supposing that, like many
persons, he was working his way up the river. Once in
the hull, among the boxes, the slave concealed himself.
Weary hours, and at last days, passed without either water or food with the hidden slave. More than once did he
resolve to let his case be known; but the knowledge that
he would be sent back to Natchez, kept him from doing
so. At last, with his lips parched and fevered to a crisp,
the poor man crawled out into the freight-room, and began wandering about. The hatches were on, and the room
dark. There happened to be on board, a wedding-party;
and a box, containing some of the bridal cake, with several bottles of port wine, was near Jerome. He found the
box, opened it, and helped himself. In eight days, the
boat tied up at the wharf at the place of her destination.
It was late at night; the boat's crew, with the single exception of the man on watch, were on shore. The hatches
were off, and the fugitive quietly made his way on deck
and jumped on shore. The man saw the fugitive, but too
late to seize him.

Still in a slave State, Jerome was at a loss to know how
he should proceed. He had with him a few dollars,
enough to pay his way to Canada, if he could find a
conveyance. The fugitive procured such food as he
wanted from one of the many eating-houses, and then,
following the direction of the North Star, he passed out
of the city, and took the road leading to Covington.
Keeping near the Ohio River, Jerome soon found an opportunity to pass over into the State of Indiana. But lib-

erty was a mere name in the latter State, and the fugitive learned, from some colored persons that he met, that it was not safe to travel by daylight. While making his way one night, with nothing to cheer him but the prospect of freedom in the future, he was pounced upon by three men who were lying in wait for another fugitive, an advertisement of whom they had received through the mail. In vain did Jerome tell them that he was not a slave. True, they had not caught the man they expected; but, if they could make this slave tell from what place he had escaped, they knew that a good price would be paid them for the slave's arrest.

Tortured by the slave-catchers, to make him reveal the name of his owner and the place from whence he had escaped, Jerome gave them a fictitious name in Virginia, and said that his master would give a large reward, and manifested a willingness to return to his "old boss."

By this misrepresentation, the fugitive hoped to have another chance of getting away.

Allured with the prospect of a large sum of the needful the slave-catchers started back with their victim. "Stopping on the second night at an inn, on the banks of the Ohio River, the kidnappers, in lieu of a suitable place in which to confine their prize during the night, chained him to the bed-post of their sleeping chamber.

The white men were late in retiring to rest, after an evening spent in drinking. At dead of night, when all was still, the slave arose from the floor, upon which he had been lying, looked around and saw that Morpheus had possession of his captors. "For once," thought he, "the brandy bottle has done a noble work." With palpitating heart and trembling limbs, he viewed his position. The door was fast, but the warm weather had compelled them to leave the window open. If he could but get the chains off, he might escape through the window to the piazza. The sleepers' clothes hung upon chairs by the bed-side. The slave thought of the padlock key, examined the pockets, and found it. the chains were soon off, and the negro stealthily making his way to the window. He stopped, and said to himself, "These men are villains, they are enemies to all who, like me, are trying to be free. Then why not teach them a lesson?" He then dressed himself in the best suit, hung his own worn-out and tattered garments on the same chair, and silently passed through the window to the piazza, and let himself down by one of the pillars, and started once more for Canada.

Daylight came upon him before he had selected a hiding-place for the day, and he was walking at a rapid rate, in hopes of soon reaching some woodland or forest. The sun had just begun to show itself, when Jerome was astonished at seeing behind him, in the distance, two men upon horseback. Taking a road to the right he saw before him a farmhouse, and so near was he to it that he observed two men in front of him looking at him. It was too late to turn back. The kidnappers were behind—strange men before. Those in the rear he knew to be enemies, while he had no idea of what principles were the farmers. The latter also saw the white men coming, and called to the fugitive to come that way.

The broad-brimmed hats that the farmers wore told the slaves that they were Quakers.

Jerome had seen some of these people passing up and down the river, when employed on a steamer between Natchez and New Orleans, and had heard that they disliked slavery. He, therefore, hastened toward the drab-coated men, who, on his approach, opened the barn-door, and told him to "run in."

When Jerome entered the barn, the two farmers closed the doors, remaining outside themselves, to confront the slave-catchers, who now came up and demanded admission, feeling that they had their prey secure.

"Thee can't enter my premises," said one of the Friends, in rather a musical voice.

The negro-catchers urged their claim to the slave, and intimated that, unless they were allowed to secure him, they would force their way in. By this time, several other Quakers had gathered around the barn-door. Unfortunately for the kidnappers, and most fortunately for the fugitive, the Friends had just been holding a quarterly meeting in the neighborhood, and a number of them had not yet returned to their homes.

After some talk, the men in drab promised to admit the hunters, provided they procured an officer and a search-warrant from a justice of the peace. One of the slave-catchers was left to see that the fugitive did not get away, while the other went in pursuit of an officer. In the mean time, the owner of the barn sent for a hammer and nails, and began nailing up the barn-door.

After an hour in search of the man of the law, they returned with an officer and a warrant. The Quaker demanded to see the paper, and, after looking at it for some time, called to his son to go into the house for his glasses. It was a long time before Aunt Ruth found the leather case, and when she did, the glasses wanted wiping before they could be used. After comfortably adjusting them on his nose, he read the warrant over leisurely.

"Come, Mr. Dugdale, we can't wait all day," said the officer.

"Well, will thee read it for me?" returned the Quaker.

The officer complied, and the man in drab said,—"Yes, thee may go in, now. I am inclined to throw no obstacles in the way of the execution of the law of the land."

On approaching the door, the men found some forty or fifty nails in it, in the way of their progress.

"Lend me your hammer and a chisel, if you please, Mr. Dugdale," said the officer.

"Please read that paper over again, will thee?" asked the Quaker.

The officer once more read the warrant.

"I see nothing there which says I must furnish thee with tools to open my door. If thee wants a hammer, thee must go elsewhere for it; I tell thee plainly, thee can't have mine."

The implements for opening the door are at length obtained, and, after another half hour, the slave-catchers are in the barn. Three hours is a long time for a slave to be in the hands of Quakers. The hay is turned over, and the barn is visited in every part; but still the runaway is not found. Uncle Joseph has a glow upon his countenance; Ephraim shakes his head knowingly; little Elijah is a perfect know-nothing, and if you look toward the house you will see Aunt Ruth's smiling face ready to announce that breakfast is ready.

"The nigger is not in this barn," said the officer.

"I know he is not," quietly remarked the Quaker.

"What were you nailing up your door for, then, as if you were afraid we would enter?" inquired one of the kidnappers.

"I can do what I please with my own door, can't I?" said the Friend.

The secret was out; the fugitive had gone in at the front door, and out at the back; and the reading of the warrant, nailing up of the door, and other preliminaries of the Quaker, was to give the fugitive time and opportunity to escape.

It was now late in the morning, and the slave-catchers were a long way from home, and the horses were jaded by the rapid manner in which they had travelled. The Friends, in high glee, returned to the house for breakfast; the officer and the kidnappers made a thorough examination of the barn and premises, and satisfied that Jerome had gone into the barn, but had not come out, and equally satisfied that he was out of their reach, the owner said, "He's gone down into the earth, and has taken an underground railroad."

And thus was christened that famous highway over which so many of the oppressed sons and daughters of African descent were destined to travel, and an account of which has been published by one of its most faithful agents, Mr. William Still, of Philadelphia.

At a later period, Cato, servant of Dr. Gaines, was sold to Captain Enoch Price, of St. Louis. The Captain took his slave with him on board the steamer *Chester*, just about sailing for New Orleans. At the latter place, the boat obtained a cargo for Cincinnati, Ohio. The master, aware that the slave might give him the slip, while in a free State, determined to leave the chattel at Louisville, Ky., till his downward return. However, Mr. Price, anxious to have the servant's services on the boat, questioned him with regard to the contemplated visit to Cincinnati.

"I don't want to go to a free State," said Cato; "fer I knowed a servant dat went up dar, once, an' dey kept beggin' him to run away; so I druther not go dar; kase I is satisfied wid my marser, an' don't want to go off, whar I'd have to take keer of mysef."

This was said in such an earnest and off-hand manner, that it removed all of the lady's suspicions in regard to his attempting to escape; and she urged her husband to take him to Ohio.

Cato wanted his freedom, but he well knew that if he

expressed a wish to go to a free State, he would never be permitted to do so. In due season, the *Chester* arrived at Cincinnati, where she remained four days, discharging her cargo, and reloading for the return trip. During the time, Cato remained at his post, attending faithfully to his duties; no one dreaming that he had the slightest idea of leaving the boat. However, on the day previous to the *Chester*'s leaving Cincinnati, Cato divulged the question to Charley, another slave, whom he wished to accompany him.

Charley heard the proposition with surprise; and although he wanted his freedom, his timid disposition would not allow him to make the trial.

"My master is a pretty good man, and treats me comparatively well; and should I be caught and taken back, he would no doubt sell me to a cotton or sugar-planter," said Charley to Cato's invitation. "But," continued he, "Captain Price is a mean man; I shall not blame you, Cato, for running away and leaving him. By the by, I am engaged to go to a surprise-party, to-night, and I reckon we'll have a good time. I've got a new pair of pumps to dance in, and I've got Jim, the cook, to bake me a pie, and I'll have some sandwiches, and I'm going with a pretty gal."

"So you won't go away with me, to-night?" said Cato to Charley.

"No," was the reply.

"It is true," remarked Cato, "your marser is a better man, an' treats you a heap better den Captain Price does me, but, den, he may get to gambling, an' get broke, and den he'll have to sell you."

"I know that," replied Charley; "none of us are safe as long as we are slaves."

It was seven o'clock at night, Cato was in the pantry, washing the supper dishes, and contemplating his flight, the beginning of which was soon to take place. Charley had gone up to the steward's hall, to get ready for the surprise, and had been away some time, which caused uneasiness to Cato, and he determined to go up into the cabin, and see that everything was right. Entering the cabin from the Social Hall, Cato, in going down and passing the Captain's room, heard a conversation which attracted his attention, and caused him to halt at his master's room door.

He was not long, although the conversation was in a low tone, in learning that the parties were his master and his fellow-servant Charley.

"And so he is going to run away, to-night, is he?" said the Captain.

"Yes, sir," replied Charley; "he's been trying to get me to go with him, and I thought it my duty to tell you."

"Very well; I'll take him over to Covington, Ky., put him in jail, for the night, and when I get back to New Orleans, I will sell the ungrateful nigger. Where is he now?" asked the Captain.

"Cato is in the pantry, sir, washing up the tea-things," was the reply.

The moving of the chairs in the room, and what he had last heard, satisfied Cato that the talk between his master and the treacherous Charley was at an end, and he at once returned to the pantry undetermined what course to pursue. He had not long been there, ere he heard the well-known squeak of the Captain's boots coming down the stairs. Just then Dick, the cook's boy, came out of the kitchen and threw a pan full of cold meat overboard. This incident seemed to furnish Cato with words, and he at once took advantage of the situation.

"What is dat you throw overboard dar?"

"None your business," replied Dick, as he slammed the door behind him and returned to the kitchen.

"You free niggers will waste everything dar is on dis boat," continued Cato. "It's my duty to watch dees niggers an' see dat dey don't destroy marser's property. Now, let me see, I'll go right off an' tell marser 'bout Charley, I won't keep his secrets any longer." And here Cato threw aside his dish towel and started for the cabin.

Captain Price, who, during Cato's soliloquy, was hid behind a large box of goods, returned in haste to his room, where he was soon joined by his dutiful servant.

In answer to the rap on the door, the Captain said "Come in."

Cato, with downcast look, and in an obsequious manner, entered the room, and said, "Marser, I is come to tell you somethin' dat hangs heavy on my mine, somethin' dat I had ought to tole you afore dis."

"Well," said the master, "what is it, Cato?"

"Now, marser, you hires Charley, don't you?"

"Yes."

"Well, den, ser, ef Charley runs away you'll have to pay fer him, won't you?"

"I think it very probable, as I brought him into a free State, and thereby giving him an opportunity to escape. Why, is he thinking of running away?"

"Yes, ser," answered Cato, "He's gwine to start to-night, an' he's bin pesterin' me all day to go wid him."

"Do you mean to say that Charley has been trying to persuade you to run away from me?" asked the Captain, rather sharply.

"Yes, ser, dats jess what he's bin a doin' all day. I axed him whar he's gwine to, an' he sed he's gwine to Canada, an' he call you some mighty mean names, an' dat made me mad."

"Why, Charley has just been here telling me that you were going to run away to-night."

With apparent surprise, and opening his large eyes, Cato exclaimed, "Well, well, well, ef dat nigger don't beat de debble!" And here the negro raised his hands, and looking upward said, "Afoe God, marser, I wouldn't leave you fer dis worl'. Now, ser, jess let me tell you how you can find out who tells de trufe. Charley has got ebry ting ready an' is a gwine right off. He's got two pies, some sweet-cake, some sandwiches, bread an' butter, an' he's got a pair of pumps to dance in when he gets to Canada. An' ef you want to kotch him in de ack of runnin' away, you jess wait out on de dock an' you'll kotch him."

This was said in such an earnest manner, and with such protestations of innocence, that Captain Price determined to follow Cato's advice and watch for Charley.

"Go see if you can find where Charley is, and come back and let me know," said the Captain.

Away went Cato, on his tip-toes, in the direction of the steward's room, where, by looking through the keyhole, he saw the treacherous fellow-servant getting ready for the surprise party that he had engaged the night previous to attend.

Cato returned almost breathless, and in a whisper said, "I foun' him ser, he's gittin' ready to start. He's got a bundle of provisions tied up all ready, ser; you'll be shur to kotch him as he's gwine away, ef you go on de dock.''

Throwing his camlet cloak over his shoulders, the Captain passed out upon the wharf, took a position behind a pile of wood, and awaited the coming of the negro; nor did he remain long in suspense.

With lighted cigar, dressed in his best apparel, and his eatables tied up in a towel, Charley was soon seen hastily leaving the boat.

Stepping out from his hiding-place, the Captain seized the negro by the collar and led him back to the steamer, exclaiming, ''Where are you going, what's that you've got in that bundle?''

''Only some washin' I is takin' out to get done,'' replied the surprised and frightened negro.

As they reached the lighted deck, ''Open that bundle,'' said the Captain.

Charley began to obey the command, and at the same time to give an explanation.

''Shut your mouth, you scoundrel,'' vociferously shouted the Captain.

As the man slowly undid the parcel, and the contents began to be seen, ''There,'' said the Captain, ''there's the pies, cake, sandwiches, bread and butter that Cato told me you had put up to eat while running away. Yes, there's the pumps, too, that you got to dance in when you reached Canada.''

Here the frightened Charley attempted again to explain, ''I was jess gwine to—''

''Shut your mouth, you villain; you were going to escape to Canada.''

''No, Marser Price, afore God I was only—''

''Shut your mouth, you black rascal; you told me you were taking some clothes to be washed, you lying scamp.''

During this scene, Cato was inside the pantry, with the door ajar, looking out upon his master and Charley with unfeigned satisfaction.

Still holding the negro by the collar, and leading him to the opposite side of the boat, the Captain called to Mr. Roberts, the second mate, to bring up the small boat to take him and the ''runaway'' over the river.

A few moments more, and the Captain, with Charley

seated by his side, was being rowed to Covington, where the negro was safely locked up for the night.

"A little longer," said the Captain to the second officer, as he returned to the boat, "a little longer and I'd a lost fifteen hundred dollars by that boy's running away."

"Indeed," responded the officer.

"Yes," continued the Commander, "my servant Cato told me, just in time to catch the rascal in the very act of running off."

One of the sailors who was rowing, and who had been attentively listening to the Captain, said, "I overheard Cato to-day, trying to persuade Charley to go somewhere with him to-night, and the latter said he was going to a 'surprise party.'"

"The devil you did," exclaimed the Captain. "Hasten up there," continued he, "for these niggers are a slippery set."

As the yawl came alongside of the steamer, Captain Price leaped on deck and went directly in search of Cato, who could nowhere be found. And even Charley's bundle, which he left where he had been opening it, was gone. All search for the tricky man was in vain.

On the following morning, Charley was brought back to the boat, saying, as they were crossing the river, "I tole de boss dat Cato was gwine to run away, but he didn't believe me. Now he sees Cato's gone."

After the Captain had learned all that he could from Charley, the latter's account of his imprisonment in the lock-up caused great merriment amongst the boat's crew.

"But I tell you dar was de biggest rats in dat jail, eber I seed in my life. Dey run aroun' dar an' make so much fuss dat I was 'fraid to set down or lay down. I had to stan' up all night."

The *Chester* was detained until in the latter part of the day, during which time every effort was made to hunt up Cato, but without success.

When upbraided by the black servants on the boat for his treachery to Cato, Charley's only plea was, "I 'speck it was de debble dat made me do it."

Dressing himself in his warmest and best clothes, and getting some provisions that he had prepared during the day, and also taking with him Charley's pies, cakes, sandwiches, and pumps, Cato left the boat and made good his escape before his master returned from Covington.

It was during the cold winter of 1834, that the fugitive travelled by night and laid by in the woods in the day. After a week's journey, his food gave out, and then came the severest of his trials, cold coupled with hunger.

Often Cato would resolve to go to some of the farmhouses and apply for food and shelter, but the fear of being captured and again returned prevented him from following his inclinations. One night a pelting rain that froze as fast as it fell, drove the fugitive into a barn, where, creeping under the hay, he remained, sleeping sweetly while his garments were drying upon his person.

Sounds of the voices of the farmer and his men feeding the cattle and doing the chores, awakened the man from his slumbers, who, seeing that it was daylight, feared he would be arrested. However, the day passed, and the fugitive coming out at nightfall, started once more on his weary journey, taking for his guide the North Star, and after travelling the entire night, he again lay by, but this time in the forest.

Three days of fasting had now forced hunger upon Cato, so that he once more determined to seek food. Waiting till night, he came upon the highway, and soon approached a farm-house, of the olden style, built of logs. The sweet savor of the supper attracted the hungry man's attention as he neared the dwelling. For once there was no dog to herald his coming, and he had an opportunity of viewing the interior of the house, through the apertures that a log cabin generally presents.

As the fugitive stood with one eye gazing through the *crack,* looking at the table, already set, and snuffing in the delicious odor from a boiling pot, he heard the mother say,—''Take off the chicken, Sally Ann, I guess the dumplings are done. Your father will be home in half an hour; if he should catch that nigger and bring him along, we'll feed him on the cold meat and potatoes.''

With palpitating heart, Cato listened to the last sentences that fell from the woman's lips. Who could the ''nigger'' be[?] thought he.

Finding only the woman and her daughter in the house, the black man had been debating in his own mind whether or not to go in and demand a part of the contents of the kettle. However, the talk about "catching a nigger," settled the question at once with him.

Seizing a sheet that hung upon the clothes-line, Cato covered himself with it; leaving open only enough to enable him to see, he rushed in, crying at the top of his voice,—"Come to judgment! Come to judgment."

Both women sprang from their seats, and, screaming, passed out of the room, upsetting the table as they went. Cato seized the pot of chicken with one hand, and a loaf of bread, that had fallen from the table, with the other; hastily leaving the house and taking to the road, he continued on his journey.

The fugitive, however, had gone but a short distance when he heard the tramp of horses and the voices of men; and, fearing to meet them, he took to the woods till they had passed by.

As he hid behind a large tree by the roadside, Cato heard distinctly:

"And what is your master's name?"

"Peter Johnson, ser," was the reply.

"How much do you think he will give to have you brought back?"

"Dunno, ser," responded a voice which Cato recognized by the language to be a negro.

It was evident that a fugitive slave had been captured, and was about to be returned for the reward. And it was equally evident to Cato that the slave had been caught by the owner of the pot of stewed chicken that he then held in his hand, and he felt a thrill of gladness as he returned to the road and pursued his journey.

CHAPTER XIV.

In the year 1850, there were fifty thousand free colored people in the slave States, the greater number residing in Louisiana, Maryland, Virginia, Tennessee, and South Carolina. In all the States these people were allowed but few privileges not given to the slaves; and in many their condition was thought to be even worse than that of the bondmen. Laws, the most odious, commonly known as the "Black Code," were enacted and enforced in every State. These provided for the punishment of the free colored people—punishment which was not mentioned in the common law for white persons; for binding out minors, a species of slavery, and naming thirty-two offences more for blacks than had been enacted for the whites, and eight of which made it capital punishment for the offences committed.

Public opinion, which is often stronger than law, was severe in the extreme. In many of the Southern cities, including Charleston, S.C., a colored lady, free, and owning the fine house in which she lived, was not allowed to wear a veil in the public streets.

In passing through the thoroughfares, blacks of both sexes were compelled to take the outside, on pain of being kicked into the street, or sent to the lock-up and whipped.

As late as 1858, a movement was made in several of the Southern States to put an exorbitant tax upon them, and in lieu of which they were to be sold into life-long slavery. Maryland led off with a bill being introduced into the Legislature by Mr. Hover, of Frederick County, for levying a tax of two dollars per annum on all colored male inhabitants of the State over twenty-one years of age, and under fifty-five, and of one dollar on every female over eighteen and under forty-five, to be collected by the collectors of the State taxes, and *devoted to the use of the Colonization Society.* In case of the refusal to pay of a property-holder or housekeeper, his or her goods were to be seized and sold; if not a property-holder, the body of the non-paying person was to be seized, and hired out to the lowest bidder who would agree to pay the tax; and in case of not being able to hire said delinquents out, they were to be sold to any person who would pay the amount of tax and costs for the lowest period of service!

Tennessee followed in the same strain. The annexed protest of one of her noblest sons, Judge Catron, appeared at the time. He said:

"My objection to the bill is, *that it proposes to commit an outrage, to perpetrate an oppression and cruelty.* This is the plain truth, and it is idle to mince words to soften the fact. Let us look the proposition boldly in the face. This depressed and helpless portion of our population is designed to be driven out, or to be enslaved for life, and their property forfeited, as no slave can hold property. The mothers are to be sold, or driven away from their children, many of them infants. The children are to be bound out until they are twenty-one years of age, and then to leave the State or be sold; which means that they are to be made slaves for life, in fact. Now, of these women and children, there is hardly one in ten that is of unmixed negro blood. Some are half-white; many have half-white mothers and white fathers, making a cast[e] of 87 1/2–100ths of white blood; many have a third cross, in whom the negro blood is almost extinct; such is the unfortunate truth. This description of people, who were born free, and lived as free persons, are to be introduced as slaves into our families, or into our negro quarters, there to be under an overseer, or they are to be sold to the negro-trader and sent South, there to be whipped by overseers—*and to preach rebellion* into the negro quarters—as they will *preach* rebellion everywhere that they may be driven to by this unjust law, whether it be amongst us here in Tennessee or south of us on the cotton and sugar plantations, or in the abolition meetings in the free States. Nor will the women be the least effective in preaching a crusade, when begging money in the North, to relieve their children, left behind in this State, in bondage.

"We are told that this 'free-negro bill' is a politic, popular measure. Where is it popular? *In what nook or corner of the State are principles of humanity so deplorably deficient that a majority of the whole inhabitants would commit an outrage not committed in a Christian country of which history gives any account?* In what country is it, this side of Africa, that the majority have enslaved the minority, sold the weak to the strong, and applied the proceeds of the sale to educate the children of the stronger side, as this bill proposes? It is an open assertion that 'might makes right.' It is re-opening the African slave trade. In that trade the strong capture the weak, and sell them; and so it will be here, if this policy is carried out."

In some of the States the law was enacted and the people driven out or sold. Those who were able to pay their way out, came away; those who could not raise the means, were doomed to languish in bondage till released by the Rebellion.

About the same time, in Georgia, Florida, and South Carolina, strong efforts were being made to re-open the African slave trade. At the Democratic State Convention, held in the city of Charleston, S. C., May 1, 1860, Mr. Gaulden made the following speech:—

"MR. PRESIDENT, AND FELLOW DEMOCRATS:—As I stated to you a few moments ago, I have been confined to my room by severe indisposition, but learning of the commotion and the intense excitement which were existing upon the questions before this body, I felt it to be my duty, feeble as I was, to drag myself out to the meeting of my delegation, and when there I was surprised to find a large majority of that delegation voting to secede at once from this body. I disagree with those gentlemen. I regret to disagree with my brethren from the South upon any of the great questions which interest our common country. I am a Southern States Rights man; I am an African slave-trader. I believe I am one of those Southern men who believe that slavery is right, morally, religiously, socially, and politically. (Applause.) I believe that the institution of slavery has done more for this country, more for civilization, than all other interests put together. I believe if it were in the power of this country to strike down the institution of slavery, it would put civilization back two hundred years. I tell you, fellow Democrats, that the African slave-trader is the true Union man. (Cheers and laughter.) I tell you that the slave-trading of Virginia is more immoral, more un-Christian in every possible point of view, than that African slave-trade which goes to Africa and brings a heathen and worthless man here, makes him a useful man, Christianizes him, and sends him and his posterity down the stream of time to join in the blessings of civilization. (Cheers and laughter.) Now, fellow-democrats, so far as any public expression of opinion of the State of Virginia—the great slave-trading State of Virginia—has been given, they are all opposed to the African slave-trade.''

DR. REED, of Indiana.—I am from Indiana, and I am in favor of it.

MR. GAULDEN.—Now, gentlemen, we are told, upon high authority, that there is a certain class of men who strain at a gnat and swallow a camel. Now, Virginia, which authorizes the buying of Christian men, separating them from their wives and children, from all the relations and association amid whom they have lived for years, rolls up her eyes in holy horror when I would go to Africa, buy a savage, and introduce him to the blessings of civilization and Christianity. (Cheers and laughter.)

MR. RYNDERS, of New York.—You can get one or two recruits from New York to join with you.

THE PRESIDENT.—The time of the gentleman has expired. (Cries of ''Go on! go on!'')

The President stated that if it was the unanimous wish of the Convention, the gentleman could proceed.

MR. GAULDEN.—Now, fellow Democrats, the slave-trade in Virginia forms a mighty and powerful reason for its opposition to the African slave-trade, and in this remark I do not intend any disrespect to my friends from Virginia. Virginia, the Mother of States and of statesmen, the Mother of Presidents, I apprehend, may err as well as other mortals. I am afraid that her error in this regard lies in the promptings of the almighty dollar. It has been my fortune to go into that noble old State to buy a few darkies, and I have had to pay from one thousand to two thousand dollars a head, when I could go to

Africa and buy better negroes for fifty dollars a-piece. (Great laughter.) Now, unquestionably, it is to the interests of Virginia to break down the African slave-trade when she can sell her negroes at two thousand dollars. She knows that the African slave-trade would break up her monopoly, and hence her objection to it. If any of you Northern Democrats—for I have more faith in you than I have in the Carpet Knight Democracy of the South—will go home with me to my plantation in Georgia, but a little way from here, I will show you some darkies that I bought in Maryland, some that I bought in Virginia, some in Delaware, some in Florida, some in North Carolina, and I will also show you the pure African, the noblest Roman of them all. (Great laughter.) Now, fellow Democrats, my feeble health and failing voice admonish me to bring the few remarks I have to make to a close. (Cries of "Go on! go on!") I am only sorry that I am not in a better condition than I am to vindicate before you to-day the words of truth, of honesty, and of right, and to show you the gross inconsistencies of the South in this regard. I came from the First Congressional District of the State of Georgia. I represent the African slave-trade interests of that section. (Applause.) I am proud of the position I occupy in that respect. I believe that the African slave-trader is a true missionary, and a true Christian. (Applause.)

Such was the feeling in a large part of the South, with regard to the enslavement of the negro.

CHAPTER XV.

The success of the slave-holders in controlling the affairs of the National Government for a long series of years, furnishing a large majority of the Presidents, Speakers of the House of Representatives, Foreign Ministers and moulding the entire policy of the nation in favor of slave-holding, and the admitted fact that none could secure an office in the national Government who were known to be opposed to the *peculiar* institution, made the Southerners feel themselves superior to the people of the free States. This feeling was often manifested by an outburst of intemperate language, which frequently showed itself in the pulpit, on the rostrum, and in the drawing-room. On all such occasions the placing of the institution of slavery above liberty, seemed to be the aim of its advocates.

"The principle of slavery is in itself right, and *does not depend on difference of complexion*,"—said the Richmond (Va.) *Enquirer.*

A distinguished Southern statesman exclaimed,—

"Make the laboring man the slave of *one* man, instead of the slave of society, and he would be far better off." "Slavery, *black or white*, is right and necessary." *"Nature has made the weak in mind or body for slaves."*

Another said:—

"Free society! We sicken of the name. What is it but a conglomeration of *greasy mechanics, filthy operators, small-fisted farmers,* and moonstruck theorists? All the Northern States, and especially the New England States, are *devoid of society fitted for well-bred gentlemen.* The prevailing class one meets with is that of mechanics struggling to be genteel, and small farmers, who do their own drudgery; and yet who are hardly fit for association with a gentleman's body servant [slave]. This is your free society."

The insults offered to John P. Hale and Charles Sumner in the United States Senate, and to Joshua R. Giddings and Owen Lovejoy in the House of Representatives, were such as no legislative body in the world would have allowed, except one controlled by slave-drivers. I give the following, which may be taken as a fair specimen of the *bulldozing* of those days.

In the National House of Representatives Hon. O. Lovejoy, member from Illinois, was speaking against the further extension of slavery in the territories, when he was interrupted by Mr. Barksdale, of Mississippi—

"Order that black-hearted scoundrel and nigger-stealing thief to take his seat."

By Mr. Boyce, of South Carolina, addressing Mr. Lovejoy—

"Then behave yourself."

By Mr. Gartrell, of Georgia, (in his seat)—

"The man is crazy."

By Mr. Barksdale, of Mississippi, again—

"No, sir; you stand there to-day, an infamous, perjured villain."

By Mr. Ashmore, of South Carolina—

"Yes; he is a perjured villain, and he perjures himself every hour he occupies a seat on this floor."

By Mr. Singleton, of Mississippi—

"And a negro thief into the bargain."

By Mr. Barksdale, of Mississippi, again—

"I hope my colleague will hold no parley with that perjured negro thief."

By Mr. Singleton, of Mississippi, again—

"No sir; any gentleman shall have time, but not such a mean, despicable wretch as that."

By Mr. Martin, of Virginia—

"And if you come among us, we will do with you as we did with John Brown—hang you as high as Haman. I say that as a Virginian."

Hon. Robert Toombs, of Georgia, made a violent speech in the Senate, January, 1860, in which he said—

"Never permit this Federal Government to pass into the traitorous hands of the Black Republican party. It has already declared war against you and your institutions. It every day commits acts of war against you; it has already compelled you to arm for your defence. Listen to 'no

vain babblings,' to no treacherous jargon about 'overt acts'; they have already been committed. Defend yourselves; the enemy is at your door; wait not to meet him at the hearthstone,—meet him at the door-sill, and drive him from the temple of liberty, or pull down its pillars and involve him in a common ruin.''

Such and similar sentiments expressed at the South, and even by Southerners when sojourning in the free States, did much to widen the breach, and to bring on the conflict of arms that soon followed.

CHAPTER XVI.

The night was dark, the rain descended in torrents from the black and overhanging clouds, and the thunder, accompanied with vivid flashes of lightning, resounded fearfully, as I entered a negro cabin in South Carolina. The room was filled with blacks, a group of whom surrounded a rough board table, and at it sat an old man holding in his hand a watch, at which all were intently gazing. A stout negro boy held a torch which lighted up the cabin, and near him stood a Yankee soldier, in the Union blue, reading the President's Proclamation of Freedom.

As it neared the hour of twelve, a dead silence prevailed and the holder of the time-piece said,—"By de time I counts ten, it will be midnight an' de lan' will be free. One, two, three, four, five, six, seven, eight, nine,—" just then a loud strain of music came from the banjo, hanging upon the wall, and at its sound the whole company, as if by previous arrangement, threw themselves upon their knees, and the old man exclaimed: "O, God, de watch was a minit' too slow, but dy promises an' dy mercy is allers in time; dou did promise dat one of dy angels should come an' give us de sign, an' shore 'nuff de sign did come. We's grateful, O, we's grateful, O, Lord, send dy angel once moe to give dat sweet sound."

At this point another strain from the banjo was heard, and a sharp flash of lightning was followed by a clap of thunder, such as is only heard in the tropics. The negroes simultaneously rose to their feet and began singing; finishing only one verse, they all fell on their knees, and Uncle Ben, the old white-haired man, again led in prayer, and such a prayer as but few outside of this injured race could have given. Rising to their feet, the leader commenced singing:—

"Oh! breth-er-en, my way, my way's cloudy, my way,
   Go send dem angels down.
Oh! breth-er-en, my way, my way's cloudy, my way,
   Go send dem angels down.
There's fire in de east an' fire in de west,
   Send dem angels down.
An' fire among de Methodist,
   O, send dem angels down.
Ole Sa-tan's mad, an' I am glad,
   Send dem angels down.
He missed the soul he thought he had,
   O, send dem angels down.
I'll tell you now as I tole afore,
   Send dem angels down.
To de promised lan' I'm bound to go,
   O, send dem angels down.
Dis is de year of Jubilee,
   Send dem angels down.
De Lord has come to set us free,
   O, send dem angels down."

One more short prayer from Uncle Ben, and they arose, clasped each other around the neck, kissed, and commenced shouting, "Glory to God, we's free."

Another sweet strain from the musical instrument was followed by breathless silence, and then Uncle Ben said, "De angels of de Lord is wid us still an' dey is watching ober us, fer ole Sandy tole us moe dan a mont ago dat dey would."

I was satisfied when the first musical strain came, that it was merely a vibration of the strings, caused by the rushing wind through the aperture between the logs behind the banjo. Fearing that the blacks would ascribe the music to some mysterious Providence, I plainly told them of the cause.

"Oh, no ser," said Uncle Ben, quickly, his eyes brightening as he spoke, "dat come fum de angels. We been specken it all de time. We know the angels struck the strings of de banjo."

The news of the music from the instrument without the touch of human hands soon spread through the entire neighborhood, and in a short time the cabin was jammed with visitors, who at once turned their attention to the banjo upon the wall.

All sorts of stories were soon introduced to prove that angelic visits were common, especially to those who were fortunate enough to carry "de witness."

"De speret of de Lord come to me lass night in my sleep an' tole me dat I were gwine to be free, an' sed dat de Lord would sen' one of His angels down to give me de warnin'. An' when de banjo sounded, I knowed dat my bressed Marster were a' keepin' His word," said Uncle Ben.

An elderly woman amongst the visitors drew a long breath, and declared that she had been lifted out of her bed three times on the previous night; "I knowed," she continued, "dat de angelic hoss was hoverin' round about us."

"I dropped a fork to-day," said another, "an' it stuck up in de floo', right afore my face, an' dat is allers good luck fer me."

"De mule kicked at me three times dis mornin' an' he never did dat afore in his life," said another, "an' I knowed good luck would come fum dat."

"A rabbit run across my path twice as I come fum de branch lass Saturday, an' I felt shor' dat somethin' mighty was gwine to happen," remarked Uncle Ben's wife.

"I had a sign that showed me plainly that all of you would be free," said the Yankee soldier, who had been silent since reading the proclamation. All eyes were instantly turned to the white man from the North, and half a dozen voices cried out simultaneously, "O, Mr. Solger, what was it? what was it? what was it?"

"Well," said the man in blue, "I saw something on a large white sheet—"

"Was it a goos?" cried Uncle Ben, before the sentence was finished by the soldier. Uncle Ben's question about a ghost, started quite a number to their feet, and many trembled as they looked each other in the face, and upon the soldier, who appeared to feel the importance of his position.

Ned, the boy who was holding the torch, began to tell a ghost story, but he was at once stopped by Uncle Ben, who said, "Shet your mouf, don't you see de gentmun ain't told us what he see in de 'white sheet?' "

"Well," commenced the soldier, again, "I saw on a large sheet of paper, a printed Proclamation from President Lincoln, like the one I've just read, and that satisfied me that you'd all be free to-day."

Every one was disappointed at this, for all were prepared for a ghost story, from the first remark about the "white sheet" of paper. Uncle Ben smiled, looked a little wise, and said, "I speck dat's a Yankee trick you's given us, Mr. Solger."

The laugh of the man in blue was only stopped by Uncle Ben's striking up the following hymn, in which the whole company joined:—

"A storm am brewin' in de Souf,
    A storm am brewin' now.
Oh! hearken den, and shut your mouf,
    And I will tell you how:
And I will tell you how, ole boy,
    De storm of fire will pour,
And make de black folks sing for joy,
    As dey neber sing afore.

"So shut your mouf as close as deafh,
And all you niggas hole your breafh,
    And do de white folks brown!

"De black folks at de Norf am ris,
    And dey am comin' down—
And comin' down, I know dey is,
    To do de white folks brown!
Dey'll tun ole Massa out to grass,
    And set de niggas free,
And when dat day am come to pass
    We'll all be dar to see!

"So shut your mouf as close as deafh,
And all you niggas hole your breafh,
    And I will tell you how.

"Den all de week will be as gay
    As am de Chris'mas time;
We'll dance all night and all de day,
    And make de banjo chime,

And make de banjo chime, I tink,
    And pass de time away,
Wid 'nuf to eat and 'nuf to drink,
    And not a bit to pay!

"So shut your mouf as close as deafh,
    And all you niggas hole your breafh,
        And make de banjo chime."

However, there was in this company a man some forty
years old, who, like a large number of the slaves, had
been separated in early life from his relatives, and was
now following in the wake of the Union army, hoping to
meet some of those dear ones.

This was Mark Myers. At the age of twenty he fled
from Winchester, Va., and although pursued by blood-
hounds, succeeded in making good his escape. The pursuers returned and reported that Mark had been killed.
This story was believed by all.

Now the war had opened the way, Mark had come
from Michigan, as a servant for one of the officers; Mark
followed the army to Harper's Ferry, and then went up
to Winchester. Twenty years had caused a vast change,
and although born and brought up there, he found but
few that could tell him anything about the old inhabitants.

"Go to an ole cabin at de edge of de town, an' darh
you'll find ole Unkel Bob Smart, an' he know ebbry-
body, man an boy, dat's lived here for forty years," said
an old woman of whom he inquired. With haste Mark
proceeded to the "ole cabin," and there he found "Unkel Bob."

"Yer say yer name is Mark Myers, an' yer mamma's
name is Nancy," responded the old man to the inquiries
put to him by Mark.

"Yes," was the reply.

"Well, sonney," continued Uncle Bob, "de Myers
niggers was all sold to traders 'bout de beginnin' ov de
war, septin some ov de ole ones dat dey couldn't sell,
an' I specks yer mamma is one ov dem dat de traders
didn't want. Now, sonney, yer go over to de Redman
place, an' it 'pers to me dat de oman yer's lookin' fer is
over darh."

Thanking Uncle Bob, Mark started for the farm designated by the old man. Arriving there, he was told that "Aunt Nancy lived over yarnder on de wess road." Proceeding to the low log hut, he entered, and found the woman.

"Is this Aunt Nancy Myers?"

"Yes, sar, dis is me."

"Had you a son named Mark?"

"Yes, dat I did, an' a good boy he were, poor feller." And here the old woman wiped the tears away with the corner of her apron.

"I have come to bring you some good news about him."

"Good news 'bout who?" eagerly asked the woman.

"Good news about your son Mark."

"Oh! no; you can't bring me no good news 'bout my son, septin you bring it from hebben, fer I feel sartin dat he is darh, fer he suffered nuff when de dogs killed him, to go to hebben."

Mark had already recognized his mother, and being unable to longer conceal the fact, he seized her by the hand and said:

"Mother, don't you know me? I am your long-lost son Mark."

Amazed at the sudden news, the woman trembled like a leaf, the tears flowed freely, and she said:

"My son, Mark, had a deep gash across the bottom of his left foot, dat he will take wid him to his grave. Ef you is my son, show me de mark."

As quick almost as thought, Mark pulled off his boot, threw himself on the floor and held up the foot. The old woman wiped her glasses, put them on, saw the mark of the deep gash; then she fainted, and fell at her son's side.

Neighbors flocked in from the surrounding huts, and soon the cabin was filled with an eager crowd, who stood in breathless silence to catch every word that should be spoken. As the old woman revived, and opened her eyes, she tremblingly said:

"My son, it is you."

"Yes, mother," responded the son, "it is me. When I ran away, old master put the dogs upon my track, but I jumped into the creek, waded down for some distance, and by that means the dogs lost the scent, and I escaped from them.''

''Well,'' said the old woman, ''in my prayers I axed God to permit me to meet you in hebben, an' He promised me I should; but He's bin better den His promise.''

''Now, mother, I have a home for you at the North, and I have come to take you to it.''

The few goods worth bringing away from the slave hut were soon packed up, and ere the darkness had covered the land, mother and son were on their way to the North.

CHAPTER XVII.

During the Rebellion and at its close, there was one question that appeared to overshadow all others; this was Negro Equality. While the armies were on the field of battle, this was the great bugbear among many who warmly espoused the cause of the Government, and who approved all its measures, with this single exception. They sincerely wished the rebels to be despoiled of their property. They wished every means to be used to secure our success on the field, including Emancipation. But they would grow pale at the words Negro Equality; just as if the liberating of a race, and securing to them personal, political, social and religious rights, made it incumbent upon us to take these people into our houses, and give them seats in our social circle, beyond what we would accord to other total strangers. No advocate of Negro Equality ever demanded for the race that they should be made pets. Protect them in their natural, lawful, and acquired rights, is all they ask.

Social equality is a condition of society that must make itself. There are colored families residing in every Southern State, whose education and social position is far above a large portion of their neighboring whites. To compel them to associate with these whites would be a grievous wrong. Then, away with this talk, which is founded in hatred to an injured people. Give the colored race in the South equal protection before the law, and then we say to them—

> "Now, to gain the social prize,
>   Paddle your own canoe."

But this hue and cry about Negro Equality generally emanates from a shoddy aristocracy, or an uneducated class, more afraid of the negro's ability and industry than of his color rubbing off against them,—men whose claims to equality are so frail that they must be fenced about, and protected by every possible guard; while the true nobleman fears not that his reputation will be compromised by any association he may choose to form. So it is with many of those men who fear negro competition. Conscious of their own inferiority to the mass of mankind, and recognizing the fact that they exist and thrive only by the aid of adventitious advantages, they look with jealousy on any new rivals and competitors, and use every means, fair and unfair, to keep them out of the market.

The same sort of opposition has been made to the introduction of female labor into any of the various branches of manufacture. Consequently, women have always been discriminated against. They have been restricted to a small range of employments; their wages have been kept down; and many who would be perfectly competent to perform the duties of clerks or accountants, or to earn good wages in some branch of manufacture, have been driven by their necessities either to suicide or prostitution.

But the nation, knowing the Southerners as they did, aware of the deep hatred to Northern whites, and still deeper hatred to their ex-slaves, who aided in blotting out the institution of slavery, it was the duty of the nation, having once clothed the colored man with the rights of citizenship and promised him in the Constitution full protection for those rights, to keep this promise most sacredly. The question, while it is invested with equities of the most sacred character, is not without its difficulties and embarrassments. Under the policy adopted by the Democrats in the late insurrectionary States, the colored citizen has been subjected to a reign of terror which has driven him from the enjoyment of his rights and leaves him as much a nonentity in politics, unless he obeys their behests, as he was when he was in slavery. Under this condition of things to-day, while he if properly protected in his rights would hold political supremacy in Mississippi, Georgia, South Carolina, Louisiana, Alabama, and Florida, he has little or no voice in either State or National Government.

Through fear, intimidation, assassination, and all the

horrors that barbarism can invent, every right of the negro in the Southern States is to-day at an end. Complete submission to the whites is the only way for the colored man to live in peace.

Some time since there was considerable talk about a "War of Races," but the war was all on the side of the whites. The freedman has succumbed to brute force, and hence the war of races is suspended; but let him attempt to assert his rights of citizenship, as the white man does at the North, according to the dictates of his own conscience and sense of duty, and the bloody hands of the Ku-Klux and White Leaguer will appear in all their horrors once more—the "dream that has passed" would become a sad reality again.

CHAPTER XVIII.

Immediately after the Rebellion ceased, the freedmen throughout the South, desiring no doubt to be fully satisfied that they were actually free and their own masters, and could go where they pleased, left their homes in the country and took up their abode in the cities and towns. This, as a matter of course, threw them out of business, and large numbers could be seen idly lolling about the steps of the court house, town hall, or other county buildings, or listlessly wandering through the streets. That they were able to do this seemed to them positive evidence that they were really free. It was not long, however, before they began to discover that they could not live without work, and that the only labor that they understood was in the country on the plantations. Consequently they returned to the farms, and in many instances to their former masters. Yet the old love for visiting the cities and towns remained, and they became habituated to leaving their work on Saturdays, and going to the place nearest to them. This caused Saturday to be called "nigger day," in most of the Southern States.

On these occasions they sell their cotton or other produce, do their trading, generally having two jugs, one for the molasses, the other for the whiskey, as indispensible to the visit. The storekeepers get ready on Saturday morning, putting their brightest and most gaudy-colored goods in the windows or on the front of their counters. Jew shops put their hawkers at their doors, and the drinking saloons, billiard saloons, and other places of entertainment, kept for their especial accommodation, either by men of their own race or by whites, are all got ready for an extra run.

Being on a visit to the State of Alabama, for a while, I had a fair opportunity of seeing the colored people in

that section under various circumstances. It was in the
autumn and I was at Huntsville. The principal business
houses of the city are situated upon a square which sur-
rounds the court house, and at an early hour in the morning this is filled with colored people of all classes and
shades. On Saturdays there are often fully two thousand
of them in the streets at one time. At noon the throng
was greatest, and up to that time fresh wagon-loads of
men, women, and children, were continually arriving.
They came not only in wagons, but on horses, and mules,
and on foot. Their dress and general appearance were
very dissimilar. Some were dressed in a queer looking
garment made of pieces of old army blankets, a few were
apparelled in faded military overcoats, which were lib-
erally supplied with patches of other material. The
women, unlike their husbands and other male relations,
were dressed in finery of every conceivable fashion. All
of them were decked out with many-colored ribbons.
They wore pinchbeck jewelry in large quantities. A few
of the young girls displayed some little taste in the arrangement of their dress; and some of them wore expensive clothes. These, however, were "city niggers," and
found but little favor in the eyes of the country girls. As
the farmers arrived they hitched their tumble-down wagons and bony mules near the court house, and then proceeded to dispose of the cotton and other products which
they had brought to town.

While the men are selling their effects, the women go
about from store to store, looking at the many gaudy
articles of wearing apparel which cunning shop-keepers
have spread out to tempt their fancy. As soon as "the
crop" is disposed of, and a negro farmer has money in
his pocket, his first act is to pay the merchant from whom
he obtained his supplies during the year. They are improvident and ignorant sometimes, but it must be said,
to their credit, that as a class they always pay their debts,
the moment they are in a position to do so. The country
would not be so destitute if a larger number of white men
followed their example in this respect. When they have
settled up all their accounts, and arranged for future bills,
they go and hunt up their wives, who are generally on
the look-out. They then proceed to a dining saloon, call
for an expensive meal, always finishing with pies, pud-

dings, or preserves, and often with all three. When they have satisfied their appetites, they go first to the dry-goods stores. Here, as in other shops, they are met by obsequious white men, who conduct them at once to a back or side room, with which most of the stores are supplied. At first I could not fathom the mystery of this ceremony. After diligent inquiry, however, I discovered that, since the war, unprincipled store-keepers, some of them northern men, have established the custom of giving the country negroes, who come to buy, as much whiskey as they wish to drink. This is done in the back rooms I have mentioned, and when the unfortunate black men and women are deprived of half their wits by the vile stuff which is served out to them, they are induced to purchase all sorts of useless and expensive goods.

In their soberest moments average colored women have a passion for bright, colored dresses which amounts almost to madness, and, on such occasions as I have mentioned, they never stop buying until their money is exhausted. Their husbands have little or no control over them, and are obliged, whether they will or not, to see most of their hard earnings squandered upon an unserviceable jacket, or flimsy bonnet, or many-colored shawl. I saw one black woman spend upward of thirty dollars on millinery goods. As she received her bundle from the cringing clerk she said, with a laugh:

"I 'clare to the Lord I'se done gone busted my old man, sure."

"Never mind," said the clerk, "he can work for more."

"To be sure," answered the woman, and then flounced out of the store.

The men are but little better than the women in their extravagance. I saw a man on the square who had bargained for a mule, which he very much needed, and which he had been intending to purchase as soon as he sold his cotton. He agreed to pay his fifty-seven dollars for the animal, and felt in his pocket for the money, but could find only sixteen dollars. Satisfying himself that he had no more, he said:

"Well, well, ef dis ain't de most stravagant nigger I ever see; I sole two bales of cotton dis bressed day, an' got one hundred and twenty-two dollars, an' now I is got only dis." Here he gave a loud laugh and said:

"Ole mule, I want you mighty bad, but I'll have to let you slide dis time."

While the large dealers were selling their products and emptying their wagons, those with vegetables and fruits were vending them in different sections of the city. A man with a large basket upon his head came along through one of the principal streets shouting:

"Hellow, dar, in de cellar, I is got fresh aggs, jess fum de hen, lay 'em dis mornin' fer de 'casion; here dey is, big hen's aggs, cheap. Now's yer time. Dees aggs is fresh an' good, an' will make fuss-rate agg-nog. Now's yer time fer agg-nogg wid new aggs in it; all laid dis mornin'." Here he set down his basket as if to rest his head. Seeing a colored servant at one of the windows, he called out:

"Here, sister, here's de fresh aggs; here dey is, big aggs fum big hen, much as she could do to lay 'em. Now's yer time; don't be foolish an' miss dis chance."

Just then, a man with a wagon-load of stuff came along, and his voice completely shut out the man with "de fresh aggs."

"Here," cried he, "Here's yer nice winter squash, taters,—Irish taters, sweet taters, Carliner taters. Big House, dar, Big House, look out de winder; here's yer nice cabbages, taters, sweet taters, squash. Now's yer time to get 'em cheap. To-morrow is Christmas, an' yer'll want 'em, shore."

The man with the basket of eggs on his head, and who had been silenced by the overpowering voice of the "tater" man, called out to the other, "Now, I reckon yer better go in anudder street. I's been totin' dees aggs all day, an' I don't get in nobody's way."

"I want to know, is dis your street?" asked the "tater" man.

"No; but I tank de Lord, I is got some manners 'bout me. But, den, I couldn't speck no more fum you, fer I knowed you afore de war; you was one of dem cheap niggers, clodhopper, never taste a bit of white bread till after de war, an' den didn't know 'twas bread."

"Well, den, ef you make so much fuss 'bout de street, I'll go out of it; it's nothin' but a second-handed street, no how,'' said the ''tater'' man, and drove off, crying, ''taters, sweet taters, Irish taters, an' squash.''

Passing into a street where the colored people are largely represented, I met another head peddler. This man had a tub on his head and with a musical voice was singing:

''Here's yer chitlins, fresh an' sweet,
    Who'll jine de Union?
Young hog's chitlins hard to beat,
    Who'll jine de Union?
Methodist chitlins, jest been biled,
    Who'll jine de Union?
Right fresh chitlins, dey ain't spiled,
    Who'll jine de Union?
Baptist chitlins by de pound,
    Who'll jine de Union?
As nice chitlins as ever was found,
    Who'll jine de Union?

''Here's yer chitlins, out of good fat hog; jess as sweet chitlins as ever yer see. Dees chitlins will make yer mouf water jess to look at 'em. Come an' see 'em.''

At this juncture the man took the tub from his head, sat it down, to answer a woman who had challenged his right to call them ''Baptist chitlins.''

''Duz you mean to say dat dem is Baptiss chitlins?''

''Yes, mum, I means to say dat dey is real Baptist chitlins, an' nuffin' else.''

''Did dey come out of a Baptiss hog?'' inquired the woman.

''Yes, mum, dem chitlins come out of a Baptist hog.''

''How duz you make dat out?''

''Well, yer see, dat hog was raised by Mr. Roberson, a hard-shell Baptist, de corn dat de hog was fatted on was also raised by Baptists, he was killed and dressed by Geemes Boone, an' you all know dat he'e as big a Baptist as ever lived.''

''Well,'' said the woman, as if perfectly satisfied, ''lem-me have two poun's.''

By the time the man had finished his explanation, and weighed out her lot, he was completely surrounded with women and men, nearly all of whom had their dishes to get the choice morsel in.

"Now," said a rather solid-looking man. "Now, I want some of de Meth-diss chitlins dat you's bin talking 'bout."

"Here dey is, ser."

"What," asked the purchaser, "you take 'em all out of de same tub?"

"Yes," quickly replied the vender.

"Can you tell 'em by lookin' at 'em?" inquired the chubby man.

"Yes, ser."

"How duz you tell 'em?"

"Well, ser, de Baptist chitlins has bin more in de water, you see, an' dey's a little whiter."

"But, how duz I know dat dey is Meth-diss?"

"Well, ser, dat hog was raised by Uncle Jake Bemis, one of de most shoutin' Methodist in de Zion connection. Well, you see, ser, de hog pen was right close to de house, an' dat hog was so knowin' dat when Uncle Jake went to prayers, ef dat hog was squeelin' he'd stop. Why, ser, you could hardly get a grunt out of dat hog till Uncle Jake was dun his prayer. Now, ser, ef dat don't make him a Methodist hog, what will?"

"Weigh me out four pounds, ser."

"Here's your fresh chitlins, Baptist chitlins, Methodist chitlins, all good an' sweet."

And in an hour's time the peddler, with his empty tub upon his head, was making his way out of the street, singing,—

"Methodist chitlins, Baptist chitlins,
    Who'll jine de Union?"

Hearing the colored cotton-growers were to have a meeting that night, a few miles from the city, and being invited to attend, I embraced the opportunity. Some thirty persons were assembled, and as I entered the room, I heard them chanting—

Sing yo' praises! Bless de Lam!
    Getting plenty money!
Cotton's gwine up—'deed it am!
    People, ain't it funny?

CHORUS.—Rise, shine, give God the glory.

[*Repeat* glory.]

Don't you tink hit's gwine to rain?
    Maybe was, a little;
Maybe one ole hurricane
    's bilin' in de kittle!—*Chorus*.

Craps done fail in Egypt lan'—
    Say so in de papers;
Maybe little slight o' hand
    'Mong de specerlaters.—*Chorus*.

Put no faith in solemn views;
    Keep yo' pot a smokin',
Stan' up squah in yo' own shoes—
    Keep de debble chokin'!—*Chorus*.

Fetch me 'roun' dat tater juice!
    Stop dat sassy grinnin'!
Turn dat stopper clean a-loose—
    Keep yo' eye a skinnin'!—*Chorus*.

Here's good luck to Egypt lan'!
    Hope she ain't a-failin'!
Hates to see my fellerman
    Straddle ob de pailin'!—*Chorus*.

The church filled up; the meeting was well conducted,
and measures taken to protect cotton-raisers, showing
that these people, newly-made free, and uneducated,
were looking to their interests.

Paying a flying visit to Tennessee, I halted at Columbia, the capital of Maury County. At Redgerford Creek,
five miles distant from Columbia, lives Joe Budge, a man
with one hundred children. Never having met one with
such a family, I resolved to make a call on the gentleman
and satisfy my own curiosity.

This distinguished individual is seventy-one years old,
large frame, of unadulterated blood, and spent his life in
slavery up to the close of the war.

"How many children have you, Mr. Budge?" I asked.

"One hundred, ser," was the quick response.

"Are they all living?"

"No, ser."

"How many wives had you?"

"Thirteen, ser."

"Had you more than one wife living at any time?"

"O, yes, ser, nearly all of dem ware livin' when de war broke out."

"How was this, did the law allow you to have more than one wife at a time?"

"Well, yer see, boss, I waren't under de law, I ware under marser."

"Were you married to all of your wives by a minister?"

"No, ser, only five by the preacher."

"How did you marry the others?"

"Ober de broomstick an' under de blanket."

"How was that performed?"

"Well, yer see, ser, dey all 'sembles in de quarters, an' a man takes hold of one en' of de broom an' a 'oman takes hole of tudder en', an' dey holes up de broom, an' de man an' de 'oman dats gwine to get married jumps ober an' den slips under a blanket, dey put out de light an' all goes out an' leabs em dar."

"How near together were your wives?"

"Marser had fore plantations, an' dey live 'bout on 'em, dem dat warn't sold."

"Did your master sell some of your wives?"

"O! yes, ser, when dey got too ole to bare children. You see, marser raised slaves fer de market, an' my stock were called mighty good, kase I ware very strong, an' could do a heap of work."

"Were your children sold away from you?"

"Yes, ser, I see three of 'em sole one day fer two thousand dollars a-piece; yer see dey ware men grown up."

"Did you select your wives?"

"Dunno what you mean by dat word."

"Did you pick out the women that you wanted?"

"O! no, ser, I had nuthin ter say 'bout dat. Marser allers get 'em, an' pick out strong, hearty young women. Dat's de reason dat de planters wanted to get my children, kase dey ware so helty."

"Did you never feel that it was wrong to get married in such a light manner?"

"No, ser, kase yer see I toted de witness wid me."

"What do you mean by that?"

"Why, ser, I had religion, an' dat made me feel dat all ware right."

"What was the witness that you spoke of?"

"De change of heart, ser, is de witness dat I totes in my bosom; an' when a man's got dat, he fears nuthin, not eben de debble himself."

"Then you know that you've got the witness?"

"Yes, ser, I totes it right here." And at this point, Mr. Budge put his hand on his heart, and looked up to heaven.

"I presume your master made no profession of religion?"

"O! yes, ser, you bet he had religion. He ware de fustest man in de church, an' he ware called mighty powerful in prayer."

"Do any of your wives live near you now, except the one that you are living with?"

"Yes, ser, dar's five in dis county, but dey's all married now to udder men."

"Have you many grand-children?"

"Yes, ser, when my 'lations am all tergedder, dey numbers 'bout fore hundred, near as I ken get at it."

"Do you know of any other men that have got as many children as you?"

"No, ser, dey calls me de boss daddy in dis part of de State."

Having satisfied my curiosity, I bade Mr. Budge "good-day."

CHAPTER XIX.

Spending part of the winter of 1880 in Tennessee, I began the study of the character of the people and their institutions. I soon learned that there existed an intense hatred on the part of the whites, toward the colored population. Looking at the past, this was easily accounted for. The older whites, brought up in the lap of luxury, educated to believe themselves superior to the race under them, self-willed, arrogant, determined, skilled in the use of side-arms, wealthy—possessing the entire political control of the State—feeling themselves superior also to the citizens of the free States—this people was called upon to subjugate themselves to an ignorant, superstitious, and poverty-stricken, race—a race without homes, or the means of obtaining them; to see the offices of State filled by men selected from this servile set made these whites feel themselves deeply degraded in the eyes of the world. Their power was gone, but their pride still remained. They submitted in silence, but "bided their time," and said: "Never mind; we'll yet make your hell a hot one."

The blacks felt their importance, saw their own power in national politics, were interviewed by obsequious and cringing white men from the North—men, many of them, far inferior morally, to the negro. Two-faced, second-class white men of the South, few in number, it is true, hung like leeches upon the blacks. Among the latter was a respectable proportion of free men—free before the Rebellion; these were comparatively well educated; to these and to the better class of freedmen the country was to look for solid work. In the different State legislatures, the great battle was to be fought, and to these the interest of the South centred. All of the Legislatures were composed mainly of colored men. The few whites that were there were not only no help to the blacks, but it would have been better for the character of the latter, and for the country at large, if most of them had been in some State prison.

Colored men went into the Legislatures somewhat as children go for the first time to a Sabbath school. They sat and waited to see "the show." Many had been elected by constituencies, of which not more than ten in a hundred could read the ballots they deposited; and a large number of these Representatives could not write their own names.

This was not their fault. Their want of education was attributable to the system of slavery through which they had passed, and the absence of the educated intelligent whites of the South, was not the fault of the colored men. This was a trying position for the recently-enfranchised blacks, but nobly did they rise above the circumstances. The speeches made by some of these men exhibited a depth of thought, flights of eloquence, and civilized statesmanship, that throw their former masters far in the back-ground. Yet, amongst the good done, bills were introduced and passed, giving State aid to unworthy objects, old, worn-out corporations re-galvanized, bills for outrageous new frauds drawn up by white men, and presented by blacks; votes of both colors bought up, bills passed, money granted, and these ignorant men congratulated as "Statesmen."

While this "Comedy of Errors" was being performed at the South, and loudly applauded at the North, these very Northern men, who had yelled their throats sore, would have fainted at the idea of a negro being elected a member of their own Legislature.

By and by came the reaction. The disfranchised whites of the South submitted, but complained. Northern men and women, the latter, always the most influential, sympathized with the dog underneath. As the tide was turning, the white adventurers returned from the South with piles of greenbacks, and said that they had been speculating in cotton; but their neighbors knew that it was stolen, for they had been members of Southern Legislatures.

While Northern carpet-baggers were scudding off to their kennels with their ill-gotten gains, the Southern colored politicians were driving fast horses, their wives in their fine carriages; and men, who, five years before were working in the cotton field under the lash, could now draw their checks for thousands.

This extravagance of black men, followed by the heavy taxes, reminded the old Southerners of their defeat in the Rebellion; it brought up thoughts of revenge; Northern sympathy emboldened them at the South, which resulted in the Ku-Klux organizations, and the reign of terror that has cursed the South ever since.

The restoring of the rebels to power and the surrendering the colored people to them, after using the latter in the war, and at the ballot box, creating an emnity between the races, is the most bare-faced ingratitude that history gives any account of.

After all, the ten years of negro Legislation in the South challenges the profoundest study of mankind. History does not record a similar instance. Five millions of un-educated, degraded people, without any preparation whatever, set at liberty in a single day, without shedding a drop of blood, burning a barn, or insulting a single female. They reconstructed the State Governments that their masters had destroyed; became Legislators, held State offices, and with all their blunders, surpassed the whites that had preceded them. Future generations will marvel at the calm forbearance, good sense, and Christian zeal of the American Negro of the nineteenth century.

Nothing has been left undone to cripple their energies, darken their minds, debase their moral sense, and obliterate all traces of their relationship to the rest of mankind; and yet how wonderfully they have sustained the mighty load of oppression under which they have groaned for thousands of years.

After looking at the past history of both races, I could easily see the cause of the great antipathy of the white man to the black, here in Tennessee. This feeling was most forcibly illustrated by an incident that occurred one day while I was standing in front of the Knoxville House, in Knoxville. A good-looking, well-dressed colored man approached a white man, in a business-like manner, and began talking to him, but ere he had finished the question, the white raised his walking stick, and with much force, knocked off the black man's hat, and with an oath said, "Don't you know better than to speak to a white man with your hat on, where's your manners?" The negro picked up his hat, held it in his hand, and resumed the conversation.

I inquired of the colored gentleman with whom I was talking, who the parties were; he replied,—"The white man is a real estate dealer, and the colored man is Hon. Mr. —, ex-member of the General Assembly."

This race feeling is still more forcibly set forth in the dastardly attack of John Warren, of Huntingdon. The wife of this ruffian, while passing through one of the streets of that town, was accidentally run against by Miss Florence Hayes, who offered ample apology, and which would have been accepted by any well-bred lady. However, Mrs. Warren would not be satisfied with anything less than the punishment of the young lady. Therefore, the two-fisted, coarse, rough, uncouth ex-slave-holder, proceeded to Miss Hayes' residence, gained admission, and without a word of ceremony seized the young lady by the hair, and began beating her with his fist, and kicking her with his heavy boots.

Not until his victim lay prostrate and senseless at his feet, did this fiend cease his blows. Miss Hayes was teaching school at Huntingdon when this outrage was committed, and so severe was the barbarous attack, that she was compelled to return to her home at Nashville, where she was confined to her room for several weeks. Yet, neither law nor public opinion could reach this monster.

A few days after the assault, the following paragraph appeared in the Huntingdon *Vindicator:*

"The occurrences of the past two weeks in the town of Huntingdon should prove conclusively to the colored citizens that there is a certain line existing between themselves and the white people which they cannot cross with impunity. The incident which prompts us to write this article, is the thrashing which a white gentleman administered to a colored woman last week. With no wish to foster a spirit of lawlessness in this community, but actuated by a desire to see the negro keep in his proper place, we advise white men everywhere to *stand up for their rights,* and in no case yield an inch to the encroachment of an inferior race.''

"Stand up for their rights," with this editor, means for the white ruffianly coward to knock down every colored lady that does not give up the entire sidewalk to him or his wife.

It was my good fortune to meet on several occasions Miss Florence T. Hayes, the young lady above alluded to, and I never came in contact with a more retiring, lady-like person in my life. She is a student of Tennessee Central College, where she bears an unstained reputation, and is regarded by all who know her to possess intellectual gifts far superior to the average white young women of Tennessee.

Spending a night in the country, we had just risen from the supper-table when mine host said:

"Listen, Mingo is telling how he re-converted his daughter; listen, you'll hear a rich story, and a true one." Mr. Mingo lived in the adjoining room.

"Yes, Mrs. Jones, my darter has bin home wissitin' me, an' I had a mighty trial wid her, I can tell yer."

"What was the matter, Mr. Mingo?" inquired the visitor.

"Well, yer see, Fanny's bin a-livin' in Philamadelfy, an' she's a mighty changed 'oman in her ways. When she come in de house, she run up to her mammy and say,— 'O! mar, I'm exquisitely pleased to greet you.' Den she run ter me an' sed,—'O! par,' an' kiss me. Well, dat was all well enuff, but to see as much as two yards of her dress a-dragin' behind her on de floor, it was too much,— an' it were silk, too. It made my heart ache. Ses I,— 'Fanny, you's very stravagant, dragin' all dat silk on de floor in dat way.' 'O!' sed she, 'That's the fashion, par.' Den, yer see, I were uneasy fer her. I were 'fraid she'd fall, fer she had on a pair of boots wid the highess heels I eber see in my life, which made her walk as ef she were walkin' on her toes. Den, she were covered all over wid ribbons and ruffles.

"When we set down to dinner, Fanny eat wid her fork, an' when she see her sister put de knife in her mouf, she ses,—'Don't put your knife in your mouth; that's vulgar.' Nex' mornin', she took out of her pocket some seeds, an' put 'em in a tin cup, an' pour bilin' hot water on

'em. Ses I,—'Fanny, is yer sick, an' gwine to take some
medicine?'

'O! no, par, it's quince seed, to make some gum-stick-
um.'

" 'What is dat fer?' I axed.

" 'Why, par, it's to make Grecian waves on my forehead. Some call them "scallopes." We ladies in the city
make them. You see, par, we comb our hair down in little
waves, and the gum makes them stick close to the forehead. All the white ladies in the city wear them; it's all
the fashion.'

"Well, yer see, Mrs. Jones, I could stand all dat, but
when we went to prayers I ax Fanny to lead in prayer;
an' when dat gal got on her knees and took out of her
pocket a gilt-edge book, and read a prayer, den I were
done, I ax myself is it possible dat my darter is come to
dat. So, when prayer were over, I sed: 'Fanny, what kind
of religion is dat yer's got?' Sed she,—'Why, par, I em
a Piscopion.' 'What is dat?' I axed. 'That's the English
Church service. Den yer's no more a Methodist?' 'O!
no,'' said she, 'to be a Piscopion is all the fashion.' ''

"Stop, Mr. Mingo," sed Mrs. Jones; "What kind of
religion is dat? Is it Baptiss?"

"No, no," replied the old man; "ef it were Baptiss,
den I could a-stood dat, kase de Baptiss religion will do
when yer can't get no better. Fer wid all dey faults, I
believe de Baptiss ken get into hebben by a tight squeeze.
Kase, yer see, Mrs. Jones, I is a Methodiss, an' I be-
lieves in ole-time religion, an' I wants my chillen to meet
me in hebben. So, I jess went right down on my knees
an' ax de Lord to show me my juty about Fanny, fer I
wanted to win her back to de ole-time religion. Well, de
Lord made it all plain to me, an' follerin' de Lord's message to me, I got right up an' went out into de woods an'
cut some switches, an' put 'em in de barn. So I sed to
Fanny: 'Come, my darter, out to de barn; I want to give
yer a present to take back to Philamadelfy wid yer.'

" 'Yes, par,' said she, fer she was a-fixin' de 'gum-
stick-um' on her hair. So I went to de barn, an' very
soon out come Fanny. I jess shut de door an' fasten it,
and took down my switches, an' ax her,—'What kind of
religion is dat yer's got?'

" 'Piscopion, par.' Den I commence, an' I did give

dat gal sech a whippen, and she cry out,—'O! par. O! par, please stop, par.' Den I ax her,—'What kind of religion yer's got?' 'Pis-co-copion,' sed she. So I give her some moo, an' I ax her again,—'What kind of religion is yer got?' She sed,—'O! par, O! par.' Sed I,—'Don't call me "par." Call me in de right way.' Den she said,—'O! daddy, O! daddy, I is a Methodiss. I is got ole-time religion; please stop an' I'll never be a Piscopion any more.'

"So, yer see, Mrs. Jones, I converted dat gal right back to de ole-time religion, which is de bess of all religion. Yes, de Lord answered my prayer dat time, wid de aid of de switches."

Whether Mingo's conversion of his daughter kept her from joining the Episcopalians, on her return to Philadelphia, or not, I have not learned.

CHAPTER XX.

The moral and social degradation of the colored population of the Southern States, is attributable to two main causes, their mode of living, and their religion. In treating upon these causes, and especially the latter, I feel confident that I shall throw myself open to the criticism of a numerous, if not an intelligent class of the people upon whom I write. The entire absence of a knowledge of the laws of physiology, amongst the colored inhabitants of the South is proverbial. Their small unventilated houses, in poor streets and dark alleys, in cities and towns, and the poorly-built log huts in the country, are often not fit for horses. A room fifteen feet square, with two, and sometimes three beds, and three or four in a bed, is common in Tennessee.

No bathing conveniences whatever, and often not a wash dish about the house, is the rule. The most inveterate eaters in the world, yet these people have no idea of cooking outside of hog, hominy, corn bread, and coffee. Yes, there is one more dish, it is the negro's sunflower in the South, cabbages.

It is usual to see a woman coming from the market about five o'clock in the evening, with a basket under her shawl, and in it a piece of pork, bacon, or half a hog's head, and one or two large heads of cabbage, and some sweet potatoes. These are put to cook at once, and the odor from the boiling pot may be snuffed in some distance off.

Generous to a fault, the host invites all who call in, to "stop to supper." They sit down to the table at about nine o'clock, spend fully an hour over the first course, then the apple dumplings, after that, the coffee and cake. Very few vegetables, except cabbages and sweet potatoes, are ever used by these people. Consequently they are not unfrequently ill from a want of the knowledge of the laws of health. The assembling of large numbers in the cities and towns has proved fatal.

Nearly all the statistics relating to the subject now accessible are those coming from the larger Southern cities, and these would seem to leave no doubt that in such centres of population the mortality of the colored greatly exceeds that of the white race. In Washington, for instance, where the negroes have enjoyed longer and more privileges than in most Southern cities, the death-rate per thousand in the year 1876 was for the whites 26.537; for the colored 49.294; and for the previous year it was a little worse for the blacks. In Baltimore, a very healthy city, the total death-rate for 1875 was 21.67 in one thousand, of which the whites showed 19.80, the colored 34.42. In a still healthier little city, Chattanooga, Tenn., the statistics of the last five years give the death-rate of the whites at 19.9; of the colored, 37. The very best showing for the latter, singularly enough, is made in Selma, Ala. It stands per one thousand, white, 14.28; colored, 18.88. In Mobile, in the same State, the mortality of the colored was just about double the rate among the whites. New Orleans for 1875 gives the record of 25.45 for the death-rate of the whites, to 39.69 for that of the colored.

Lecturers of their own race, male and female, upon the laws of health, is the first move needed.

After settling the question with his bacon and cabbage, the next dearest thing to a colored man, in the South, is his religion. I call it a "thing," because they always speak of getting religion as if they were going to market for it.

"You better go an' get religion, dat's what you better do, fer de devil will be arter you one of dees days, and den whar will yer be?" said an elderly Sister, who was on her way to the "Revival," at St. Paul's, in Nashville, last winter. The man to whom she addressed these words of advice stopped, raised his hat, and replied:

"Anty, I ain't quite ready to-night, but I em gwine to get it before the meetins close, kase when that getting-up day comes, I want to have the witness; that I do."

"Yes, yer better, fer ef yer don't, dar'll be a mighty stir 'mong de brimstone down dar, dat dey will, fer yer's bin bad nuff; I knows yer fum A to izzard,'' returned the old lady.

The church was already well filled, and the minister had taken his text. As the speaker warmed up in his subject, the Sisters began to swing their heads and reel to and fro, and eventually began a shout. Soon, five or six were fairly at it, which threw the house into a buzz. Seats were soon vacated near the shouters, to give them more room, because the women did not wish to have their hats smashed in by the frenzied Sisters. As a woman sprung up in her seat, throwing up her long arms, with a loud scream, the lady on the adjoining seat quickly left, and did not stop till she got to a safe distance.

''Ah, ha!'' exclaimed a woman near by, '' 'fraid of your new bonnet! Ain't got much religion, I reckon. Specks you'll have to come out of that if you want to save your soul.''

''She thinks more of that hat now, than she does of a seat in heaven,'' said another.

''Never mind,'' said a third, ''when she gets de witness, she'll drap dat hat an' shout herself out of breath.''

The shouting now became general; a dozen or more entering into it most heartily. These demonstrations increased or abated, according to movements of the leaders, who were in and about the pulpit; for the minister had closed his discourse, and first one, and then another would engage in prayer. The meeting was kept up till a late hour, during which, four or five sisters becoming exhausted, had fallen upon the floor and lay there, or had been removed by their friends.

St. Paul is a fine structure, with its spire bathed in the clouds, and standing on the rising land in South Cherry Street, it is a building that the citizens may well be proud of.

In the evening I went to the First Baptist Church, in Spruce Street. This house is equal in size and finish to St. Paul. A large assembly was in attendance, and a young man from Cincinnati was introduced by the pastor as the preacher for the time being. He evidently felt that to set a congregation to shouting, was the highest point to be attained, and he was equal to the occasion. Failing to raise a good shout by a reasonable amount of exertion, he took from his pocket a letter, opened it, held it up and began, "When you reach the other world you'll be hunting for your mother, and the angel will read from this paper. Yes, the angel will read from this paper."

For fully ten minutes the preacher walked the pulpit, repeating in a loud, incoherent manner, "And the angel will read from this letter." This created the wildest excitement, and not less than ten or fifteen were shouting in different parts of the house, while four or five were going from seat to seat shaking hands with the occupants of the pews. "Let dat angel come right down now an' read dat letter," shouted a Sister, at the top of her voice. This was the signal for loud exclamations from various parts of the house. "Yes, yes, I want's to hear the letter." "Come, Jesus, come, or send an angel to read the letter." "Lord, send us the power." And other remarks filled the house. The pastor highly complimented the effort, as one of "great power," which the audience most cordially endorsed. At the close of the service the strange minister had hearty shakes of the hand from a large number of leading men and women of the church. And this was one of the most refined congregations in Nashville.

It will be difficult to erase from the mind of the negro of the South, the prevailing idea that outward demonstrations, such as, shouting, the loud "amen," and the most boisterous noise in prayer, are not necessary adjuncts to piety.

A young lady of good education and refinement, residing in East Tennessee, told me that she had joined the church about a year previous, and not until she had one shouting spell, did most of her Sisters believe that she had "the Witness."

"And did you really shout?" I inquired.

"Yes. I did it to stop their mouths, for at nearly every meeting, one or more would say, 'Sister Smith, I hope to live to see you show that you've got the Witness, for where the grace of God is, there will be shouting, and the sooner you comes to that point the better it will be for you in the world to come.'"

To get religion, join a benevolent society that will pay them "sick dues" when they are ill, and to bury them when they die, appears to be the beginning, the aim, and the end of the desires of the colored people of the South. In Petersburg I was informed that there were thirty-two different secret societies in that city, and I met persons who held membership in four at the same time. While such associations are of great benefit to the improvident, they are, upon the whole, very injurious. They take away all stimulus to secure homes and to provide for the future.

As a man observed to me, "I b'longs ter four s'ieties, de 'Samaritans,' de 'Gallalean Fisherman,' de 'Sons of Moses,' an' de 'Wise Men of de East.' All of dees pays me two dollars a week when I is sick, an' twenty-five dollars ter bury me when I dies. Now ain't dat good?"

I replied that I thought it would be far better, if he put his money in a home and educated himself.

"Well," said he, "I is satisfied, kas, ef I put de money in a house, maybe when I got sick some udder man might be hangin' roun' wantin' me ter die, an' maybe de ole 'oman might want me gone too, an' not take good kere of me, an' let me die an' let de town bury me. But, now, yer see, de s'iety takes kere of me and burries me. So, now, I am all right fer dis worl' an' I is got de Witness, an' dat fixes me fer hebben."

This was all said in an earnest manner, showing that the brother had an eye to business.

The determination of late years to ape the whites in the erection of costly structures to worship in, is very injurious to our people. In Petersburg, Va., a Baptist society pulled down a noble building, which was of ample size, to give place to a more fashionable and expensive one, simply because a sister Church had surpassed them in putting up a house of worship. It is more consistent with piety and Godly sincerity to say that we don't believe there is any soul-saving and God-honoring element in such expensive and useless ornaments to houses in which to meet and humbly worship in simplicity and sincerity the true and living God, according to his revealed will. Poor, laboring people who are without homes of their own, and without (in many instances) steady remunerative employment, can ill afford to pay high for useless and showy things that neither instruct nor edify them. The manner, too, in which the money is raised, is none of the best, to say the least of it. For most of the money, both to build the churches and to pay the ministers, is the hard earnings of men in the fields, at service, or by our women over the wash-tub. When our people met and worshipped in less costly and ornamental houses, their piety and sincerity was equally as good as now, if not better. With more polish within and less ornament without, we would be more spiritually and less worldly-minded.

Revival meetings, and the lateness of the hours at which they close, are injurious to both health and morals. Many of the churches begin in October, and continue till the holidays; and commencing again the middle of January, they close in April. They often keep the meetings in till eleven o'clock; sometimes till twelve; and in some country places, they have gone on later. I was informed of a young woman who lost her situation—a very good one—because the family could not sit up till twelve o'clock every night to let her in, and she would not leave her meeting so as to return earlier. Another source of moral degradation lies in the fact that a very large number of men, calling themselves "missionaries," travel the length and breadth of the country, stopping longest where they are best treated. The "missionary" is usually armed with a recommendation from some minister in charge, or has a forged one, it makes but little difference which. He may be able to read enough to line a hymn, but that is about all.

His paper that he carries speaks of him as a man "gifted in revival efforts," and he at once sets about getting up a revival meeting. This tramp, for he cannot be called anything else, has with him generally a hymn-book, and an old faded, worn-out carpet-bag, with little or nothing in it. He remains in a place just as long as the people will keep him, which usually depends upon his ability to keep up an excitement. I met a swarm of these lazy fellows all over the South, the greatest number, however, in West Virginia.

The only remedy for this great evil lies in an educated ministry, which is being supplied to a limited extent. It is very difficult, however, to induce the uneducated, superstitious masses to receive and support an intelligent Christian clergyman.

The great interest felt in the South for education amongst the colored people often produce scenes of humor peculiar to the race. Enjoying the hospitality of a family in West Virginia, I was not a little amused at the preparation made for the reception of their eldest son, who had been absent six months at Wilberforce College. A dinner with a turkey, goose, pair of fowls, with a plentiful supply of side dishes, and apple dumplings for dessert, was on the table at the hour that the son was expected from the train.

An accident delayed the cars to such an extent that we were at the table and dinner half through, when suddenly the door flew open, and before us stood the hope of the family. The mother sprang up, raised her hands and exclaimed, "Well, well, ef dar ain't Peter, now. De Lord bress dat chile, eh, an' how college-like he seems. Jess look at him, don't he look educated? Come right here dis minit an' kiss your mammy."

During this pleasant greeting, Peter stood near the door where he had entered; dressed in his college rig, small cap on his head, bag swung at his side, umbrella in the left hand, and a cigar in the right, with a smile on his countenance, he looked the very personification of the Harvard student. The father of the family, still holding his knife and fork, sat with a glow upon his face, while the two youngsters, taking advantage of the occasion, were helping themselves to the eatables.

At the bidding, "Come an' kiss your mammy," Peter came forward and did the nice thing to all except the youngest boy, who said, "I can't kiss yer now, Pete, wait till I eat dees dumplins, den I'll kiss yer."

Dinner over, and Peter gave us some humorous accounts of college life, to the great delight of his mother, who would occasionally exclaim, "Bress de chile, what a hard time he muss hab dar at de college. An' how dem boys wory's him. Well, people's got to undergo a heap to git book larnin', don't dey?"

At night the house was filled, to see the young man from college.

CHAPTER XXI.

In the olden time, ere a blow was struck in the Rebellion, the whites of the South did the thinking, and the blacks did the work; the master planned, and the slave executed. This unfitted both for the new dispensation that was fast coming, and left each helpless, without the other.

But the negro was the worst off of the two, for he had nothing but his hands, while the white man had his education, backed up by the lands that he owned. Who can wonder at the negro's improvidence and his shiftlessness, when he has never had any systematic training—never been compelled to meet the cares of life?

This was the black man's misfortune on gaining his freedom, and to learn to save, and to manage his own affairs, appeared to all to be his first duty.

The hope of every one, therefore, seemed to centre in the Freedman's Saving Bank. "This is our bank," said they; and to this institution the intelligent and the ignorant, the soldier fresh from the field of battle, the farmer, the day laborer, and the poor washerwoman, all alike brought their earnings and deposited them in the Freedman's Bank. This place of safety for their scanty store seemed to be the hope of the race for the future. It was a stimulus for a people who had never before been permitted to enter a moneyed institution, except at his master's heels, to bring or to take away the bag of silver that his owner was too proud or too lazy to "tote."

So great was the negro's wish to save, that the deposits in the Freedman's Bank increased from three hundred thousand dollars in 1866, to thirty-one million dollars, in 1872, and to fifty-five million dollars, in 1874. This saving of earnings became infectious throughout the South, and the family that had no bank-book was considered poorly off. These deposits were the first instalments toward purchasing homes, or getting ready to begin some mercantile or mechanical business. The first announcement, therefore, of the closing of the Freedman's Saving Bank had a paralyzing effect upon the blacks everywhere.

Large numbers quit work; the greater portion sold their bank-books for a trifle, and general distrust prevailed throughout the community. Many who had purchased small farms, or cheap dwellings in cities and towns, and had paid part of the purchase money, now became discouraged, surrendered their claims, gave up the lands, and went about as if every hope was lost. It was their first and their last dealings with a bank.

These poor people received no sympathy whatever, from the whites of the South. Indeed, the latter felt to rejoice, for the negro obtained his liberty through the Republican party, and the Freedmen's Bank was a pet of that party.

The negro is an industrious creature, laziness is not his chief fault, and those who had left their work, returned to it. But the charm for saving was gone.

"No more Banks for me, I'll use my money as I get it, and then I'll know where it has gone to," said an intelligent and well-informed colored man to me.

This want of confidence in the saving institutions of the country, has caused a general spending of money as soon as obtained; and railroad excursions, steamboat rides, hiring of horses and buggies on Sabbath, and even on week days, have reaped large sums from colored people all over the South. Verily, the failure of the Freedman's Saving Bank was a National calamity, the influence of which will be felt for many years.

Not satisfied with robbing the deluded people out of the bulk of their hard earnings, commissioners were appointed soon after the failure, with "appropriate" salaries, to look after the interest of the depositors, and these leeches are eating up the remainder.

Whether truly or falsely, the freedmen were led to believe that the United States Government was responsible to them for the return of their money with interest. Common justice would seem to call for some action in the matter.

CHAPTER XXII.

Those who recollect the standing of Virginia in days gone by, will be disappointed in her at the present time. The people, both white and black, are poor and proud, all living on their reputation when the "Old Dominion" was considered the first State in the Union.

I viewed Richmond with much interest. The effect of the late Rebellion is still visible everywhere, and especially amongst those who were leaders in society thirty years ago. I walked through the market and observed several men with long, black cloth cloaks, beneath which was a basket. Into this they might be seen to deposit their marketing for the day.

I noticed an old black man bowing very gracefully to one of these individuals, and I inquired who he was. "Ah, massa," said the negro, "dat is Major ———, he was berry rich before de war, but de war fotch him right down, and now he ain't able to have servants, and he's too proud to show his basket, so he covers it up in his cloak." And then the black man smiled and shook his head significantly, and walked on. Standing here in the market place, one beholds many scenes which bring up the days of slavery as seen by the results. Here is a girl with a rich brown skin; after her comes one upon whose cheek a blush can just be distinguished; and I saw one or two young women whose cream-like complexion would have justly excited the envy of many a New York belle. The condition of the women of the latter class is most deplorable. Beautiful almost beyond description, many of them educated and refined, with the best white blood of the South in their veins, it is perhaps only natural that they should refuse to mate themselves with coarse and ignorant black men. Socially, they are not recognized by the whites; they are often without money enough to buy the barest necessaries of life; honorably they can never procure sufficient means to gratify their luxurious tastes; their mothers have taught them how to sin; their fathers they never knew; debauched white men are ever ready to take advantage of their destitution, and after living a short life of shame and dishonor they sink into early and unhallowed graves. Living, they were despised by whites and blacks alike; dead, they are mourned by none.

I went to hear the somewhat celebrated negro preacher, Rev. John Jasper. The occasion was one of considerable note, he having preached, and by request, a sermon to prove that the "Sun do move," and now he was to give it at the solicitation of forty-five members of the Legislature, who were present as hearers.

Those who wanted the sermon repeated were all whites, a number of whom did it for the fun that they expected to enjoy, while quite a respectable portion, old fogy in opinion, felt that the preacher was right.

On reaching the church, I found twelve carriages and two omnibuses, besides a number of smaller vehicles, lining the street, half an hour before the opening of the doors. However, the whites who had come in these conveyances had been admitted by the side doors, while the streets were crowded with blacks and a poorer class of whites.

By special favor I was permitted to enter before the throng came rushing in. Members of the Legislature were assigned the best seats, indeed, the entire centre of the house was occupied by whites, who, I was informed, were from amongst the F. F. Vs [First Families of Virginia]. The church seats one thousand, but it is safe to say that twelve hundred were present at that time.

Rev. John Jasper is a deep black, tall, and slim, with long arms and somewhat round-shouldered, and sixty-five years old. He has preached in Richmond for the last forty-five years, and is considered a very good man. He is a fluent speaker, well versed in Scriptures, and possesses a large amount of wit. The members of Jasper's church are mainly freedmen, a large number of whom are from the country, commonly called "corn-field niggers."

The more educated class of the colored people, I found, did not patronize Jasper. They consider him behind the times, and called him "old fogy." Jasper looked proudly upon his audience, and well he might, for he had before him some of the first men and women of Virginia's capital. But these people had not come to be instructed, they had really come for a good laugh and were not disappointed.

Jasper had prepared for the occasion, and in his opening service saved himself by calling on "Brother Scogin" to offer prayer. This venerable Brother evidently felt the weight of responsibility laid upon him, and discharged the duty, at least to the entire satisfaction of those who were there to be amused. After making a very sensible prayer, Scogin concluded as follows:—"O Lord, we's a mighty abused people, we's had a hard time in slavery, we's been all broken to pieces, we's bow-legged, knock-kneed, bandy-shanked, cross-eyed, and a great many of us is hump-backed. Now, Lord, we wants to be mendid up, an' we wants you to come an' do it. Don't send an angel, for dis is too big a job for an angel. You made us, O Lord, an' you know our wants, an' you can fix us up as nobody else can. Come right down yourself, and come quickly." At this sentence Jasper gave a loud groan, and Scogin ceased. After service was over I was informed that when Jasper finds any of his members a little too long-winded in prayer, singing, or speaking, he gives that significant groan, which they all well understand. It means " enough."

The church was now completely jammed, and it was said that two thousand people sought admission in vain. Jasper's text was "God is a God of War." The preacher, though wrong in his conclusions, was happy in his quotations, fresh in his memory, and eloquently impressed his views upon his hearers.

He said, "If the sun does not move, why did Joshua command it to 'stand still?' Was Joshua wrong? If so, I had rather be wrong with Joshua than to be right with the modern philosophers. If this earth moves, the chimneys would be falling, tumbling in upon the roofs of the houses, the mountains and hills would be changing and levelling down, the rivers would be emptying out. You and I would be standing on our heads. Look at that mountain standing out yonder; it stood there fifty years ago when I was a boy. Would it be standing there if the earth was running round as they tell us?''

"No, blessed God," cried a Sister. Then the laugh came, and Jasper stood a moment with his arms folded. He continued: "The sun rises in the east and sets in the west; do you think any one can make me believe that the earth can run around the world in a single day so as to give the sun a chance to set in the west?''

"No, siree, that doctrine don't go down with Jasper."

At this point the preacher paused for breath, and I heard an elderly white in an adjoining pew, say, in a somewhat solemn tone—"Jasper is right, the sun moves."

Taking up his bandanna, and wiping away the copious perspiration that flowed down his dusky cheeks, the preacher opened a note which had just been laid upon the desk, read it, and continued,—"A question is here asked me, and one that I am glad to answer, because a large number of my people, as well as others, can't see how the children of Israel were able to cross the Red Sea in safety, while Pharaoh and his hosts were drowned. I have told you again and again that everything was possible with God. But that don't seem to satisfy you.

"Those who doubt these things that you read in Holy Writ are like the infidel,—won't believe unless you can see the cause. Well, let me tell you. The infidel says that when the children of Israel crossed the Red Sea, it was in winter, and the sea was frozen over. This is a mistake, or an intentional misrepresentation." Here the preacher gave vivid accounts of the sufferings and flight of the children of Israel, whose case he likened to the colored people of the South. The preacher wound up with an eloquent appeal to his congregation not to be led astray by "these new-fangled notions."

Great excitement is just now taking hold of the people upon the seeming interest that the colored inhabitants are manifesting in the Catholic religion. The Cathedral in Richmond is thrown open every Sunday evening to the blacks, when the bishop himself preaches to them, and it is not strange that the eloquent and persuasive voice of Bishop Kean, who says to the negro, "My dear beloved brethren," should captivate these despised people. I attended a meeting at the large African Baptist Church, where the Rev. Moses D. Hoge, D. D., was to preach to the colored people against Catholicism. Dr. Hoge, though noted for his eloquence, and terribly in earnest, could not rise higher in his appeals to the blacks than to say "men and women" to them.

The contrast was noticeable to all. After hearing Dr. Hoge through I asked an intelligent colored man how he liked his sermon. His reply was: "If Dr. Hoge is in earnest, why don't he open his own church and invite us in and preach to us there? Before he can make any impression on us, he must go to the Catholic Church and learn the spirit of brotherly love."

One Sunday, Bishop Kean said to the colored congregation, numbering twelve hundred, who had come to hear him: "There are distinctions in the business and in the social world, but there are no distinctions in the spiritual. A soul is a soul before God, may it be a black or a white man's. God is no respecter of persons, the Christian Church cannot afford to be. The people who would not let you learn to read before the war, are the ones now that accuse me of trying to use you for political purposes.

"Now, my dear beloved brethren, when I attempt to tell you how to vote, you need not come to hear me preach any more."

The blacks have been so badly treated in the past that kind words and social recognition will do much to win them in the future, for success will not depend so much upon their matter as upon their manner; not so much upon their faith as upon the more potent direct influence of their practice. In this the Catholics of the South have the inside track, for the prejudice of the Protestants seems in a fair way to let the negro go anywhere except to heaven, if they have to go the same way.

CHAPTER XXIII.

Norfolk is the place above all others, where the "old-Verginny-never-tire" colored people of the olden time may be found in their purity. Here nearly everybody lives out of doors in the warm weather. This is not confined to the blacks. On the sidewalks, in front of the best hotels, under the awnings at store-doors, on the door-sills of private houses, and on the curbstones in the streets, may be seen people of all classes. But the blacks especially give the inside of the house a wide berth in the summer.

I went to the market, for I always like to visit the markets on Saturday, for there you see "life among the lowly," as you see it nowhere else. Colored men and women have a respectable number of stalls in the Norfolk market, the management of which does them great credit.

But the costermongers, or street-vendors, are the men of music. "Here's yer nice vegables—green corn, butter beans, taters, Irish taters, new, jess bin digged; come an' get 'em while dey is fresh. Now's yer time; squash, Calafony quash, bess in de worl'; come an' git 'em now; it'll be Sunday termorrer, an' I'll be gone to church. Big fat Mexican peas, marrer fat squash, Protestant squash, good Catholic vegables of all kinds."

> Now's yer time to git snap-beans,
> Okra, tomatoes, an' taters gwine by;
> Don't be foolish virgins;
> Hab de dinner ready
> When de master he comes home,
> Snap-beans gwine by.

Just then the vender broke forth in a most musical voice:

Oh! Hannah, boil dat cabbage down.
  Hannah, boil 'em down,
And turn dem buckwheats round and round,
  Hannah, boil 'em down.
It's almost time to blow de horn,
  Hannah, boil 'em down,
To call de boys dat hoe de corn,
  Hannah, boil 'em down.

Hannah, boil 'em down,
  De cabbage just pulled out de ground,
Boil 'em in de pot,
  And make him smoking hot.

. . . .

Some like de cabbage made in krout,
  Hannah, boil 'em down,
Dey eat so much dey get de gout,
  Hannah, boil 'em down,
Dey chops 'em up and let dem spoil,
  Hannah, boil 'em down;
I'd rather hab my cabbage boiled,
  Hannah, boil 'em down.

Some say dat possum's in de pan,
  Hannah, boil 'em down,
Am de sweetest meat in all de land,
  Hannah, boil 'em down;
But dar is dat ole cabbage head,
  Hannah, boil 'em down,
I'll prize it, children, till I's dead,
  Hannah, boil 'em down.

This song, given in his inimitable manner, drew the women to the windows, and the crowd around the vegetable man in the street, and he soon disposed of the contents of his cart. Other venders who "toted" their commodities about in baskets on their heads, took advantage of the musical man's company to sell their own goods. A woman with some really fine strawberries, put forth her claims in a very interesting song; the interest, however, centered more upon the manner than the matter:—

"I live fore miles out of town,
  I am gwine to glory.
My strawberries are sweet an' soun',
  I am gwine to glory.
I fotch 'em fore miles on my head,
  I am gwine to glory.
My chile is sick, an' husban' dead,
  I am gwine to glory.
Now's de time to get 'em cheap,
  I am gwine to glory.
Eat 'em wid yer bread an' meat,
  I am gwine to glory.
Come sinner get down on your knees,
  I am gwine to glory.
Eat dees strawberries when you please,
  I am gwine to glory."

Upon the whole, the colored man of Virginia is a very favorable physical specimen of his race; and he has peculiarly fine, urbane manners. A stranger judging from the surface of life here, would undoubtedly say that they were a happy, well-to-do people. Perhaps, also, he might say: "Ah, I see. The negro is the same everywhere—a hewer of wood, a peddler of vegetables, a wearer of the waiter's white apron. Freedom has not altered his status."

Such a judgment would be a very hasty one. Nations are not educated in twenty years. There are certain white men who naturally gravitate also to these positions; and we must remember that it is only the present generation of negroes who have been able to appropriate any share of the nobler blessings of freedom. But the colored boys and girls of Virginia are to-day vastly different from what the colored boys and girls of fifteen or twenty years ago were. The advancement and improvement is so great that it is not unreasonable to predict from it a very satisfactory future.

The negro population here are greatly in the majority, and formerly sent a member of their own color to the State Senate, but through bribery and ballot-box stuffing, a white Senator is now in Richmond. One negro here at a late election sold his vote for a barrel of sugar. After he had voted and taken his sugar home, he found it to be a barrel of sand. I learn that his neighbors turned the laugh upon him, and made him treat the whole company, which cost him five dollars.

I would not have it supposed from what I have said about the general condition of the blacks in Virginia that there are none of a higher grade. Far from it, for some of the best mechanics in the State are colored men. In Richmond and Petersburg they have stores and carry on considerable trade, both with the whites and their own race. They are doing a great deal for education; many send their sons and daughters North and West for better advantages; and they are building some of the finest churches in this State. The Second Baptist Church here pulled down a comparatively new and fine structure, last year, to replace it with a more splendid place of worship, simply because a rival church of the same denomination had surpassed them. I viewed the new edifice, and feel confident it will compare favorably with any church on the Back Bay, Boston.

The new building will seat three thousand persons, and will cost, exclusive of the ground, one hundred thousand dollars, all the brick and wood work of which is being done by colored men.

CHAPTER XXIV.

The education of the negro in the South is the most important matter that we have to deal with at present, and one that will claim precedence of all other questions for many years to come. When, soon after the breaking out of the Rebellion, schools for the freedmen were agitated in the North, and teachers dispatched from New England to go down to teach the "poor contrabands," I went before the proper authorities in Boston, and asked that a place be given to one of our best-educated colored young ladies, who wanted to devote herself to the education of her injured race, and the offer was rejected, upon the ground that the "time for sending colored teachers had not come." This happened nearly twenty years ago. From that moment to the present, I have watched with painful interest the little progress made by colored men and women to become instructors of their own race in the Southern States.

Under the spur of the excitement occasioned by the Proclamation of Freedom, and the great need of schools for the blacks, thousands of dollars were contributed at the North, and agents sent to Great Britain, where generosity had no bounds. Money came in from all quarters, and some of the noblest white young women gave themselves up to the work of teaching the freedmen.

During the first three or four years, this field for teachers was filled entirely by others than members of the colored race, and yet it was managed by the "New England Freedmen's Association," made up in part by some of our best men and women.

But many energetic, educated colored young women and men, volunteered, and, at their own expense, went South and began private schools, and literally forced their way into the work. This was followed by a few appointments, which in every case proved that colored teachers for colored people was the great thing needed. Upon the foundations laid by these small schools, some of the most splendid educational institutions in the South have sprung up. Fisk, Howard, Atlanta, Hampton, Tennessee Central, Virginia Central, and Straight, are some of the most prominent. These are all under the control and management of the whites, and are accordingly conducted upon the principle of whites for teachers and blacks for pupils. And yet each of the above institutions are indebted to the sympathy felt for the negro, for their very existence. Some of these colleges give more encouragement to the negro to become an instructor, than others; but, none however, have risen high enough to measure the black man independent of his color.

At Petersburg I found a large, fine building for public schools for colored youth; the principal, a white man, with six assistants, but not one colored teacher amongst them. Yet Petersburg has turned out some most excellent colored teachers, two of whom I met at Suffolk, with small schools. These young ladies had graduated with honors at one of our best institutions, and yet could not obtain a position as teacher in a public school, where the pupils were only their own race.

At Nashville, the School Board was still more unjust, for they employed teachers who would not allow their colored scholars to recognize them on the streets, and for doing which, the children were reprimanded, and the action of the teachers approved by the Board of Education.

It is generally known that all the white teachers in our colored public schools feel themselves above their work; and the fewest number have any communication whatever with their pupils outside the school-room. Upon receiving their appointments and taking charge of their schools some of them have been known to announce to their pupils that under no circumstances were they to recognize or speak to them on the streets. It is very evident that these people have no heart in the work they are doing, and simply from day to day go through the mechanical form of teaching our children for the pittance they receive as a salary. While teachers who have no interest in the children they instruct, except for the salary they get, are employed in the public schools and in the Freedman's Colleges, hundreds of colored men and women, who are able to stand the most rigid examination, are idle, or occupying places far beneath what they deserve.

It is to be expected that the public schools will, to a greater or less extent, be governed by the political predilections of the parties in power; but we ought to look for better things from Fisk, Hampton, Howard, Atlanta, Tennessee Central and Virginia Central, whose walls sprung up by money raised from appeals made for negro education.

There are, however, other educational institutions of which I have not made mention, and which deserve the patronage of the benevolent everywhere. These are: Wilberforce, Berea, Payne Institute, in South Carolina, Waco College, in Texas, and Storer College, at Harper's Ferry.

Wilberforce is well known, and is doing a grand work. It has turned out some of the best of our scholars,—men whose labors for the elevation of their race cannot be too highly commended.

Storer College, at Harper's Ferry, looks down upon the ruins of "John Brown's Fort." In the ages to come, Harper's Ferry will be sought out by the traveller from other lands. Here at the confluence of the Potomac and the Shenandoah Rivers, on a point just opposite the gap through which the united streams pass the Blue Ridge, on their course toward the ocean, stands the romantic town, and a little above it, on a beautiful eminence, is Storer, an institution, and of whose officers I cannot speak too highly.

I witnessed, with intense interest, the earnest efforts of these good men and women, in their glorious work of the elevation of my race. And while the benevolent of the North are giving of their abundance, I would earnestly beg them not to forget Storer College, at Harper's Ferry.

The other two, of which I have made mention, are less known, but their students are numerous and well trained. *Both these schools are in the South,* and both are owned and managed by colored men, free from the supposed necessity of having white men to do their *thinking,* and therein ought to receive the special countenance of all who believe in giving the colored people a chance to paddle their own canoe.

I failed, however, to find schools for another part of our people, which appear to be much needed. For many years in the olden time the South was noted for its beautiful Quadroon women. Bottles of ink, and reams of paper, have been used to portray the "finely-cut and well-moulded features," the "silken curls," the "dark and brilliant eyes," the "splendid forms," the "fascinating smiles," and "accomplished manners" of these impassioned and voluptuous daughters of the two races,—the unlawful product of the crime of human bondage. When we take into consideration the fact that no safeguard was ever thrown around virtue, and no inducement held out to slave-women to be pure and chaste, we will not be surprised when told that immorality pervaded the domestic circle in the cities and towns of the South to an extent unknown in the Northern States. Many a planter's wife has dragged out a miserable existence, with an aching heart, at seeing her place in the husband's affections usurped by the unadorned beauty and captivating smiles of her waiting-maid. Indeed, the greater portion of the colored women, in the days of slavery, had no greater aspiration than that of becoming the finely-dressed mistress of some white man. Although freedom has brought about a new order of things, and our colored women are making rapid strides to rise above the dark scenes of the past, yet the want of protection to our people since the old-time whites have regained power, places a large number of the colored young women of the cities and towns at the mercy of bad colored men, or worse white men. To save these from destruction, institutions ought to be established in every large city.

Mrs. Julia G. Thomas, a very worthy lady, deeply interested in the welfare of her sex, has a small institution for orphans and friendless girls, where they will have a home, schooling, and business training, to fit them to enter life with a prospect of success. Mrs. Thomas' address is 190 High Street, Nashville, Tennessee.

CHAPTER XXV.

Among the causes of that dissatisfaction of the colored people in the South which has produced the exodus therefrom, there is one that lies beneath the surface and is concealed from even an astute observer, if he is a stranger to that section. This cause consists in certain legislative enactments that have been passed in most of the cotton States, ostensibly for other purposes, but really for the purpose of establishing in those States a system of peonage similar to, if not worse than, that which prevails in Mexico. This is the object of a statute passed by the Legislature of Mississippi, in March, 1878. The title of the act, whether intentionally so or not, is certainly misleading. It is entitled "An act to reduce the judiciary expenses of the State." But how it can possibly have that effect is beyond human wisdom to perceive. It, however, does operate, and is used in such a way as to enslave a large number of negroes, who have not even been convicted of the slightest offence against the laws.

The act provides that "all persons convicted and committed to the jail of the county, except those committed to jail for contempt of court, and except those sentenced to imprisonment in the Penitentiary, shall be delivered to a contractor, to be by him kept and worked under the provisions of this act; and all persons committed to jail, except those not entitled to bail, may also, with their consent, be committed to said contractor and worked under this act before conviction." But Sect. 5, of the act provides ample and cogent machinery to produce the necessary consent on the part of the not yet convicted prisoner to work for the contractor. In that section it is provided "that if any person committed to jail for an offence that is bailable shall not consent to be committed to the safe keeping and custody of said contractor, and to work for said contractor, and to work for the same under this act, the prisoner shall be entitled to receive only six ounces, of the bacon, or ten ounces of beef, and one pound of bread and water.''

This section also provides that any prisoner not consenting to work before his conviction for the contractor, and that too, without compensation, "If said prisoner shall afterward be convicted, he shall, nevertheless, work under said contractor a sufficient term to pay all cost of prosecution, including the regular jail fees for keeping and feeding him. The charge for feeding him, upon the meagre bill of fare above stated, is twenty cents a day. Now, it cannot be denied that the use made of this law is to deprive the negro of his natural right to choose his own employer; and in the following manner: Let us suppose a case and such cases are constantly occurring. A is a cotton planter, owns three or four thousand acres of land, and has forty, fifty, or one hundred negro families on his plantation. At the expiration of the year, a negro proposes to leave the plantation of A, and try to better his condition by making a more advantageous bargain with B, or C, for another year. If A can prevent the negro from leaving him in no other way, this statute puts full power in his hands. A trumps up some petty charge against the negro, threatens to have him arrested and committed to jail. The negro knows how little it will take to commit him to jail, and that then he must half starve on a pound of bread and water and six ounces of bacon a day, or work for the contractor for nothing until he can be tried; and when tried he must run the risk of conviction, which is not slight, though he may be ever so innocent. Avarice—unscrupulous avarice—is pursuing him, and with little power to resist, there being no healthy public sentiment in favor of fair play to encourage him, he yields, and becomes the peon of his oppressor.

I found the whipping-post in full operation in Virginia, and heard of its being enforced in other States. I inquired of a black man what he thought of the revival of that mode of punishment. He replied, "Well, sar, I don't ker for it, kase dey treats us all alike; dey whips whites at de poss jess as dey do de blacks, an' dat's what I calls equality before de law."

A friend of mine meeting a man who was leaving Arkansas, on account of the revival of her old slave laws, the following conversation occurred, showing that the oppression of the blacks extends to all the States South.

"You come from Arkansas, I understand?"

"Yes."

"What wages do you generally get for your work?"

"Since about '68, we've been getting about two bits a day—that's twenty cents. Then there are some people that work by the month, and at the end of the month they are either put off or cheated out of their money entirely. Property and goods are worth nothing to a black man there. He can't get his price for them; he gets just what the white man chooses to give him. Some people who raise from ten to fifteen bales of cotton sometimes have hardly enough to cover their body and feet. This goes on while the white man gets the price he asks for his goods. This is unfair, and as long as we pay taxes we want justice, right, and equality before the people."

"What taxes do you pay?"

"A man that owns a house and lot has to pay about twenty-six dollars a year; and if he has a mule worth about one hundred and fifty dollars they tax him two dollars and a half extra. If they see you have money—say you made three thousand dollars—you'd soon see some bill about taxes, land lease and the other coming in for about two thousand of it. They charge a black man thirteen dollars where they would only charge a white man one or two. Now, there's a man," pointing to a portly old fellow, "who had to run away from his house, farm, and all. It is for this we leave Arkansas. We want freedom, and I say, 'Give me liberty or give me death.' We took up arms and fought for our country, so we ought to have our rights."

"How about the schooling you receive?"

"We can't vote, still we have to pay taxes to support schools for the others. I got my education in New Orleans and paid for it, too. I have six children, and though I pay taxes not one of them has any schooling from the public schools. The taxes and rent are so heavy that the children have to work when they are as young as ten years. That's the way it is down there."

"Did you have any teachers from the North?"

"There were some teachers from the North who came

down there, but they were run out. They were paid so badly and treated so mean that they had to go.''

''What county did you live in?''

''Phillips County.''

''How many schools were in that county?''

''About five.''

''When do they open?''

''About once every two years and keep open for two or three weeks. And then they have a certain kind of book for the children. Those that have dogs, cats, hogs, cows, horses, and all sorts of animals in them. They keep the children in these and never let them get out of them.''

''Have you any colleges in the State for colored men?''

''No, they haven't got any colleges and don't allow any. The other day I asked a Republican how was it that so many thousands of dollars were taken for colleges and we didn't get any good of it. He said, 'The bill didn't pass, somehow.' And now I guess those fellows spent all that money.''

''As a general thing, then, the people are very ignorant?''

''Yes, sir; the colored man that's got education is like some people that's got religion—he hides it under a bushel; if he didn't, and stood up for his rights as a citizen, he would soon become the game of some of the Ku-Klux clubs.''

Having succeeded in getting possession of power in the South, and driving the black voters from the polls at elections, and also having them counted in National Representation, the ex-rebels will soon have a power which they never before enjoyed. Had the slaveholders in 1860 possessed the right of representing their slaves fully instead of partly in Congress and in the Electoral College, they would have ruled this country indefinitely in the interest of slavery. It was supposed that by the result of the war, freedom profited and the slaveholding class lost power forever. But the very act which conferred the full right of representation upon the three million freedmen, by the help of the policy, has placed an instrument in the hands of the rebel conspirators which they will use to pervert and defeat the objects of the Constitutional amendments. Through this policy the thirty-five additional electoral votes given to the freedmen have been "turned over to the Democratic party." Aye, more than that; they have been turned over to the ex-rebels, who will use them in the cause of oppression scarcely second in hatefulness to that of chattel slavery. In a contest with the solid South, therefore, the party of freedom and justice will have greater odds to overcome than it did in 1860, and the Southern oligarchs hold a position which is well nigh impregnable for whatever purpose they choose to use it.

Of the large number of massacres perpetrated upon the blacks in the South, since the ex-rebels have come into power, I give one instance, which will show the inhumanity of the whites. This outrage occurred in Gibson County, Tennessee. The report was first circulated that the blacks in great numbers were armed, and were going to commit murder upon the whites. This created the excitement that it was intended to, and the whites in large bodies, armed to the teeth, went through Gibson, and adjoining counties, disarming the blacks, taking from them their only means of defence, and arresting all objectionable blacks that they could find, taking them to Trenton and putting them in jail.

The following account of the wanton massacre, is from the *Memphis Appeal:*—

"About four hundred armed, disguised, mounted men entered this town at two o'clock this morning, proceeded to the jail, and demanded the keys of the jailor, Mr. Alexander. He refused to give up the keys. Sheriff Williams, hearing the noise, awoke and went to the jail, and refused to surrender the keys to the maskers, telling them that he did not have the keys. They cocked their pistols, and he refused again to give them the keys, whereupon the Captain of the company ordered the masked men to draw their pistols and cock them, swearing they would have the keys or shoot the jailor. The jailor dared them to shoot, and said they were too cowardly to shoot. They failed to do this. Then they threatened to tear down the jail or get the prisoners. The jailor told them that rather than they should tear down the jail he would give them the keys if they would go with him to his office. The jailor did this because he saw that the men were determined to break through. 'They were all disguised. Then they came,' says the Sheriff, 'and got the keys from my office, and giving three or four yells, went to the jail, unlocked it, took out the sixteen negroes who had been brought here from Pickettsville (Gibson), and, tying their hands, escorted them away. They proceeded on the Huntingdon road without saying a word, and in fifteen minutes I heard shots. In company with several citizens I proceeded down the road in the direction taken by the men and prisoners, and just beyond the river bridge, half a mile from town, I found four negroes dead, on the ground, their bodies riddled with bullets, and two wounded. We saw no masked men. Ten negroes yet remain unaccounted for. Leaving the dead bodies where we found them, we brought the two wounded negroes to town, and summoned medical aid. Justice J. M. Caldwell held an inquest on the bodies, the verdict being in accordance with the facts that death resulted from shots inflicted by guns in the hands of unknown parties. The inquest was held about eight o'clock this morning. These are all the facts relative to the shooting I can give you. I did my duty to prevent the rescue of the negroes, but found it useless to oppose the men, one of whom said there were four hundred in the band.'

"Night before last the guard that brought the prisoners from Pickettsville remained. No fears or intimations of the attempted rescue were then heard of or feared. This morning, learning that four or five hundred armed negroes, on the Jackson road, were marching into town to burn the buildings and kill the people, the citizens immediately organized, armed, and prepared for active defence, and went out to meet the negroes, scouted the whole country around but found no armed negroes. The citizens throughout the country commenced coming into town by hundreds. Men came from Union City, Kenton, Troy, Rutherford, Dyer Station, Skull Bone, and the whole country, but found no need of their services. The two wounded negroes will die. The bodies of the ten other negroes taken from the jail were found in the river bottom about a mile from town.

"We blush for our State, and with the shame of the bloody murder, the disgraceful defiance of law, of order, and of decency full upon us, are at a loss for language with which to characterize a deed that, if the work of Comanches or Modocs, would arouse every man in the

Union for a speedy vengeance on the perpetrators. To-day, we must hold up to merited reprobation and con-demnation the armed men who besieged the Trenton Jail, and wantonly as wickedly, without anything like justifi-cation, took thence the unarmed negroes there awaiting trial by the courts, and brutally shot them to death; and, too, with a show of barbarity altogether as unnecessary as the massacre was unjustifiable. To say that we are not, in any county in the State, strong enough to enforce the law, is to pronounce a libel upon the whole Common-wealth. We are as a thousand to one in moral and phys-ical force to the negro; we are in possession of the State, of all the machinery of Government, and at a time more momentous than any we ever hope to see again have proved our capacity to sustain the law's executive officers and maintain the laws. Why, then, should we now, in time of profound peace, subvert the law and defy its ad-ministrators? Why should we put the Government of our own selection under our feet, and defy and set at naught the men whom we have elected to enforce the laws, and this ruthlessly and savagely, without any of the forms, even, that usually attend on the administration of the wild behests of Judge Lynch? And all without color of exten-uation; for no sane man who has regard for the truth will pretend to say that because the unfortunate negroes were arrested as the ringleaders of a threatening and armed band that had fired upon two white men, they were, therefore, worthy of death, and without the forms of law, in a State controlled and governed by law-abiding men.''

No one was ever punished, or even an attempt made to ferret out the perpetrators of this foul murder. And the infliction of the death punishment, by ''Lynch Law,'' on colored persons for the slightest offence, proves that there is really no abatement in this hideous race prejudice that prevails throughout the South.

CHAPTER XXVI.

Years ago, when the natural capabilities of the races were more under discussion than now, the negro was always made to appear to greater disadvantage than the rest of mankind. The public mind is not yet free from this false theory, nor has the colored man done much of late years to change this opinion. Long years of training of any people to a particular calling, seems to fit them for that vocation more than for any other. Thus, the Jews, inured to centuries of money-lending and pawn-broking, they, as a race, stick to it as if they were created for that business alone.

The training of the Arabs for long excursions through wild deserts, makes them the master roamers of the world. The Gypsies, brought up to camping out and trading in horses, send forth the idea that they were born for it. The black man's position as a servant, for many generations, has not only made the other races believe that is his legitimate sphere, but he himself feels more at home in a white apron and a towel on his arm, than with a quill behind his ear and a ledger before him.

That a colored man takes to the dining-room and the kitchen, as a duck does to water, only proves that like other races, his education has entered into his blood. This is not theory, this is not poetry; but stern truth. Our people prefer to be servants.

This may be to some extent owing to the fact that the organ of alimentativeness is more prominently formed in the negro's make-up, than in that of almost any other people.

During several trips in the cars between Nashville and Columbia, I noticed that the boy who sold newspapers and supplied the passengers with fruit, had a basket filled with candy and cakes. The first time I was on his car he

offered me the cakes, which I declined, but bought a
paper. Watching him I observed that when colored persons entered the car, he would offer them the cakes which
they seldom failed to purchase. One day as I took from
him a newspaper, I inquired of him why he always offered cakes to the colored passengers. His reply was:—
"Oh! they always buy something to eat."

"Do they purchase more cakes than white people?"

"Yes," was the response.

"Why do they buy your cakes and candy?" I asked.

"Well, sir, the colored people seem always to be hungry. Never see anything like it. They don't buy papers,
but they are always eating."

Just then we stopped at Franklin, and three colored
passengers came in. "Now," continued the cake boy,
"you'll see how they'll take the cakes," and he started
for them, but had to pass their seats to shut the door that
had been left open. In going by, one of the men, impatient to get a cake, called, "Here, here, come here wid
yer cakes."

The peddler looked at me and laughed. He sold each
one a cake, and yet it was not ten o'clock in the morning.

Not long since, in Massachusetts, I succeeded in getting a young man pardoned from our State prison, where
he has been confined for more than ten years, and where
he had learned a good trade.

I had already secured him a situation where he was to
receive three dollars per day to commence with, with a
prospect of an advance of wages.

As we were going to his boarding place, and after I
had spent some time in advising him to turn over a new
leaf and to try and elevate himself, we passed one of our
best hotels. My ward at once stopped, began snuffing as
if he "smelt a mice." I looked at him, watched his countenance as it lighted up and his eyes sparkled; I inquired
what was the matter. With a radiant smile he replied, "I
smell good wittles; what place is that?"

"It is the Revere House," I said.

"Wonder if I could get a place to wait on table there?"
he asked.

I thought it a sorry comment on my efforts to instil
into him some self-respect. This young man had learned
the shoemaking trade, and at a McKay machine, I un-

derstood that he could earn from three dollars and a half to five dollars per day.

A dozen years ago, two colored young men commenced the manufacture of one of the necessary commodities of the day. After running the establishment some six or eight months successfully, they sold out to white men, who now employ more than one hundred hands. Both of the colored men are at their legitimate callings; one is a waiter in a private house, the other is a porter on a sleeping car.

The failure of these young men to carry on a manufacturing business was mainly owing to a want of training, in a business point of view. No man is fit for a profession or a trade, unless he has learned it.

Extravagance in dress is a great and growing evil with our people. I am acquainted with a lady in Boston who wears a silk dress costing one hundred and thirty dollars. She lives in two rooms, and her husband is a hair-dresser.

Since the close of the war, a large number of freedmen settled in Massachusetts, where they became servants, the most of them. These people surpass in dress, the wealthiest merchants of the city.

A young man, now a servant in a private house, sports a sixty-dollar overcoat while he works for twenty dollars per month.

A woman who cooks for five dollars per week, in Arlington Street, swings along every Sunday in a hundred-dollar silk dress, and a thirty-dollar hat. She cannot read or write.

Go to our churches on the Sabbath, and see the silk, the satin, the velvet, and the costly feathers, and talk with the uneducated wearers, and you will see at once the main hindrance to self-elevation.

To elevate ourselves and our children, we must cultivate self-denial. Repress our appetites for luxuries and be content with clothing ourselves in garments becoming our means and our incomes. The adaptation and the deep inculcation of the principles of total abstinence from all intoxicants. The latter is a pre-requisite for success in all the relations of life.

Emerging from the influence of oppression, taught from early experience to have no confidence in the whites, we have little or none in our own race, or even in ourselves.

We need more self-reliance, more confidence in the ability of our own people; more manly independence, a higher standard of moral, social, and literary culture. Indeed, we need a union of effort to remove the dark shadow of ignorance that now covers the land. While the barriers of prejudice keep us morally and socially from educated white society, we must make a strong effort to raise ourselves from the common level where emancipation and the new order of things found us.

We possess the elements of successful development; but we need live men and women to make this development. The last great struggle for our rights; the battle for our own civilization, is entirely with ourselves, and the problem is to be solved by us.

We must use our spare time, day and night, to educate ourselves. Let us have night schools for the adults, and not be ashamed to attend them. Encourage our own literary men and women; subscribe for, and be sure and pay for papers published by colored men. Don't stop to inquire if the paper will live; but encourage it, and make it live.

With the exception of a few benevolent societies, we are separated as far from each other as the east is from the west.

CHAPTER XXVII.

Union is strength, has long since passed into a proverb. The colored people of the South should at once form associations, combine and make them strong, and live up to them by all hazards. All civilized races have risen by means of combination and co-operation. The Irishman, the German, the Frenchman, all come to this country poor, and they stay here but a short time before you see them succeeding in some branch of business. This success is not the result of individual effort—it is the result of combination and co-operation. Whatever an Irishman has to spend he puts in the till of one of his own countrymen, and that accounts for Irish success.

A German succeeds in this country because all his fellow-countrymen patronize him in whatever business he engages. A German will put himself to inconvenience, and go miles out of his way to spend money with one of his own race and nationality.

With all his fickleness, the Frenchman never forgets to find out and patronize one of his own people. Italians flock together and stand by each other, right or wrong. The Chinese are clannish, and stick by one another. The Caucasian race is the foremost in the world in everything that pertains to advanced civilization,—simply owing to the fact that an Englishman never passes the door of a countryman to patronize another race; and a Yankee is a Yankee all the days of his life, and will never desert his colors. But where is the Negro?

A gentlemanly and well-informed colored man came to me a few days since, wishing to impart to me some important information, and he commenced by saying: "Now, Doctor, what I am going to tell you, you may rely on its being true, because I got it from a white man—no nigger told me this."

On Duke Street, in Alexandria, Va., resides an Irishman, who began business in that place a dozen years ago, with two jugs, one filled with whiskey, the other with molasses, a little pork, some vegetables, sugar and salt. On the opposite side of the street was our good friend, Mr. A. S. Perpener. The latter had a respectable provision store, minus the whiskey. Colored people inhabited the greater part of the street. Did they patronize their own countryman? Not a bit of it. The Irishman's business increased rapidly; he soon enlarged his premises, adding wood and coal to his salables. Perpener did the same, but the blacks passed by and went over on the other side, gave their patronage to the son of Erin, who now has houses "to let," but he will not rent them to colored tenants.

The Jews, though scattered throughout the world, are still Jews. Their race and their religion they have maintained in all countries and all ages. They never forsake each other. If they fall out, over some trade, they make up in time to combine against the rest of mankind. Shylock says: "I will buy with you, sell with you, talk with you, walk with you, and so following; but I will not eat with you, drink with you, nor pray with you." Thus, the Jew, with all his love of money, will not throw off his religion to satisfy others, and for this we honor him.

It is the misfortune of our race that the impression prevails that "one nigger is as good as another." Now this is a great error; there are colored men in this country as far ahead of others of their own race as Webster and Sumner were superior to the average white man.

Then, again, we have no confidence in each other. We consider the goods from the store of a white man necessarily better than can be purchased from a colored man.

No man ever succeeded who lacked confidence in himself. No race ever did or ever will prosper or make a respectable history which has no confidence in its own nationality.

Those who do not appreciate their own people will not be appreciated by other people. If a white man will pat a colored man on the shoulder, bow to him, and call him "Mr.," he will go a mile out of his way to patronize him, if in doing so he passes a first-class dealer of his own race. I asked a colored man in Columbia if he patronized Mr. Frierson. He said, "No." I inquired, "Why?" "He never invited me to his house in his life," was the reply.

"Does the white man you deal with invite you?"

"No."

"Then, why do you expect Mr. Frierson to do it?"

"Oh! he's a nigger and I look for more from him than I do from a white man." So it is clear that this is the result of jealousy.

The recent case of the ill-treatment of Cadet Whittaker, at West Point, shows most clearly the unsuspecting character of the negro, when dealing with whites. Although Whittaker had been repeatedly warned that an attack was to be made upon him, and especially told to look out for the assault the very night that the crime was committed, he laid down with his room-door unfastened, went off into a sound sleep, with no weapon or means of defence near him. This was, for all the world, like a negro. A Yankee would have had a revolver with every chamber loaded; an Irishman would have slept with one eye open, and a stout shillalah in his right hand, and in all probability somebody would have had a nice funeral after the attack. But that want of courage and energy, so characteristic of the race, permitted one of the foulest crimes to be perpetrated which has come to light for years.

But the most disgraceful part in this whole transaction lies with the Court of Investigation, now being conducted at West Point under the supervision of United States officials. The unfeeling and unruly cadets that outraged Whittaker, no doubt, laid a deep plan to cover up their tracks, and this was to make it appear that their victim had inflicted upon himself his own injuries. And acting upon this theory, one of the young scamps, who had no doubt been rehearsing for the occasion, volunteered to show the Court how the negro could have practised the imposition.

And, strange to say these sage *investigators* sat quietly and looked on while the young ruffian laid down upon the floor, tied himself, and explained how the thing was done.

If the victim had been a white man and his persecutors

black, does any one believe for a moment that such a theory would have been listened to?

Generations of oppression have done their work too thoroughly to have its traces wiped away in a dozen years. The race must be educated out of the ignorance in which it at present dwells, and lifted to a level with other races. Colored lawyers, doctors, artisans and mechanics, starve for patronage, while the negro is begging the white man to do his work. Combinations have made other races what they are to-day.

The great achievements of scientific men could not have been made practical by individual effort. The great works of genius could never have benefited the world, had those who composed them been mean and selfish. All great and useful enterprises have succeeded through the influence and energy of numbers.

I would not have it thought that all colored men are to be bought by the white man's smiles, or to be frightened by intimidation. Far from it. In all the Southern States we have some of the noblest specimens of mankind,— men of genius, refinement, courage and liberality, ready to do and to die for the race.

CHAPTER XXVIII.

Advice upon the formation of Literary Associations, and total abstinence from all intoxications is needed, and I will give it to you in this chapter. The time for colored men and women to organize for self-improvement has arrived. Moral, social, and intellectual development, should be the main attainment of the negro race. Colored people have so long been in the habit of aping the whites, and often not the better class either, that I fear this characteristic in them, more than anything else. A large percentage of them being waiters, they see a great deal of drinking in white society of the "Upper Ten." Don't follow their bad example. Take warning by their degradation.

During the year 1879, Boston sent four hundred drunken women to the Sherborn prison; while two private asylums are full, many of them from Boston's first families. Therefore, I beseech you to never allow the intoxicant to enter your circles.

It is bad enough for men to lapse into habits of drunkenness. A drunken husband, a drunken father—only those patient, heart-broken, shame-faced wives and children on whom this great cross of suffering is laid, can estimate the misery which it brings.

But a drunken girl—a drunken wife—a drunken mother—is there for woman a deeper depth? Home made hideous—children disgraced, neglected, and maltreated.

Remember that all this comes from the first glass. The wine may be pleasant to the taste, and may for the time being, furnish happiness; but it must never be forgotten that whatever degree of exhiliration may be produced in a healthy person by the use of wine, it will most certainly be succeeded by a degree of nervous depression proportioned to the amount of previous excitement. Hence the immoderate use of wine, or its habitual indulgence, debilitates the brain and nervous system, paralyzes the intellectual powers, impairs the functions of the stomach, produces a perverted appetite for a renewal of the deleterious beverage, or a morbid imagination, which destroys man's usefulness.

The next important need with our people, is the cultivation of habits of business. We have been so long a dependent race, so long looking to the white as our leaders, and being content with doing the drudgery of life, that most who commence business for themselves are likely to fail, because of want of a knowledge of what we undertake. As the education of a large percentage of the colored people is of a fragmentary character, having been gained by little and little here and there, and must necessarily be limited to a certain degree, we should use our spare hours in study and form associations for moral, social, and literary culture. We must aim to enlighten ourselves and to influence others to higher associations.

Our work lies primarily with the inward culture, at the springs and sources of individual life and character, seeking everywhere to encourage, and assist to the fullest emancipation of the human mind from ignorance, inviting the largest liberty of thought, and the utmost possible exaltation of life into approximation to the loftier standard of cultivated character. Feeling that the literature of our age is the reflection of the existing manners and modes of thought, etherealized and refined in the alembic of genius, we should give our principal encouragement to literature, bringing before our associations the importance of original essays, selected readings, and the cultivation of the musical talent.

If we need any proof of the good that would accrue from such cultivation, we have only to look back and see the wonderful influence of Homer over the Greeks, of Virgil and Horace over the Romans, of Dante and Ariosto over the Italians, of Goethe and Schiller over the Germans, of Racine and Voltaire over the French, of Shakespeare and Milton over the English. The imaginative powers of these men, wrought into verse or prose, have been the theme of the king in his palace, the lover in his dreamy moods, the farmer in the harvest field, the mechanic in the work-shop, the sailor on the high seas, and the prisoner in his gloomy cell.

Indeed, authors possess the most gifted and fertile minds who combine all the graces of style with rare, fascinating powers of language, eloquence, wit, humor, pathos, genius and learning. And to draw knowledge from such sources should be one of the highest aims of man. The better elements of society can only be brought together by organizing societies and clubs.

The cultivation of the mind is the superstructure of the moral, social and religious character, which will follow us into our every-day life, and make us what God intended us to be—the noblest instruments of His creative power. Our efforts should be to imbue our minds with broader and better views of science, literature, and a nobleness of spirit that ignores petty aims of patriotism, glory, or mere personal aggrandizement. It is said, never a shadow falls that does not leave a permanent impress of its image, a monument of its passing presence. Every character is modified by association. Words, the image of the ideas, are more impressive than shadows; actions, embodied thoughts, more enduring than aught material. Believing these truths, then, I say, for every thought expressed, ennobling in its tendency and elevating to Christian dignity and manly honor, God will reward us. Permanent success depends upon intrinsic worth. The best way to have a public character is to have a private one.

The great struggle for our elevation is now with ourselves. We may talk of Hannibal, Euclid, Phyllis Wheatly, Benjamin Banneker, and Toussaint L'Overture, but the world will ask us for our men and women of the day. We cannot live upon the past; we must hew out a reputation that will stand the test, one that we have a legitimate right to. To do this, we must imitate the best examples set us by the cultivated whites, and by so doing we will teach them that they can claim no superiority on account of race.

The efforts made by oppressed nations or communities to throw off their chains, entitles them to, and gains for them the respect of mankind. This, the blacks never made, or what they did, was so feeble as scarcely to call for comment. The planning of Denmark Vesey for an insurrection in South Carolina, was noble, and deserved a better fate; but he was betrayed by the race that he was attempting to serve.

Nat Turner's strike for liberty was the outburst of feelings of an insane man,—made so by slavery. True, the negro did good service at the battles of Wagner, Honey Hill, Port Hudson, Millikin's Bend, Poison Springs, Olustee and Petersburg. Yet it would have been far better if they had commenced earlier, or had been under leaders of their own color. The St. Domingo revolution brought forth men of courage. But the subsequent course of the people as a government, reflects little or no honor on the race. They have floated about like a ship without a rudder, ever since the expulsion of Rochambeau.

The fact is the world likes to see the exhibition of pluck on the part of an oppressed people, even though they fail in their object. It is these outbursts of the love of liberty that gain respect and sympathy for the enslaved. Therefore, I bid God speed to the men and women of the South, in their effort to break the long spell of lethargy that hangs over the race. Don't be too rash in starting, but prepare to go, and "don't stand upon the order of going, but go." By common right, the South is the negro's home. Born, and "raised" there, he cleared up the lands, built the cities, fed and clothed the whites, nursed their children, earned the money to educate their sons and daughters; by the negro's labor churches were built and clergymen paid.

For two hundred years the Southern whites lived a lazy life at the expense of the negro's liberty. When the rebellion came, the blacks, trusted and true to the last, protected the families and homes of white men while they were away fighting the Government. The South is the black man's home; yet if he cannot be protected in his rights he should leave. Where white men of liberal views can get no protection, the colored man must not look for it. Follow the example of other oppressed races, strike out for new territory. If suffering is the result, let it come; others have suffered before you. Look at the Irish, Germans, French, Italians, and other races, who have come to this country, gone to the West, and are now enjoying the blessings of liberty and plenty; while the negro is discussing the question of whether he should leave the South or not, simply because he was born there.

While they are thus debating the subject, their old oppressors, seeing that the negro has touched the right chord, forbid his leaving the country. Georgia has made it a penal offence to invite the blacks to emigrate, and one negro is already in prison for wishing to better the condition of his fellows. This is the same spirit that induced the people of that State to offer a reward of five thousand dollars, in 1835, for the head of Garrison. No people has borne oppression like the negro, and no race has been so much imposed upon. Go to his own land. Ask the Dutch boor whence comes his contempt and inward dislike to the negro, the Hottentot, and Caffre; ask him for his warrant to reduce these unhappy races to slavery; he will point to the fire-arms suspended over the mantle-piece—"There is my right."

Want of independence is the colored man's greatest fault. In the present condition of the Southern States, with the lands in the hands of a shoddy, ignorant, superstitious, rebellious, and negro-hating population, the blacks cannot be independent. Then emigrate to get away from the surroundings that keep you down where you are. All cannot go, even if it were desirable; but those who remain will have a better opportunity. The planters will then have to pursue a different policy. The right of the negroes to make the best terms they can, will have to be recognized, and what was before presumption that called for repression will now be tolerated as among the privileges of freedom. The ability of the negroes to change their location will also turn public sentiment against bull-dozing.

Two hundred years have demonstrated the fact that the negro is the manual laborer of that section, and without him agriculture will be at a stand-still.

The negro will for pay perform any service under heaven, no matter how repulsive or full of hardship, He will sing his old plantation melodies and walk about the cotton fields in July and August, when the toughest white man seeks an awning. Heat is his element. He fears no malaria in the rice swamps, where a white man's life is not worth sixpence.

Then, I say, leave the South and starve the whites into

a realization of justice and common sense. Remember that tyrants never relinquish their grasp upon their victims until they are forced to.

Whether the blacks emigrate or not, I say to them, keep away from the cities and towns. Go into the country. Go to work on farms.

If you stop in the city, get a profession or a trade, but keep in mind that a good trade is better than a poor profession.

In Boston there are a large number of colored professionals, especially in the law, and a majority of whom are better fitted for farm service, mechanical branches, or for driving an ash cart.

Persons should not select professions for the name of being a "professional," nor because they think they will lead an easy life. An honorable, lucrative and faithfully-earned professional reputation, is a career of honesty, patience, sobriety, toil and Christian zeal.

No drone can fill such a position. Select the profession or trade that your education, inclination, strength of mind and body will support, and then give your time to the work that you have undertaken, and work, work.

Once more I say to those who cannot get remunerative employment at the South, emigrate.

Some say, "stay and fight it out, contend for your rights, don't let the old rebels drive you away, the country is as much yours as theirs." That kind of talk will do very well for men who have comfortable homes out of the South, and law to protect them; but for the negro, with no home, no food, no work, the land-owner offering him conditions whereby he can do but little better than starve, such talk is nonsense. Fight out what? Hunger? Poverty? Cold? Starvation? Black men, emigrate.

CHAPTER XXIX.

In America, the negro stands alone as a race. He is without mate or fellow in the great family of man. Whatever progress he makes, it must be mainly by his own efforts. This is an unfortunate fact, and for which there seems to be no remedy.

All history demonstrates the truth that amalgamation is the great civilizer of the races of men. Wherever a race, clan, or community have kept themselves together, prohibiting by law, usage, or common consent, intermarriage with others, they have made little or no progress. The Jews, a distinct and isolated people, are good only at driving a bargain and getting rich. The Gipsies commence and stop with trading horses. The Irish, in their own country, are dull. The Coptic race form but a handful of what they were—those builders, unequalled in ancient or modern times. What has become of them? Where are the Romans? What races have they destroyed? What races have they supplanted? For fourteen centuries they lorded it over the semi-civilized world; and now they are of no more note than the ancient Scythians, or Mongols, Copts, or Tartars. An un-amalgamated, inactive people will decline. Thus it was with the Mexicans, when Cortes marched on Mexico, and the Peruvians, when Pizarro marched on Peru.

The Britons were a dull, lethargic people before their country was invaded, and the hot, romantic blood of Julius Caesar and William of Normandy coursed through their veins.

Caractacus, king of the Britons, was captured and sent to Rome in chains. Still later, Hengist and Horsa, the Saxon generals, imposed the most humiliating conditions upon the Britons, to which they were compelled to submit. Then came William of Normandy, defeated Harold

at Hastings, and the blood of the most renowned land-
pirates and sea-robbers that ever disgraced humanity,
mixed with the Briton and Saxon, and gave to the world
the Anglo-Saxon race, with its physical ability, strong
mind, brave and enterprising spirit. And, yet, all that this
race is, it owes to its mixed blood. Civilization, or the
social condition of man, is the result and test of the qualities of every race. The benefit of this blood mixture, the
negro is never to enjoy on this continent. In the South
where he is raised, in the North, East, or West, it is all
the same, no new blood is to be infused into his sluggish
veins.

His only hope is education, professions, trades, and
copying the best examples, no matter from what source
they come.

This antipathy to amalgamation with the negro, has
shown itself in all of the States. Most of the Northern
and Eastern State Legislatures have passed upon this
question years ago. Since the coming in of the present
year, Rhode Island's Senate refused to repeal the old law
forbidding the inter-marriage of whites and blacks. Thus
the colored man is left to "paddle his own canoe" alone.
Where there is no law against the mixture of the two
races, there is a public sentiment which is often stronger
than law itself. Even the wild blood of the red Indian
refuses to mingle with the sluggish blood of the negro.
This is no light matter, for race hate, prejudice and common malice all die away before the melting power of
amalgamation. The beauty of the half-breeds of the
South, the result of the crime of slavery, have long
claimed the attention of writers, and why not a lawful
mixture? And then this might help in

> "Making a race far more lovely and fair,
>   Darker a little than white people are:
>   Stronger, and nobler, and better in form,
>   Hearts more voluptuous, kinder, and warm;
>   Bosoms of beauty, that heave with a pride
>   Nature had ever to white folks denied."

Emigration to other States, where the blacks will come
in contact with educated and enterprising whites, will do
them much good. This benefit by commercial intercourse

is seen in the four thousand colored people who have come to Boston, where most of them are employed as servants. They are sought after as the best domestics in the city. Some of these people, who were in slavery before the war, are now engaged in mercantile pursuits, doing good business, and showing what contact will do. Many of them rank with the ablest whites in the same trades. Indeed, the various callings are well represented by Southern men, showing plainly the need of emigration. Although the colored man has been sadly at fault in not vindicating his right to liberty, he has, it is true, shown ability in other fields. Benjamin Banneker, a negro of Maryland, who lived a hundred years ago, exhibited splendid natural qualities. He had a quickness of apprehension, and a vivacity of understanding, which easily took in and surmounted the most subtile and knotty parts of mathematics and metaphysics. He possessed in a large degree that genius which constitutes a man of letters; that quality without which judgment is cold, and knowledge is inert; that energy which collects, combines, amplifies, and animates.

The rapid progress made in acquiring education and homesteads by the colored people of the South, in the face of adverse circumstances, commends the highest admiration from all classes.

The product of their native genius and industry, as exhibited at county and State Agricultural Fairs, speak well for the race.

At the National Fair, held at Raleigh, N.C., in the autumn of 1879, the exhibition did great credit to the colored citizens of the South, who had the matter in charge. Such manifestations of intellectual and mechanical enterprise will do much to stimulate the people to further development of their powers, and higher facilities.

The colored people of the United States are sadly in need of a National Scientific Association, to which may be brought yearly reports of such investigations as may be achieved in science, philosophy, art, philology, ethnology, jurisprudence, metaphysics, and whatever may tend to *unite* the race in their moral, social, intellectual and physical improvement.

We have negro artists of a high order, both in painting

and sculpture; also, discoverers who hold patents, and yet the world knows little or nothing about them. The time for the negro to work out his destiny has arrived. Now let him show himself equal to the hour.

In this work I frequently used the word "negro," and shall, no doubt, hear from it when the negro critics get a sight of the book. And why should I not use it? Is it not honorable? What is there in the word that does not sound as well as "English," "Irish," "German," "Italian," "French?"

"Don't call me a negro; I'm an American," said a black to me a few days since.

"Why not?" I asked.

"Well, sir, I was born in this country, and I don't want to be called out of my name."

Just then, an Irish-American came up, and shook hands with me. He had been a neighbor of mine in Cambridge. When the young man was gone, I inquired of the black man what countryman he thought the man was.

"Oh!" replied he, "he's an Irishman."

"What makes you think so?" I inquired.

"Why, his brogue is enough to tell it."

"Then," said I, "why is not your color enough to tell that you're a negro?"

"Arh!" said he, "that's a horse of another color," and left me with a "Ha, ha, ha!"

Black men, don't be ashamed to show your colors, and to own them.

BIBLIOGRAPHY

Andrews, William L. "Mark Twain, William Wells Brown, and the Problem of Authority in New South Writing," in Jefferson Humphries, ed., *Southern Literature and Literary Theory*. Athens: University of Georgia Press, 1990.

———. *To Tell a Free Story: The First Century of Afro-American Autobiography, 1760–1865*. Urbana: University of Illinois Press, 1986.

Butterfield, Stephen. *Black Autobiography in America*. Amherst: University of Massachusetts Press, 1974.

Farrison, William Edward. *William Wells Brown: Author and Reformer*. Chicago: University of Chicago Press, 1969.

Foster, Frances Smith. *Witnessing Slavery: The Development of Ante-bellum Slave Narratives*. Westport, CT: Greenwood, 1979.

Jackson, Blyden. *A History of Afro-American Literature. Vol. 1. The Long Beginning, 1746–1895*. Baton Rouge: Louisiana State University Press, 1989.

Loggins, Vernon. *The Negro Author in America: His Development to 1900*. New York: Columbia University Press, 1931.

Redding, J. Saunders. *To Make a Poet Black*. Chapel Hill: University of North Carolina Press, 1939.

Stepto, Robert B. *From Behind the Veil: A Study of Afro-American Narrative*. Urbana: University of Illinois Press, 1979.

Yellin, Jean Fagan. *The Intricate Knot: Black Figures in American Literature, 1776–1863*. New York: New York University Press, 1972.

AFRICAN AMERICAN
STUDIES

☐ **AFRICANS AND THEIR HISTORY by Joseph E. Harris.** A landmark reevaluation of African cultures by a leading black historian. "A major brief summary of the history of Africa."—Elliot P. Skinner, *Columbia University* (625560—$4.99)

☐ **THE CLASSIC SLAVE NARRATIVES edited by Henry Louis Gates, Jr.** One of America's foremost experts in black studies, presents a volume of four classic slave narratives that illustrate the real nature of the black experience with the horrors of bondage and servitude. (627261—$5.99)

☐ **BEFORE FREEDOM edited and with an Introduction by Belinda Hurmence.** The oral history of American slavery in the powerful words of former slaves. Including the two volumes *Before Freedom, When I Can Just Remember* and *My Folks Don't Want Me to Talk About Slavery*. "Eloquent . . . historically valuable."—*Los Angeles Times Book Review* (627814—$4.99)

☐ **BLACK LIKE ME by John Howard Griffin.** The startling, penetrating, first-hand account of a white man who learned what it is like to live as a black in the South. Winner of the *Saturday Review* Anisfield-Wolf Award. (163176—$4.99)

☐ **THE SOULS OF BLACK FOLK by W.E.B. DuBois.** A passionate evaluation of the blacks' bitter struggle for survival and self-respect, and a classic in the literature of the civil rights movement. Introduction by Nathan Hare and Alvin F. Poussaint. (523970—$4.95)

Prices slightly higher in Canada.

Buy them at your local bookstore or use this convenient coupon for ordering.

NEW AMERICAN LIBRARY
P.O. Box 999 – Dept. #17109
Bergenfield, New Jersey 07621

Please send me the books I have checked above.
I am enclosing $_____ (please add $2.00 to cover postage and handling).
Send check or money order (no cash or C.O.D.'s) or charge by Mastercard or
VISA (with a $15.00 minimum). Prices and numbers are subject to change without
notice.

Card # _____ Exp. Date _____
Signature_____
Name_____
Address_____
City _____ State _____ Zip Code _____

For faster service when ordering by credit card call **1-800-253-6476**

Allow a minimum of 4-6 weeks for delivery. This offer is subject to change without notice.